Discover
Switzerland

Contents

Throughout this book, we use these icons to highlight special recommendations:

The Best...
Lists for everything from bars to wildlife – to make sure you don't miss out

Don't Miss
A must-see – don't go home until you've been there

Local Knowledge Local experts reveal their top picks and secret highlights

Detour
Special places a little off the beaten track

If you like...
Lesser-known alternatives to world-famous attractions

These icons help you quickly identify reviews in the text and on the map:

Sights

Eating

Drinking

Sleeping

Information

This edition written and researched by

Ryan Ver Berkmoes,
Kerry Christiani, Sally O'Brien, Damien Simonis,
Nicola Williams

Bern, Jura &
Mittelland p91

Zürich,
Lake Constance
& the Northeast
p193

Bernese
Oberland
& Central
Switzerland p119

p49

p229

Geneva &
the West

St Moritz,
Graubünden
& the Southeast

p165

Valais & Zermatt

Contents

Plan Your Trip | On the Road

●●●

Geneva &
the West   49

●●●

Bern, Jura &
Mittelland   91

● Valais &
Zermatt

Contents

On the Road

In Focus

Survival Guide

This is Switzerland

No one has a hard time conjuring images of Switzerland:
Alps, chocolate, cows with bells, cable cars, mountain
meadow hikes, tidy old villages, yodelling, lake steamers,
cheese (lots of tasty cheese!) and much more. And the
reality lives up to the iconography. This orderly nation –
where a train is officially late if it's three minutes off – is
a splendid place to explore winter or summer, whether
you're cliché-hunting or ready for a surprising adventure.

What giddy romance Zermatt, St Moritz and other legendary names evoke.

From the intoxicating chink of Verbier glitterati hobnobbing
over champagne in ice-carved flutes to the reassuring bell
jangle of cows coming home in Kandersteg, Switzerland is
a harmonious tableau of beautiful images. This small, landlocked country is so darn easy to step into and experience.

Switzerland begs outdoor escapades with its larger-than-life canvas of hallucinatory landscapes.

Skiing and snowboard-
ing in the winter wonderlands of Graubünden, Bernese
Oberland and Central Switzerland are obvious choices. Or
you can hop an engineering marvel of a train and travel to
the crevassed ice on Jungfraujoch (3454m), at what seems
like the top of the world. But there is also plenty to do when
pastures are green. Hiking and biking trails abound in both
glacier-encrusted mountain areas and lower down along
lost valleys, mythical lakeshores and pea-green vines.

The perfect antidote to this rich Alpine land is a surprise set of cities.

There's the
capital Bern, with its Old Town and world-class modern
art; Germanic Basel and its bold architecture; shopping-
chic Geneva astraddle Europe's largest lake; and ubercool
Zürich with its rooftop bars and atypical Swiss street grit.

Smaller but equally beguiling are Lucerne, St Gallen, Chur and Lausanne.

Here medieval wooden structures complement ancient
stones, and old towns beg exploration. You may be
charmed by a castle or simply a scrumptious slice of cake.
Either way, Switzerland never fails to reward.

> **"** This
> small,
> landlocked
> country
> is so darn
> easy to step
> into and
> experience **"**

The fairytale Château de Chillon (p87) on Lake Geneva
PHOTOGRAPHER: ANDY CHRISTIANI / GETTY IMAGES ©

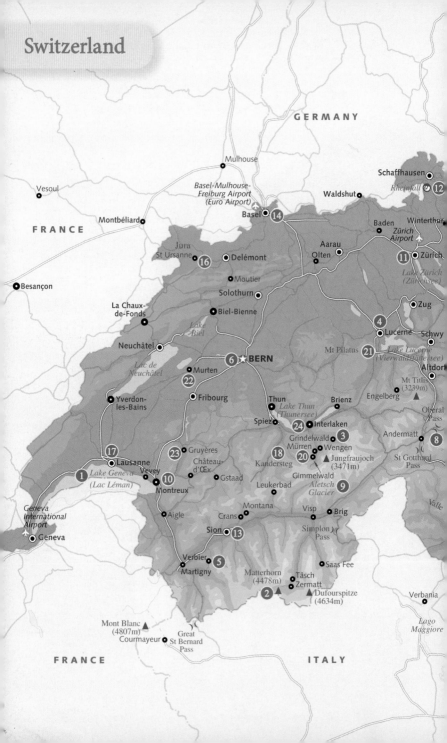

Switzerland

GERMANY

FRANCE

ITALY

Vesoul

Montbéliard

Besançon

Mulhouse

Basel-Mulhouse-
Freiburg Airport
(Euro Airport)

Basel 14

Delémont 16

Jura
St Ursanne

Moutier

Solothurn

Biel-Bienne

La Chaux-
de-Fonds

Neuchâtel

Lac de
Neuchâtel

Lake
Biel

Yverdon-
les-Bains

Murten 22

BERN 6

Fribourg

Aarau
Olten

Baden

Waldshut

Schaffhausen 12

Rheinfall

Winterthur

Zürich
Airport

Zürich 11

Lake Zürich
(Zürichsee)

Zug

Schwy

Lucerne 4

Mt Pilatus 21

Lake Lucerne
(Vierwaldstättersee)

Altdorf

Mt Titlis
(3239m)

Engelberg

Oberal
Pass

Andermatt 8

St Gotthard
Pass

Lausanne 17

Vevey

Montreux 10

Aigle

Geneva
International
Airport

Geneva

Lake Geneva
(Lac Léman) 1

Gruyères 23

Château-
d'Œx

Gstaad

Thun

Spiez

Lake Thun
(Thunersee)

Brienz

Interlaken 24

Grindelwald 3

Mürren

Wengen

Gimmelwald

Aletsch
Glacier 9

Jungfraujoch
(3471m) 20

Kandersteg 18

Leukerbad

Montana

Crans

Sion 13

Verbier 5

Martigny

Mont Blanc
(4807m)

Courmayeur

Great
St Bernard
Pass

Matterhorn
(4478m) 2

Täsch
Zermatt

Dufourspitze
(4634m)

Saas Fee

Visp

Brig

Simplon
Pass

Valle

Verbania

Lago
Maggiore

25
Top Experiences

25 Switzerland's Top Experiences

Lake Geneva

The emerald vines marching uphill in perfect unison from the shores of Lake Geneva in Lavaux (p83) are staggering. But the urban viewpoint from which to admire Europe's largest lake is Geneva (p62), French-speaking Switzerland's most cosmopolitan city, where canary-yellow *mouettes* (seagulls) ferry locals across the water and Mont Blanc peeps in on the action. Strolling Old Town streets, savouring a vibrant cafe society and making the odd dash beneath its iconic pencil fountain is what life's about for the 180 nationalities living here.

1

Matterhorn

This charismatic peak has more pulling power than most; a precocious beauty who demands to be admired, ogled and repeatedly photographed at sunset, sunrise, in different seasons and from every last angle. There is no finer place to base yourself to explore the Matterhorn than Zermatt (p183), one of Europe's most-desirable Alpine resorts, in fashion with the skiing, climbing, hiking and hip hobnobbing set since the 19th century. Darling, you'll love it.

Grindelwald's Jungfrau Region

No trio is more immortalised in mountaineering legend than Switzerland's 'big three' – Eiger (Ogre), Mönch (Monk) and Jungfrau (Virgin) – peaks that soar to the sky above the gorgeous, traditional 19th-century resort of Grindelwald (p138). And whether you choose to schuss around on skis, shoot down Europe's longest toboggan run on the back of an old-fashioned sledge, bungee jump in the Gletscherschlucht or ride the train up to Europe's highest station at 3454m, your pulse will race. James Bond, eat your heart out.

The Best...
Mountain Vistas

EIGER, JUNGFRAU & MÖNCH
Hike from Grindelwald/ Wengen or ride the cable car or train to Kleine Scheidegg for dramatic close-ups of Switzerland's big trio. (p137)

ALETSCH GLACIER
A shimmering 23km-long glacier, best seen from Bettmerhorn. (p190)

SCHILTHORN
This 360-degree vista takes in 200 peaks stretching from Mt Titlis to Mont Blanc in France. (p148)

JUNGFRAUJOCH
An uplifting lookout to 4000m peaks, the Aletsch Glacier and as far as the Black Forest beyond. (p142)

The Best...
Serious Ski Runs

VERBIER
Almost vertical and pummelled with moguls; off-piste, some of Switzerland's best powder. (p179)

JUNGFRAU REGION
It just doesn't get better than Inferno, a 16km black run. (p149)

LAAX
Snowboarding mecca with Europe's smallest and largest half-pipes. (p244)

WENGEN
Aptly named black run 'Oh God' and legendary off-piste White Hare at the foot of the Eiger north face. (p145)

ST MORITZ
Spectacular and jaw-dropping glacier descents at 3000m. (p242)

4 Lakeside Lucerne

Medieval bridge strolling is the principal charm of this irresistible Romeo in Central Switzerland. Throw sparkling lake vistas, an alfresco cafe life, candy-coloured architecture and Victorian curiosities into the cooking pot and lakeside Lucerne (p155) could well be the start of a very beautiful love affair. The town under your belt, step back to savour the ensemble from a wider perspective: views across the lake of green hills, meadows and hidden lake resorts from atop Mt Pilatus (p161) or Mt Rigi (p163). Kapellbrücke (p155)

5 Skiing Verbier

Switzerland never looks better than on a crisp winter's day, when the Alpine heights and forests are blanketed in snow. Nowhere else in Europe has higher peaks or better views. Shaking up this snow-globe scene are the skiers, snowboarders, sledders, skaters, and snowshoers. There are plenty of ski resorts to choose from but Verbier (p179) combines the best of all: legendary powder, glitz, great nightlife and activities for every taste and budget.

Capital Bern

Medieval cobbled streets, arcaded boutiques, a dancing clock and 16th-century folk figures frolicking in fountains: Switzerland's capital, Bern (p102), does not fit the quintessential 'capital city' image. Indeed, few realise this small town *is* the capital, situated as it is in the flat, unassuming middle bit of the country. Yet its unexpectedness, cemented by the new millennium 'hills' of Renzo Piano's Zentrum Paul Klee (p102), is precisely its charm.

Hiking in the Swiss National Park

No country in Europe is more synonymous with magnificent and mighty hiking than Switzerland, and its high-altitude national park (p247), with eagle-dotted skies, is the place to do it. Follow trails through flower-strewn meadows to piercing blue lakes, knife-edge ravines, rocky outcrops and Alpine huts where shepherds make summertime cheese with cows' milk, fresh that morning from the bell-clad herd. Nature gone wild and on the rampage, this park provides a rare and privileged glimpse of Switzerland before the dawn of tourism.

Glacier Express to St Moritz

It's one of the world's most-mythical train rides, linking two of Switzerland's glitziest Alpine resorts. Hop aboard the iconic red train with floor-to-ceiling windows in Zermatt, and sit back and savour shot after cinematic shot of green peaks, glistening Alpine lakes, glacial ravines and other hallucinatory landscapes. Pulled by steam engine when it first puffed out of the station in 1930, the Glacier Express (p245) traverses 91 tunnels and 291 bridges on its journey to St Moritz (p242). The icing on the cake: lunch in the vintage restaurant car.

The Best...
Hikes

GLACIER HIKE
Be blown away by the frosty landscape surrounding the Aletsch Glacier. (p190)

CASTLE HIKE
Follow the Chemin Fleuri (Flower Path) 4km from Montreux to lakeside Château de Chillon. (p87)

VINEYARD WALK
The Bisse de Clavau walk through the vine-strewn Rhône Valley is especially beautiful on a golden September day. (p182)

ALPS CLOSE-UPS
Walk downhill from Kleine Scheidegg to Wengen. (p138)

Aletsch Glacier

One of the world's natural marvels, this mesmerising glacier (p190) of gargantuan proportions in the Upper Valais is like a 23km-long, five-lane highway powering between mountain peaks at altitude. Its ice is glacial-blue and 900m thick at its deepest point. The view of Aletsch from Jungfraujoch will make your heart sing, but for the hardcore adrenalin surge, nothing beats getting up close: hike between crevasses with a mountain guide from Riederalp, or ski above it on snowy pistes in Bettmeralp.

The Best...
Castles & Abbeys

CHILLON
Follow the Flower Path from Montreux to this huge stone castle on Lake Geneva's shore. (p87)

THUN
No *schloss* (castle) in Germanic Switzerland is as fairy tale as Thun's red-turreted beauty. (p148)

ST GALLEN
This grand abbey safeguards an extraordinary rococo library. (p223)

BELLINZONA
Unesco-listed trio of medieval castles in Italianate Ticino. (p253)

SION
Bewitching pair of 13th-century chateaux on rocky outcrops above vines. (p181)

Romance in Montreux

10

As if one of the world's most-legendary jazz festivals (p88) with open-air concerts on the shore of Lake Geneva is not enough, Montreux has a castle to add to the French-style romance. From the well-known lakeside town with a climate so mild that palm trees grow, a flower-framed footpath follows the water south to Château de Chillon (p87). Historic, sumptuous and among Switzerland's oldest, this magnificent stone château built by the Savoys in the 13th century is everything a castle should be.

Zürich Lifestyle

One of Europe's most liveable cities, Zürich (p204), in German-speaking Switzerland, is an ode to urban renovation. It's also hip (yes, this is where Google employees shoot down a slide to lunch). With enough of a rough edge to resemble Berlin at times, Zürich is all about drinking in waterfront bars, dancing until dawn in Züri-West (p211), shopping for recycled fashion accessories in Kreis 5 and boogying with the best of them at Europe's largest street party, the city's wild and wacky, larger-than-life Street Parade (p43) in August.

LOOK DIE BILDAGENTUR DER FOTOGRAFEN GMBH / ALAMY ©

Splash of the Rheinfall

So moved were Goethe and Lord Byron by the wispy waterfalls of Staubbach Falls, fairytale threads of spray ensnaring the cliffside in Lauterbrunnen, that they composed poems exalting their ethereal beauty. Yet it is the theatrical, crash-bang-wallop splash of the thunderous Rheinfall (p220), guarded by a twin set of medieval castles, in northeastern Switzerland that really takes your breath away.

Sion & Valaisian Wine

Swiss vintages aren't plentiful outside Switzerland, making their tasting and discovery a joyous experience. Gentle walking trails tread through steeply terraced vineyards in Valais, producer of the country's best wines, and many *vignerons* (winegrowers) open their doors for tasting and buying. Pair a vineyard walk near Sion (p181) with the region's autumnal *brisolée*, the traditional feast built around local chestnuts, cheese, cold meats and *vin nouveau*.

GÜNTER GRÄFENHAIN / 4CORNERS ©

Art & Architecture in Basel

Contemporary architecture of world-class standing is Basel's golden ticket – seven winners of the Pritzker Prize have a living design in or around this city, which sits plump on the Rhine. Kick off with a hop across the German border to the Vitra Design Museum, designed by architect Frank Gehry; and devote the rest of the day to Switzerland's best private collection of modern art in a long, light-flooded building by Renzo Piano – the dream fusion of art and architecture at Fondation Beyeler (p107).

Vitra Design Museum

14

The Best...
Art Museums

KUNSTHAUS
As you'd expect, Zürich's main art gallery has a vast collection of masterpieces. (p207)

SAMMLUNG OSKAR REINHART AM RÖMERHOLZ
Combines a grand collection of old masters with big modern names in Winterthur. (p215)

FONDATION PIERRE GIANADDA
The star of Martigny has Picasso, Cézanne et al. (p178)

FONDATION BEYELER
Switzerland's best collection of contemporary art is in Basel. (p107)

ZENTRUM PAUL KLEE
Bern's answer to the Guggenheim. (p102)

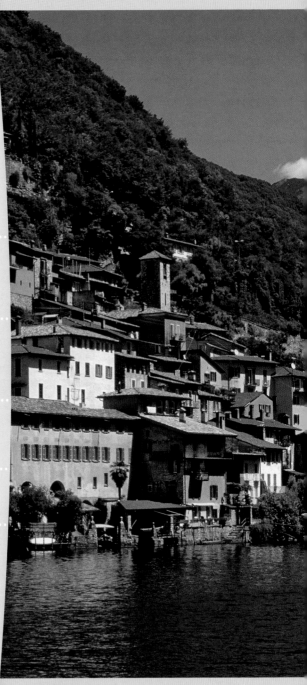

The Best...
Lakes

LAKE GENEVA
This vast body of water has boats linking oodles of cute towns and cities. (p73)

LAKE LUCERNE
The medieval city's front yard is this stunning lake surrounded by green hillsides. (p161)

LAKE ZÜRICH
Beautiful Lake Zürich saves the city from being a big sprawl. (p204)

LAGO DI LUGANO
A sinuous lake in the sun-drenched south. (p259)

LAKE THUN
Along with Lake Brienz, this startlingly turquoise lake provides a dramatic entrance to Interlaken. (p148)

Lago di Lugano

An intrinsic part of Switzerland's unique charm is its mixed bag of languages and cultures. And no spot on Swiss earth exalts the country's Italianate soul with such gusto as Lago di Lugano (p259) in Ticino, a shimmering Alpine lake fringed with palm-tree promenades and pretty-girl villages of delicate pastel hues. Lugano (p255), the biggest town on the lake and the country's third-largest affluent banking centre to boot, is vivacious and busy with porticoed alleys, cafe-packed piazzas and boats yo-yoing to other places on the lake.

ABOVE: JAN GREUNE / GETTY IMAGES © LEFT: GLENN VAN DER KNIJFF / GETTY IMAGES ©

Rural Jura's St Ursanne

Tiptoe off the tourist map and into clover-shaped Jura, a fascinating backwater on the French–Swiss border woven from thick dark forests, gentle rolling hills, medieval villages and a go-slow vibe. No piece of scenery is too large, too high or too racy here. Rather, travel in the rural Jura is an exquisite sensory experience, and nowhere is this more true than in its most evocative village, St Ursanne (p117), which has a 16th-century town square and a great Gothic church.

SIEGFRIED EIGSTLER / 4CORNERS ©

Lausanne

To this day the night watch scales the bell tower inside the Gothic cathedral in Lausanne (p74) to call out the hour. This hilly place in the heart of the Lake Geneva wine country has an Old Town dominated by a great cathedral. Narrow lanes meander up and down the hills and where bridges cross over streets, summertime bars let you imbibe under massive stone arches. Down on the waterfront is one of Lake Geneva's prettiest promenades. Visit via train or lake steamer.

Vie Ferrate in Kandersteg

Anyone who fancies mountaineering but with the security of being attached to the rock face should clip onto a *via ferrata* (Klettersteig in German). Though safer and easier for beginners than climbing, these vertigo-inducing fixed-cable traverses involving ladders, zip-lines and tightrope-style bridges aren't for the faint-hearted. This hiking and climbing hybrid is all the rage in Switzerland and you can try it at resorts throughout the Alps, but for real knuckle-whitening stuff, clamp on to the one in Kandersteg (p150). Climbing in Kandersteg

18

The Best...
Hotels

HÔTEL BEL'ESPERANCE
A rooftop terrace only adds to the charms of this simple gem. (p68)

HÔTEL BEAU-RIVAGE PALACE
Easily the most stunningly located hotel in Lausanne, this luxury lakeside address is suitably sumptuous. (p77)

HOTEL SCHWEIZERHOF
A top five-star option in Bern. (p104)

GLETSCHERGARTEN
A rustic timber chalet in beautiful Grindelwald. (p139)

GASTHAUS BARGIS
Quaint dark-wood chalet in Klosters dating to the 18th century. (p250)

St Gallen

What a feast: St Gallen (p221) has an extraordinary rococo library that is a top Unesco site, a zany red square to chill in and taverns in half-timbered houses – all rooted in a deeply Germanic, rural world. As a bonus it has a fine Alps setting that gives you a panoply of peaks from which to choose, either for mere gazing or surmounting, or some sort of hike in between. At night you can get cosy in a traditional Swiss restaurant and let the cheese work its magic. Stiftsbibliothek (p223)

STUART DEE / ROBERT HARDING ©

The Best...
Family Travel

VERKEHRSHAUS
Fly a plane or travel to the moon at Lucerne's Transport Museum. (p157)

ZENTRUM PAUL KLEE
Interactive art exhibits and workshops in Bern. (p102)

ALIMENTARIUM
Fun cookery workshops at Nestlé's Vevey home. (p85)

GSTAAD
Loop-the-loop Alpine Coaster, husky rides and guided llama and goat hikes. (p152)

GRINDELWALD
Summer scooter trail, gentle walks and ski pistes for every age and ability. (p138)

(20) Mürren & Gimmelwald

Heidi may be fictional, but her Alpine village lifestyle isn't. Switzerland will meet all your storybook fantasies: the hilltop hamlets in the Bernese Oberland offer cowbells as your wake-up call, and when it turns crisp at night, you can snuggle by a crackling fire. Sound idyllic? You bet. Mürren (p147) has scenery, skiing and hiking to make your heart sing. Pick a log chalet for dress-circle views of the Eiger, Mönch and Jungfrau. To be at one with nature, tiptoe away from the crowds to cute-as-a-button Gimmelwald (p147) nearby.

Mürren (p147)

FERGUS KENNEDY / GETTY IMAGES ©

Mt Pilatus Circle

This is one of Switzerland's great day trips. At 2132m, Mt Pilatus (p161) not only has good views but it lets you enjoy almost every form of transport the country offers. Leave Lucerne by steamer and glide across the namesake lake to the village of Alpnachstad. Here you catch a cog railway to the summit. Catch sweeping views through the trees as the train's gears grind away pulling you up the steepest railway of its kind in the world. Heading back, take a cable car and a bus. Fun!

Murten

Once upon a time villages across Europe were encircled by walls to keep out marauding bands looking to loot, pillage and worse. Almost every town tore down its walls by the 19th century with very few exceptions. An easy day trip from Bern, Murten (p112) is just such a town. Its medieval walls still encircle its handful of streets and you can romp from one tower to the next, imagining the night watch on guard for invaders. It's the perfect castle fantasy.

Fondue in Gruyères

Why not enjoy one of Switzerland's favourite meals right at the source of its main ingredient, Gruyère cheese? The village of Gruyères (p114; it carries an 's', the cheese doesn't) is an appealing place in its own right, with houses hundreds of years old tumbling down the side of a mountain to a classic cobblestoned heart. You can visit local cheese factories to enjoy tastes of the savoury, nutty cheese and then choose the perfect spot for a classic pot of oozing, luxurious fondue.

23

The Best...
Swiss Restaurants

MICHEL'S STALLBEIZLI
Dining doesn't get more back-to-nature than at this converted barn in luxe Gstaad. (p154)

WIRTSHAUS GALLIKER
An old-style tavern dating to 1856. (p159)

LE NAMASTÉ
This cosy mountain cabin is always packed. (p180)

ALPENROSE
Fine cuisine from regions all over the country. (p209)

BÄUMLI
Timeless eatery that showcases all the typical specialities. (p224)

Interlaken Adventures

With the heart of the Alps a beckoning vista and two lakes serving as watery bookends, Interlaken (p132) may be the sportiest place in a very sporty country. Adventure guides and outfitters seem as common as majestic vistas. What's your fancy? Pulse-stirring options include white-water rafting, canyoning, paragliding, ice climbing, mountain climbing, hikes of every theme and difficulty, skiing, snowboarding – and the list just goes on. Chances are someone has thought of an adventure for you that you haven't thought of yet.

The Best...
Chocolate

ST GALLEN
Hot chocolate, pralines and truffles to die for at Chocolaterie. (p224)

LUGANO
A spin through the history of chocolate and tastings at the Museo del Cioccolato Alprose. (p257)

BROC
Watch Swiss chocolate being made at the Cailler chocolate factory. (p114)

FRIBOURG
Villars chocolate at factory prices and creamy hot chocolate with chocolate shavings. (p114)

ZÜRICH
Café Sprüngli, epicentre of sweet Switzerland, in business since 1836. (p209)

Lake Constance

Serving as a liquid nexus between Switzerland, Germany and Austria, Central Europe's third largest lake, Lake Constance (p221), is an ideal way to connect all three of these closely linked cultures. A network of boats criss-cross its usually smooth waters. You can hop from one town – and country – to the next (and there's a lot of good ones to hop to) or you can settle back up on deck and enjoy sweeping Alpine views reflected on the cool, blue waters. Best perhaps is some combination of the two.

Switzerland's Top Itineraries

Zürich to Lucerne
Classic
Switzerland

5 DAYS

Short on time? Spend two days exploring Switzerland's main city and then two in beautiful Lucerne, many people's favourite Swiss city. That saves you time for a return day trip from Lucerne, which includes fun boat and train trips and a taste of the Alps.

ZÜRICH ①

Lake Zürich

LUCERNE ②   Lake Lucerne

③

MT PILATUS (2132M)

SWITZERLAND

① Zürich (p204)

Start with the city's must-see sights. The 13th-century **Fraumünster** is a Zürich landmark with a modern touch: stained-glass windows by Marc Chagall. Wander the heart of the **old town**, noticing the stolid Swiss banks hiding their secrets, and amble along the **lakefront**, with distant mountains hinting at things to come. On day two stop into the **Kunsthaus**, which has an unsurpassed collection of masterpieces; bone up on a little bit of the nation's fascinating history at the **Schweizerisches Landesmuseum**. Along the way, enjoy fine coffee at **cafes** and hearty Swiss fare in any of many **restaurants**.

ZÜRICH ⟶ LUCERNE

🚆 **One scenic hour** From Zürich's Hauptbahnhof to Lucerne's Hauptbahnhof. 🚗 **One hour** Depending on traffic on the A4 and A14.

② Lucerne (p155)

A swan gliding past the **Kapellbrücke**, Lucerne's iconic wooden bridge, is likely to be one of your first impressions of this beautiful city, which sits right on its

namesake lake. As you walk though the old town, you'll find a good mix of urban buzz and historic charm. Pause for a glimpse of the **Lion Monument**, which moved 19th-century visitors including Mark Twain. On your second day, stroll the lakefront with its posh cafes and sweeping views. After an easy 3km you'll find the **Verkehrshaus**, the most popular museum in Switzerland. Thrill to learn all the ways the Swiss have cleverly knitted their Alp-covered country with trains, cable cars, boats and more.

LUCERNE ⟶ MT PILATUS

This is a circular day trip that combines many forms of transport; see p161 for details.

③ Mt Pilatus (p161)

A lake boat, the world's steepest cog railway and a cable car are all part of this day trip that takes you from Lucerne to the 2132m peak of **Mt Pilatus** and back again in one fun circular route. From the summit, you'll see the Alps and Lake Lucerne spread out around and below you. There are many good well-marked short hikes from the top.

Views over Zürich (p204)
PHOTOGRAPHER: TIBOR BOGNAR / ALAMY ©

Zermatt to St Moritz
The Glacier Express

This mythical 290km train journey has been a traveller-must ever since the birth of winter tourism in the Alps. Do it any time of year – in one glorious 7½-hour stretch or as several sweet nuggets interspersed with overnights in Switzerland's most glamorous Alpine mountain resorts.

AUSTRIA

LIECHTENSTEIN

SWITZERLAND

CHUR ③ DAVOS ④

BETTMERALP ②

ST MORITZ ④

ZERMATT ①

ITALY

1 Zermatt (p183)

The looming Matterhorn almost seems to wave farewell as you head off on your great railway adventure from **Zermatt**, the ski and holiday town at its base. From here, the narrow-gauge railway winds north down the valley to **Visp** and **Brig**. Both are important crossroads and have been for centuries.

From here, the train swings northeast along the pretty eastern stretch of the Rhône Valley through attractive villages such as **Betten** and **Fiesch**.

2 Bettmeralp (p190)

Hop off in Betten and catch a cable car up to car-free village **Bettmeralp**, where you can spend the night and enjoy a beguiling Alpine town that has activities for visitors winter and summer. From here you can go onwards up to **Bettmerhorn** or **Eggishorn** via cable cars for a look at the Unesco-listed **Aletsch Glacier**. This ribbon of ice stretches all the way back 23km to the Jungfrau region.

Back in the valley on the Glacier Express, the train trundles towards the **Furka Pass** (which it circumvents by tunnel) and descends on the new mega ski resort of **Andermatt**. In winter you can stop here and hit the slopes with their ultra-modern facilities.

3 Chur (p248)

Heading towards Chur, the stretch of tracks that climbs up and through the **Oberalp Pass** (2033m) is the literal high point of the Glacier Express journey. Expect everybody in the cars to be snapping pics like mad. From here it meanders alongside the Vorderrhein River, through Disentis/Mustér to **Chur**, where the train splits for its dual end points (St Moritz and Davos). Chur has a charmer of an old town – Switzerland's oldest – and is a good overnight stop to wander around, have a fine meal and possibly go for an Alpine meadow hike the next day.

4 St Moritz (p242) or Davos (p251)

The glamour of Switzerland's original ski resort is a suitable finish for such a famous journey. In winter you can join the famous on the **St Moritz** powder. In summer you can hike the surrounding Alps. The alternative end point for the Glacier Express, **Davos** is a modern and vibrant resort town.

ZERMATT ➋ ST MORITZ/DAVOS

🚃 In one go, the Glacier Express takes 7½ hours from Zermatt to St Moritz or Davos (the train splits), but you can do it in little nibbles and easily take five days by overnighting at some of the great little towns on the way.

Scenic Switzerland
PHOTOGRAPHER: CHRIS PARKER / GETTY IMAGES ©

Basel to Wengen
Reaching Ever Higher

Start at Basel, the nexus for France, Germany and Switzerland. From the banks of the Rhine, travel through rolling hills to Bern, then cut across to lovely Lucerne, heading ever more upwards. Finally make the big climb to Grindewald and eye- and ear-popping Wengen.

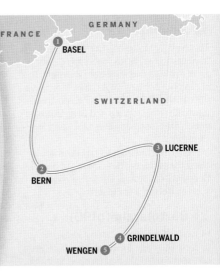

1 Basel (p107)

Basel mixes ancient architecture with cutting-edge design. It has a commanding position on the banks of the Rhine and its train station is linked by fast trains to Paris, Frankfurt and beyond. You can spend a full day here wandering. If you drive to Bern, stop at **Augusta Raurica**, an ancient Roman town.

BASEL ⟶ BERN

🚆 **70 minutes** From Basel's main station to Bern's main station. 🚗 **Two hours** On the A1.

2 Bern (p102)

Albert Einstein worked as a bureaucrat here at the dawn of the 20th century, but he was obviously bored as his mind turned to solving the mysteries of the universe. While you may not find the same sort of inspiration in **Bern**, you'll likely find yourself lingering for at least a day in ancient **arcades** and fine **museums**.

BERN ⟶ LUCERNE

🚆 **One hour** From Bern's main station to Lucerne's main station. 🚗 **1¾ hours** On the scenic Route 10.

3 Lucerne (p155)

Often topping polls ranking Switzerland's favourite cities, **Lucerne** combines its too-beautiful-for-words lakeside location with some urban charms. Museums

include the wildly popular **Verkehrshaus**, which explores all the ways the Swiss have knitted their country together, the Alps notwithstanding. The old town has fine restaurants or you can pick from the many **lakeside cafes**.

LUCERNE ⟶ GRINDELWALD

🚆 **2½ hours** From Lucerne's main station to Grindelwald. 🚗 **1½ hours** On the A8.

4 Grindelwald (p138)

Grindelwald is the kind of place where you can just let your feet choose a direction in the morning and it's bound to end well. Cable cars, trains and footpaths take you right up into the Alps where the **walking** is simply superb. You can let a couple of days drift by in a blur of beautiful scenery. When you move on to Wengen, the train goes via **Kleine Scheidegg**, where you can veer off for the fabled **Jungfraujoch** day trip.

GRINDELWALD ⟶ WENGEN

🚆 **One hour** From Grindelwald to Wengen via Kleine Scheidegg.

5 Wengen (p145)

Perfectly perched on a mountainside, **Wengen** has sweeping views across to Jungfrau and its siblings. Opportunities for **skiing** and **hiking** abound (depending on the season) but perhaps its greatest allure is sitting and soaking up one of the world's great views.

Basel's Rathaus (town hall; p111)
PHOTOGRAPHER: OWEN FRANKEN/CORBIS ©

10 DAYS

Montreux to Klosters
French and Italian Switzerland

Although much of Switzerland speaks German (64%), the French (19%) and Italian (8%) minorities are sizeable and have influence across the country. This tour takes in wine-growing regions, the Matterhorn, sunny Lugano and famous ski resorts.

GERMANY

FRANCE

AUSTRIA

LIECHTENSTEIN

SWITZERLAND

KLOSTERS 6

1 MONTREUX

2 SION

4 BELLINZONA

3 ZERMATT

▲ 5 LUGANO

MATTERHORN
(4478M)

ITALY

1 Montreux (p86)

Genteel **Montreux** brims with posh lakeside cafes where you can sample wines that come from the surrounding hillside vineyards. Go for a lakeside stroll to one of Switzerland's best castles, **Château de Chillon**. It's everything a kid of any age could hope for in the cool-fortification department. Get lost amidst the towers and courtyards, and learn its history.

MONTREUX ➲ SION

🚆 **45 minutes** From Montreux's main station to Sion's main station. 🚘 **One hour** Via the A9.

2 Sion (p181)

French Switzerland continues through this riverside town, which is surrounded by yet more **vineyards**. Take a day to go hiking among the grapes and indulge in some delicious tastings.

SION ➲ ZERMATT

🚆 **1½ hours** From Sion's main station to Visp (30 minutes), then change trains for Zermatt (one hour). 🚘 **1½ hours** Via the A9 to Visp (30 minutes), then transfer to the train for car-free Zermatt (one hour).

3 Zermatt (p183)

Even Walt Disney couldn't ignore the **Matterhorn**. And once you're in this quaint mountain resort, your gaze will be pulled ever-upwards to its sheer granite sides. There's plenty of winter skiing, but summer hikes past flower-strewn meadows and looming glaciers are tops. Back in **Zermatt**, enjoy nightlife more lively than your typical mountain hamlet.

ZERMATT ➲ BELLINZONA

Return by train to Visp. 🚆 **3¾ hours** From Visp to Bellinzona. 🚘 **Two hours** Via Route 19 and the A2.

4 Bellinzona (p253)

What could be more evocative than **three medieval stone castles** guarding this ancient city? Bellinzona has always been a gateway to Italy from the north, and even the squares are called piazzas thanks to the Italian heritage.

BELLINZONA ➲ LUGANO

🚆 **20 minutes** From Bellinzona main station to Lugano main station. 🚘 **30 minutes** Via the A2.

5 Lugano (p255)

Lugano is filled with surprises, especially on market days when food browsing is like going on a treasure hunt. But don't waste too much time ashore: head out onto **Lago di Lugano** for gentle boat trips amid beautiful mountain vistas.

LUGANO ➲ KLOSTERS

🚆 **Four hours** From Lugano main station to Klosters. 🚘 **2½ hours** Via the A13.

6 Klosters (p250)

One of the first Swiss winter resorts, **Klosters** has always held on to traditions that have hints of a Victorian past. Here you'll find yourself in German-speaking Switzerland. The skiing (here and at neighbouring **Davos**) is fab, and in summer those famed Swiss hiking paths spread out in all directions.

A lakeside view of Château de Chillon (p87)
PHOTOGRAPHER: MICHELE FALZONE / GETTY IMAGES ©

2 WEEKS

Geneva to St Gallen
Switzerland's Top Sights

Switzerland may be small but seeing the best it has to offer is truly a grand tour. Geneva, Bern, the heart of the Alps, fabulous Lucerne and Zürich are just some of the stops, and there are many options for day trips.

① Geneva (p62)

The international city of **Geneva** is a fine introduction to all that is genteel about Switzerland. Its old town beguiles and it has great dining thanks to all the diplomats stationed here. Head out for a lake cruise and gaze up France's **Mont Blanc**.

GENEVA ➡ LAUSANNE

🚃 **40 minutes** From Geneva's main station to Lausanne's main station. 🚗 **One hour** On the A1.

② Lausanne (p74)

From its beautiful lakeside location – you can get here by boat – **Lausanne** climbs the hills up to the main train station and beyond. Lanes wander hither and yon and **cafes** shelter under soaring arched stone bridges. Enjoy the famous **vineyard views**.

LAUSANNE ➡ BERN

🚃 **65 minutes** From Lausanne's main station to Bern's main station. 🚗 **1¼ hours** On the A1.

③ Bern (p102)

The Swiss capital harks back to the middle ages with old buildings spilling down to the river. **Museums** vie with a historic riverside park where bears roam. There are good day trips from here, including ancient walled **Murten** and the home of Switzerland's best cheese: **Gruyères**.

BERN ➡ INTERLAKEN

🚃 **One hour** From Bern's main station to Interlaken Ost station. 🚗 **One hour** On the A6.

④ Interlaken (p132)

The adventure capital of Switzerland, **Interlaken** is beautifully surrounded by lakes. But it's easy to quickly be drawn to towns and villages that dot the sides of the **magnificent Alps** stretching out before you. Names like **Grindelwald**, **Wengen** and **Mürren** are the stuff of summer and winter legends.

INTERLAKEN ➡ JUNGFRAUJOCH

🚃 **2¼ hours** From Interlaken Ost station to the top of Jungfraujoch. The return takes the same amount of time.

Stunning views over the French border to Mont Blanc
PHOTOGRAPHER: MENNO BOERMANS / GETTY IMAGES ©

⑥ Lucerne (p155)

Old medieval **wooden bridges** link the old town of this fabled city of cuteness. Wander the lakefront for lovely views and take in plenty of attractions along the way. If you have time there are more Alpine day trips here (such as **Mt Pilatus** and **Mt Titlis**).

LUCERNE ➡ ZÜRICH

🚊 **One hour** From Lucerne's main station to Zürich's main station. 🚗 **One hour** Depending on traffic on the A4 and A14.

⑦ Zürich (p204)

Another place that makes full use of its namesake lake, the largest city in Switzerland combines conservative tradition with cutting-edge fun. In summer, swim in the lake from one of many **lakeside cafes** and **clubs** or head to trendy districts and watch movies outside. At any time you can get lost in the city's excellent **museums**.

ZÜRICH ➡ ST GALLEN

🚊 **One hour** From Zürich's main station to St Gallen's main station. 🚗 **One hour** On the A1.

⑧ St Gallen (p221)

Step back to the past at this town set among the Alps, which boasts the remarkable and Unesco-recognised **Stiftsbibliothek**.

⑤ Jungfraujoch (p142)

One of the world's great journeys takes three trains from Interlaken, each surmounting tracks more precipitous than the last. You start in a beautiful river valley to **Lauterbrunnen** and then change trains for a ride filled with views to the Alpine outpost of **Kleine Scheidegg**. A final switch and you are on a train that bores up through the mountain to the summit of **Jungfraujoch**. Once at the top, you won't be able to get enough of the **Alpine wonderland views** (although you'll need to return to Interlaken before the last trains.)

INTERLAKEN ➡ LUCERNE

🚊 **Two hours** From Interlaken Ost station to Lucerne's main station. 🚗 **One hour** On the A8 and Route 4.

Switzerland Month by Month

Top Events

⭐ **Lucerne Festival,** April

⭐ **Montreux Jazz,** July

❄️ **Swiss National Day,** 1 August

❄️ **Zürich Street Parade,** August

🍴 **L'Escalade,** December

January

🏃 **Cartier Polo World Cup**

Upper-crust St Moritz is the chic venue for this four-day event that sees world-class polo players saddle up and battle it out on a frozen lake. Buy tickets online (www.polomoritz.com), dress up and don't forget your shades.

❄️ **Harder Potschete**

What a devilish day it is on 2 January in Interlaken when warty ogre-like *Potschen* run around town causing folkloric mischief. The party ends on a high with cockle-warming drinks, upbeat folk music and fiendish merrymaking.

❄️ **Vogel Gryff**

Another old folkloric celebration, this street party sees a larger-than-life savage, griffin and lion chase away winter in Basel with a drum dance on a city bridge.

February

❄️ **Carnival**

Never dare call the Swiss goody two-shoes again: pre-Lenten parades, costumes, music and all the fun of the fair sweep through Catholic cantons during *Fasnacht* (carnival). Catch the party – stark raving bonkers – in Lucerne or Basel.

March

🏃 **Engadine Ski Marathon**

Watching 11,000 cross-country skiers warming up to the rousing sound of *Chariots of Fire* is unforgettable – as is, no doubt, the iconic 42km cross-country ski marathon for the athletes who ski across frozen lakes and through

Cartier Polo World Cup, St Moritz

pine forests and picture-perfect snow scenes in the Engadine.

mer music fests. Nyon in late July is the date to put in the diary.

April

✪ Sechseläuten

Winter's end is celebrated in Zürich on the third Monday of the month with costumed street parades and the burning of a firework-filled 'snowman', aka the terrifying *Böögg*. Be prepared to be scared.

☆ Lucerne Festival

Easter ushers in this world-class music festival with chamber orchestras, pianists and other musicians from all corners of the globe performing in Lucerne. True devotees of the festival can return in summer and November.

June

☆ St Galler Festspiele

It's apt that Switzerland's 'writing room of Europe', aka St Gallen, should play host to this wonderful two-week opera season. The curtain rises in late June with performances spilling into July.

July

☆ Montreux Jazz

A fortnight of jazz, pop and rock in early July is reason enough to slot elegant Montreux into your itinerary. Some concerts are free, some ticketed, and dozens are staged alfresco with lake views from heaven.

☆ Paléo Festival

Another Lake Geneva goodie, this six-day open-air world-music extravaganza – a 1970s child – is billed as the king of sum-

August

✪ Swiss National Day

Fireworks light up lakes, mountains, towns and cities countrywide on this national holiday celebrating Switzerland's very creation.

✪ Sertig Schwinget

This high-entertainment festival in Davos sees thickset men with invariably large tummies battle it out in sawdust for the title of *Schwingen* (Swiss Alpine wrestling) champion.

✪ Street Parade

Mid-August brings with it Europe's largest street party in the form of Zürich's famous Street Parade, established in 1992.

October

✪ Foire du Valais

Cows battle for the title of bovine queen on the last day of the cow-fighting season at this 10-day regional fair in Martigny in the lower Valais. Everyone rocks up for it, a great excuse to drink and feast.

December

✕ L'Escalade

Torch-lit processions in the Old Town, fires, a run around town for kids and adults alike and some serious chocolate-cauldron smashing and scoffing make Geneva's biggest festival on 11 December a riot of fun.

What's New

For this new edition of Discover Switzerland, our authors have hunted down the fresh, the revamped, the hot and the happening. These are some of our favourites. For up-to-the-minute recommendations, see lonelyplanet.com/switzerland.

1 CITY BEACH
Zürich's City Beach (p211), a trendy rooftop beach in the Kreis 5 district, features 500 tons of sand, swimming pools and a bar on the roof of a city car park.

2 COW TREKKING
Riding at cow pace through bucolic countryside is hot in northeastern Switzerland thanks to one farmer's experiential approach to organic dairy farming. Saddle, riding crop and optional picnic provided. Bolderhof (☎ 052 742 40 48; www.bolderhof.ch) in Hemishofen, 3km west of Stein am Rhein.

3 RIGI KALTBAD
Ticino architect Mario Botta will knock your socks off with his latest Swiss work, these stunning mineral baths and spa with designer views of Lake Lucerne from their Mt Rigi lookout (p163).

4 LAVAUX VINORAMA
Pea-green vines cascading into Lake Geneva are a magnificent sight and Lavaux's latest wine-tasting address, cut out of concrete beneath vineyards, adds a new dimension to visiting the Unesco-listed wine region (p84).

5 ICE WORLD
Why glacial ice is blue, what asexual glacial fleas do, how fast glacial ice moves: the new Eiswelt exhibition above the Aletsch Glacier on Bettmerhorn (2856m) is absolutely riveting (admission free; ☺ 9am-4pm Jun–mid-Oct & Dec-Apr).

6 URBAN TAPAS
It's not a patch on Spanish tapas, but a dozen different 'tapas' is what Geneva bars chalk on the blackboard these days – dining on the cheap in one of Europe's priciest cities. Yvette de Marseille (Rue Henri Blanvalet 13, Geneva; ☺ 11am-late Tue-Fri, from 5pm Sat).

7 FLOATING OLYMPIC MUSEUM
Part of Lausanne's Olympic Museum, the most-visited *musée* in Suisse Romande (French-speaking Switzerland) is afloat in a belle époque steamer moored in front of the lakeside mansion (p75).

Get Inspired

📖 Books

○ **Green Henry** (Gottfried Keller, 1854) A massive tome revolving around a Zürich student's reminiscences is considered one of the masterpieces of Germanic literature.

🎬 Films

○ **Heidi** The 1937 version with Shirley Temple is considered the definitive cliché, although there are versions from 1954 (also a favourite), 1968, 1993 and 2005.

○ **James Bond** Several 007 movies have been filmed at least partially in Switzerland. *Goldfinger* (1964) is an early example, followed a short time later by *On Her Majesty's Secret Service* (1969), which memorably uses Schilthorn in the Jungfrau region.

🎵 Music

○ **Monday's Ghost** (2008) and **1983** (2010) are popular folk ballads featuring the fragile voice of Bern-born singer Sophie Hunger (www. sophiehunger.com) who flips between English,

German and Swiss German.

○ **Alpenhorn** This pastoral wind instrument, used to herd cattle in the mountains, is 2m to 4m long with a curved base and a cup-shaped mouthpiece. The shorter the horn, the harder it is to play. Catch a symphony of a hundred-odd alpenhorn players blowing in unison on the 'stage' – usually alfresco and invariably lakeside between mountain peaks – and you'll be won over forever.

○ **Stress** Switzerland's hottest hip-hop artist, known for his occasional political and controversial lyrics.

🖱 Websites

○ **SBB CFF FFS** (www. sbb.ch) The Swiss railways official site.

○ **Switzerland Travel Centre** (www. swisstravelsystems.ch) Transport info, including travel passes.

○ **Swiss Info** (www. swissinfo.ch) Swiss news and current affairs.

○ **Swiss World** (www. swissworld.org) People,

culture, lifestyle and the environment.

○ **Lonely Planet** (www. lonelyplanet.com/ switzerland) Information, hotel bookings, traveller forum.

🕐 Short on time?

This list will give you an instant insight into the country.

Read *Heidi* by Johanna Spyri. The most-famous Swiss novel is about an orphan living with her grandfather in the Swiss Alps who is ripped away to the city.

Listen Yodelling is a traditional form of Swiss 'music' that began in the Alps as a means of communication between peaks.

Log on www.myswitzerland. com is the main website for Swiss tourism.

Restaurant at the top of Schilthorn (p148)
PHOTOGRAPHER: MICHELE FALZONE / AWL ©

Need to Know

Currency
Swiss franc (in this book Sfr)

Languages
German, French, Italian, Romansch

ATMs
ATMs at every airport, most train stations and every second street corner.

Credit Cards
Visa, MasterCard and Amex widely accepted.

Visas
Not needed with passports from the EU, Iceland, Norway, USA, Canada, Australia or New Zealand.

Mobile Phones
European and Australian phones work. Use a Swiss SIM card for cheaper calls.

Wi-Fi
Wi-Fi is widely available at most accommodation, train stations (pay) and cafes.

Internet Access
Smartphones and wi-fi have closed many internet cafes.

Driving
Drive on right; steering wheel is on left side of car.

Tipping
At sit-down restaurants round up your bill by 5% to 10%.

When to Go

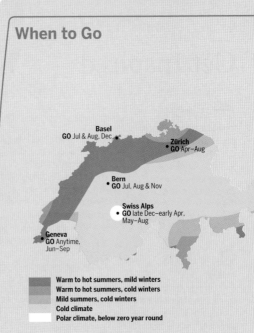

Basel
GO Jul & Aug, Dec

Zürich
GO Apr–Aug

Bern
GO Jul, Aug & Nov

Swiss Alps
GO late Dec–early Apr, May–Aug

Geneva
GO Anytime, Jun–Sep

Warm to hot summers, mild winters
Warm to hot summers, cold winters
Mild summers, cold winters
Cold climate
Polar climate, below zero year round

High Season
(Jul & Aug, Dec–Apr)
o In July and August, walkers and cyclists hit high-altitude trails.
o Christmas and New Year see lots of ski activity.
o Late December to early April is high season in ski resorts.

Shoulder
(Apr–Jun & Sep)
o Look for deals in ski resorts and traveller hotspots.
o Spring is idyllic with warm temperatures, flowers and local produce.
o Watch the grape harvest in autumn.

Low Season
(Oct–Mar)
o Mountain resorts go into snooze mode from mid-October to early December.
o Prices are up to 50% less than in high season.
o Sights and restaurants are open fewer days and shorter hours.

Advance Planning
o **Six months before** Reserve ski-resort accommodation if you're visiting during holidays.
o **Three months before** Reserve your accommodation in popular summer destinations such as Lucerne and the Jungfrau region.
o **One month before** For summer travel, reserve your seats on the Glacier Express.
o **One week before** Ponder the weather, whether walking in summer or skiing in winter.

Your Daily Budget

Budget less than Sfr200
o Dorm bed: Sfr30–60
o Free admission to some museums first Saturday or Sunday of every month
o Lunch out (Sfr15–30) and self-cater after dark

Midrange Sfr200–300
o Double room in two- or three-star hotel: Sfr150–350
o Dish of the day *(tagesteller, plat du jour, piatto del giorno)* or fixed two-course menu: Sfr40–70

Top End more than Sfr300
o Double room in four- or five-star hotel: from Sfr350
o Lower rates Friday to Sunday in city business hotels
o Three-course dinner in an upmarket restaurant: from Sfr100

Exchange Rates

Australia	A$1	Sfr1.03
Canada	C$1	Sfr0.98
Europe	€1	Sfr1.20
Japan	¥100	Sfr1.24
New Zealand	NZ$1	Sfr0.79
UK	UK£1	Sfr1.52
US	US$1	Sfr0.97

For current exchange rates see www.xe.com.

Important Numbers

Swiss telephone numbers start with an area code that must be dialled every time, even when making local calls.
o **Switzerland country code** ☎41
o **International access code** ☎00
o **Ambulance** ☎144
o **Police** ☎117
o **Swiss Mountain Rescue** ☎1414

What to Bring

o **Sunglasses and hat** Needed year-round; all that snow makes for sharp glare.
o **Sturdy walking shoes** Should be comfortable, broken in and at least water-resistant.
o **Warm socks** Needed for summer Alpine hikes.
o **Jacket** Even in summer, glaciers are cold.
o **Sweet tooth** A love of cheese helps too.

Arriving in Switzerland

o Zürich Airport
SBB trains – Up to nine hourly to Hauptbahnhof from 6am to midnight.

Taxis – Around Sfr60 to the centre.

Coaches – During winter ski season, to Davos and other key resorts.

o Geneva Airport
SBB trains – At least every 10 minutes to Gare de Cornavin.

Taxis – Sfr30–50 to the centre.

Coaches & minibuses – In winter to Verbier, Saas Fee, Crans-Montana and French ski resorts.

Getting Around

o **Trains** You can use Switzerland's fast, efficient and integrated railway for your entire trip.
o **Boats** Use scenic boats to link your journey, especially on Lakes Geneva, Lucerne and Zürich.
o **Bus** The postal-bus system goes where trains don't, is efficient and integrated with the railways.
o **Car** More hindrance than pleasure. Hard to park in cities, and many resorts such as Zermatt and Wengen are car-free.

Accommodation

o **Hotels** Everywhere and in all price ranges. Top-end properties are often legendary.
o **Rental Accommodation** Common at winter resorts; with a kitchen, one or more private bedrooms and a common room. Great for groups.

Be Forewarned

o It's a safe and healthy place to travel. Enjoy!

Geneva & the West

Lake Geneva, Western Europe's biggest lake, stretches like a giant liquid mirror between the French-speaking Swiss canton of Vaud (north) and France (south). Its west end is Geneva, Europe's most urbane city. Museums, cafes and famous international agencies cluster around the lakeside, with its exclamation point of a fountain. Further east Lake Geneva is lined by the elegant student city of Lausanne and a phalanx of pretty smaller towns, and the Swiss side of the lake presents the marvellous emerald spectacle of tightly ranked vineyards spreading in terraces up the steep hillsides of the Lavaux area – the source of some very fine tipples.

Down by the water, the lake is lined by fairy-tale châteaux, luxurious manor houses and modest beaches, often backed by peaceful woodland. In the mild climate around Montreux, palm trees grow.

Château de Chillon (p87) on Lake Geneva

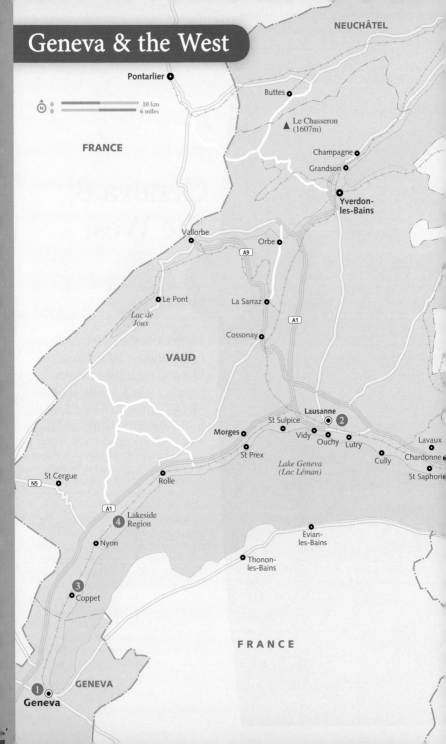

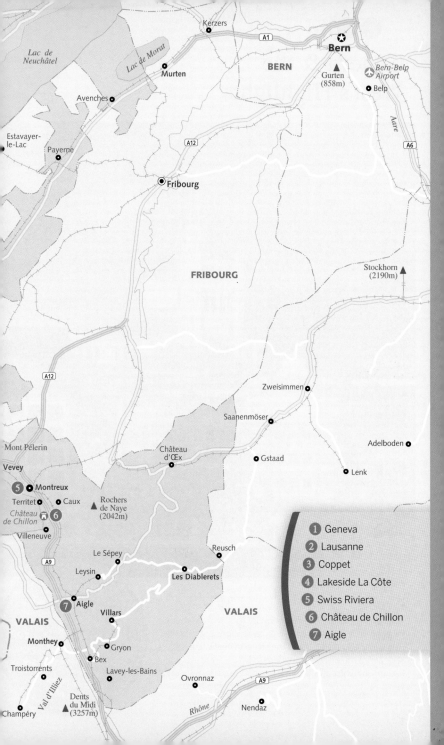

Geneva & the West's Highlights

Geneva

Switzerland's most-international city (p62) has a fabulous location on its namesake lake. Organisations such as the Red Cross and the UN keep the streets filled with people speaking a multitude of languages and enjoying every luxury. Still, you can sense the past in the old town. Above: Cathédrale St-Pierre (p63); Bottom right: Fireworks during the Geneva Festival

Need to Know

BEST TIME TO VISIT Geneva is a year-round city but in summer it comes alive along the lakefront. **TOP TIP** Prepare for Mont Blanc views everywhere. **For further coverage, see p62.**

Geneva Don't Miss List

ISABELLA FOLETTI,
TOURISM EXPERT

1 LAKE

It's one of Switzerland's most outstanding landscapes. You immediately see the **Jet d'Eau** (p68), our huge fountain in the middle of the lake. **Lake boats** (p67) docked at the lakefront will take you for a cruise with Mont Blanc for a backdrop. Sit back on a sunny day and enjoy.

2 SHOPPING

We love our shopping in Geneva. If you wander the **Rue du Rhône** and the **Rue de Rive** (p72), you'll see what seems like every famous luxury brand in the world. Of course, the Swiss ones have huge boutiques. And if you want a **watch**, we're the birthplace of high-end watch manufacturing (p74).

3 PEACE & FREEDOM

There are more than 150 international organisations here, and we are world-famous for our role in diplomacy and mediation. Geneva is the birthplace of the Red Cross and Red Crescent Movement. You can visit the **museum** (p66) and see all the incredible work the organisation does. The UN is also a huge presence locally.

4 FESTIVALS

We have a ball at **L'Escalade** (www.escalade.ch) when we break candy containers and eat the contents! It happens on 11 December and everybody parties. In early August, we have **Fêtes de Genève** (www.fetes-de-geneve. ch), which is a 10-day blowout. There's food, dancing and huge amounts of fun. There's a big techno parade and on the last night a huge fireworks show over the lake.

5 CHURCHES

With all the international organisations, it shouldn't surprise that Geneva is also a multifaith meeting place. But the city is one of the key religious places in the history of Protestantism. Jean Calvin's influence and legacy gave the city the name of 'Protestant Rome' in the 1600s. You can learn more at the **International Museum of the Reformation** (p63).

Lausanne

The lake may be flat (albeit mirror smooth and beautifully flat) but Lausanne (p74) is wonderfully hilly. Vast stone bridges soar over narrow chasms of building and you can find cafes tucked into the arches. It just begs for random, wanton exploration. Top right: Place de la Palud (p75); Bottom right: Sauvabelin's wooden tower

Need to Know

BEST TIME TO VISIT In summer you can fully enjoy the lakefront, but in fall the hills are filled with colour as the vineyard leaves change. **For further coverage, see p74.**

Lausanne Don't Miss List

NATHALIE NINI REY,
LAUSANNE GUIDE

1 CATHÉDRALE DE NOTRE DAME

The **cathedral** (p79) of Lausanne is a masterpiece of early Gothic style: do not miss the painted portal dated 1235 and its impressive polychromatic sculptures, the rose window with its medieval symbolism, the new organ (2002) and its fantastic design. On certain Friday evenings, you may attend a concert.

2 CENTRE & MARKET

From the cathedral, a lovely walk down 174 stairs leads you to **Place de la Palud** (p75). A must is the open air market on Wednesday and Saturday morning. Local products like cheese, charcuterie, pastries, and seasonal fruits and vegetables show that the Lausanne people love their market!

3 SAUVABELIN & HERMITAGE

A short bus ride (No 16; 15 minutes) from St-François square brings you to **Sauvabelin**, a 60-hectare forest in the northern part of Lausanne, located at an elevation of 670m. Climb the wooden tower and its 150 steps for a 360° breathtaking view. Walk downhill to the **Fondation de l'Hermitage museum** (☎ 021 320 50 01; www.fondation-hermitage.ch; Route du Signal 2; adult/child Sfr18/free; ⏰10am-6pm Tue-Wed & Fri-Sun, to 9pm Thu), an exhibition of paintings in a beautiful 19th-century mansion.

4 LAVAUX VINEYARDS

The nearest **Lavaux vineyards** (p83; Unesco World Heritage listed since 2007) are easy to reach by train from Lausanne and are a fun day trip. A 15-minute train ride to **Grandvaux** brings you to the steep terraces of this wine area; from there you can walk down to the picturesque village of **Lutry** (p83) on the lake in an hour. Return to Lausanne by bus (No 9) or enjoy a walk (flat and easy) back.

5 ART BRUT MUSEUM

This very special **museum** (p76) shows the creative works of people living in psychiatric hospitals, in prisons or outside society. Away from artistic standards, these artists invented a personal universe. Paintings, sculptures, collage and patchworks made from all kinds of materials will astonish you.

Coppet

This compact medieval village (p82) offers lots of strolling pleasures along its narrow old lanes. Save time for a walk up to the hilltop, 18th-century Château de Coppet, the one-time home of French swells who ran a vibrant salon graced by the likes of Edward Gibbon and Lord Byron. Château de Coppet (p82)

Lakeside La Côte

In the region of La Côte (p81), between Geneva and Lausanne, villages are strung along the lake like bunches of grapes in the hillside vineyards. Heading west on a walk from Lausanne, one of the first villages you reach is St Sulpice, which has a noted cathedral. Another 6km an you're in Morges, where you can ponde its harbourside 13th-century castle. Another worthwhile stop is Nyon for splendid ice cream. Nyon (p82)

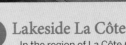

Sailing the Swiss Riviera

The east end of Lake Geneva has the marketing-friendly name of the Swiss Riviera (p84), but it's no hype. The walks here seem especially sun-drenched during summer and you can sense an inner peace that comes from living in such a genteel patch of loveliness. In Vevey, you can explore a world of food and fun at the Alimentarium, while in Montreux you can simply luxuriate in the good life.

5

6

Château de Chillon

While you might think twice about being led along the garden path, don't hesitate to take the Flower Path (Chemin Fleuri) from Montreux, which stretches some 4km southeast along the water to the magnificent Château de Chillon (p87), one of Switzerland's most-famous castles. It presents a grim fortified visage to the shore and a gentler face to the lake. Wander through a maze of rooms and courtyards, and enjoy fine art and furnishings.

7

Aigle

Lake Geneva's reputation for wine and castles is perfectly combined in Aigle (p88) where you can learn about wine making through the millennia and taste wine inside a fairytale palace at the Musée de la Vigne et du Vin. The vineyards here are spread over hills more gentle than elsewhere along the lake, and they produce some of Switzerland's finest whites. Languid lunch opportunities abound.

Geneva & the West's Best...

Ancient Places

◦ **Cathédrale St-Pierre** (p63) Geneva's lovely cathedral is mainly Gothic and dates back to the 11th century.

◦ **Place de la Palud** (p75) This 9th-century medieval market square in Lausanne includes the 17th-century town hall.

◦ **Cathédrale de Notre Dame** (p79) Switzerland's finest Gothic cathedral stands proudly at the heart of Lausanne's Old Town.

◦ **Coppet** (p82) A lakeside medieval village.

Lakeside Scenes

◦ **Jardin Anglais** (p62) Geneva's garden features a huge clock, crafted from 6500 plants.

◦ **Quai du Mont-Blanc** (p63) Flowers, statues, outdoor art exhibitions and views of Mont Blanc abound on this promenade.

◦ **Château de Chillon** (p87) This oval-shaped 13th-century fortress is a maze of courtyards, towers and halls, plus there's a dungeon.

◦ **Aigle** (p88) The capital of the Chablais wine-producing region has castles too.

Museums

◦ **Musée International de la Réforme** (p63) Historical exhibits bring to life all things Reformation.

◦ **Musée Olympique** (p75) A real must for sports buffs, this beautiful museum recounts the Olympic story from its inception to the present day.

◦ **Alimentarium** (p85) Nestlé's museum is dedicated to all things edible, past and present.

◦ **Musée de l'Art Brut** (p76) Remarkable art created by society's disadvantaged.

Need to Know

Tours

○ **CGN** (p73, p81) Lake cruises, some aboard beautiful belle époque steamers, by Lake Geneva's main boat operator.

○ **Swissboat** (p67) Thematic cruises – castles, nature and so on – around the lake and along the Rhône River.

○ **Lavaux Express** (p86) Tractor-pulled tourist train chugs through Lavaux' vineyards and villages.

○ **Les Baladeurs** (p77) Themed cycling tours cater to everyone.

ADVANCE PLANNING

○ **Two months before** Book hotels in Geneva and Lausanne, which are always popular.

○ **One month before** Start plotting how you'll bounce around the region – when you'll take the train, float along on a boat or set off on foot.

RESOURCES

○ **City of Geneva** (www. ville-ge.ch) Where to start for the region's premier city.

○ **Canton de Vaud Tourist Office** (www.lake-geneva -region.ch) Covers the region.

○ **Glocals** (www.glocals. com) Globals and locals share their Geneva region tips.

○ **Lonely Planet** (www. lonelyplanet.com/ switzerland/geneva)

GETTING AROUND

○ **Ferry** Sail scenically between Lake Geneva cities, including Geneva and Lausanne. The best way to get around the region.

○ **Train** Fast and frequent trains link every important city and town in the region. No reservations necessary; just turn up and go.

○ **Car** Not needed unless you want to putter about the tiny villages of the wine region around Aigle.

○ **Walk** Spectacular shoreline promenades abound, linking towns and sights on the lake.

BE FOREWARNED

○ **Winter** When the rest of Switzerland is revelling in winter sports, things get very quiet on the shores of Lake Geneva. Lake boats and tours are sharply curtailed or don't sail at all. The walks on the waterfront, and those among the wineries, can be bitterly cold.

○ **Weather** Even in August, cold winds can wash down from glacier-clad mountains, so be prepared for anything nature dishes out.

○ **Festivals** Hugely popular events like Montreux Jazz (p88) can soak up every spare room in the region.

Left: Rue du Rhône, Geneva;
Above: Festival-goers at Montreux Jazz (p88)

Geneva & the West Itineraries

Lake Geneva is the focus of the region and these itineraries show you the best places to stop along its shores. Boats will take you out on the water to see the gorgeous towns backed by vine-covered hillsides.

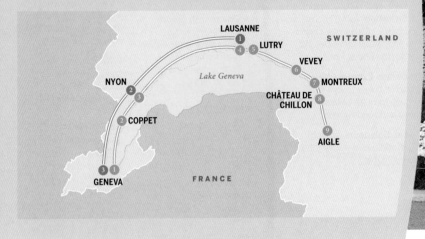

LAUSANNE
1
LUTRY
4 5
VEVEY
6
MONTREUX
7
CHÂTEAU DE CHILLON
8
AIGLE
9
NYON
2
3
COPPET
2
Lake Geneva
SWITZERLAND
3 1
GENEVA
FRANCE

3
DAYS

LAUSANNE TO GENEVA
Best of Lake Geneva

(1) Lausanne is a lakeside favourite for most visitors, with a medieval centre that is evocative even by Swiss standards. Start at the **Place de la Palud**, the beautiful main square, and head over to the Gothic **Cathédrale de Notre Dame**. Vault or hurdle over to the **Musée Olympique** (the city is home to the International Olympic Committee). Stroll the lakefront and enjoy some creative modern-European fare for dinner.

On day two, catch a lake boat to **(2) Nyon**, which dates back to Roman times. Wander the hilly streets and explore the **castle**. No matter what the weather, take time for the fab frozen fare

at **Gelateria Venezia** and **La Yogourterie**. Board a lake boat for Geneva and settle back to enjoy the sensational views of the French Alps across Lake Geneva. You might even see Mont Blanc.

Once ashore in beguiling, smart and stylish **(3) Geneva**, take time to wander the lakefront at **Quai du Mont-Blanc**. Explore its many pleasures and then ponder the **Jet d'Eau** from every angle. Walk the streets of the **Old Town** and peek into the **Cathédrale St-Pierre**. When night falls, take your pick of cuisines and dine at one of the world-class cafes or restaurants Geneva is renowned for.

GENEVA TO AIGLE
Lake Geneva Ramble

5 DAYS

Synchronise your watch in **(1) Geneva** at the flowery **Horloge Fleurie** in the **Jardin Anglais**. Then catch a train to **(2) Coppet**, a little medieval town on the shores of Lake Geneva. From here catch a boat or train or even walk to **(3) Nyon**, another ancient town that tumbles down the hillside to the lake.

A quick train ride and you are in **(4) Lausanne**. Wander the hilly streets, pause for a drink at a bar built into a bridge and revel in the wild creativity of the **Musée de l'Art Brut**. In the morning, catch a lake boat to **(5) Lutry** in the heart of the **Lavaux wine region**. You can ride tourist trains or hike about the vineyards for views and tastings. Catch another boat to **(6) Vevey** where you can tour the engaging lakeside museum run by local big-shot Nestlé.

It's a quick train to **(7) Montreux**. Chill at the waterfront and then enjoy the fine local cuisine. After a good night's rest, go for a morning stroll along the Chemin Fleuri (Flower Path) to **(8) Château de Chillon**, an evocative old castle. Spend another night in Montreux and then train it to **(9) Aigle** for wine and castles, and a final overnight stay.

The Horloge Fleurie (flower clock) in the Jardin Anglais (p62), Geneva
WONJIN KIM / GETTY IMAGES ©

Discover
Geneva & the West

GENEVA

Sleek, slick and cosmopolitan, Geneva is a rare breed of a city: it's one of Europe's priciest, its people chatter in every language under the sun and it's constantly perceived as the Swiss capital (it isn't). Superbly strung around the shores of Europe's largest Alpine lake, this is only Switzerland's third-largest city.

Yet the whole world is here: 200-odd governmental and nongovernmental international organisations fill the city's plush hotels, feast on its incredible choice of international cuisine, and help prop up Geneva's famed overload of banks, luxury jewellers and chocolate shops.

◉ Sights

Geneva's major sights are split by the Rhône, which flows through the city to create its greatest attraction – the lake – and several distinct neighbourhoods. On the left bank (*rive gauche*), mainstream shopping districts Rive and Eaux-Vives climb uphill from the water to Plainpalais and Vieille Ville (Old Town), while the right bank (*rive droite*) holds grungy bar- and club-hot Pâquis, the train-station area and the international quarter that houses most world organisations.

Vieille Ville

Geneva's Old Town is a short walk south from the lakeside.

JARDIN ANGLAIS   Garden
(Quai du Général-Guisan) Before tramping up the hill, join the crowds getting snapped in front of the flower clock in the **Jardin**

Cathédrale St-Pierre, Geneva
TIBOR BOGNAR / ALAMY ©

Anglais, Geneva's flowery waterfront garden landscaped in 1854 on the site of an old lumber-handling port and merchant yard. The **Horloge Fleurie**, Geneva's most photographed clock, is crafted from 6500 plants and has ticked since 1955 in the garden. Its second hand, 2.5m long, claims to be the world's longest.

CATHÉDRALE ST-PIERRE   Cathedral
(Cour St-Pierre; admission free; ⏱9.30am-6.30pm Mon-Fri, to 5.30pm Sat, noon-6.30pm Sun) Started in the 11th century, Geneva's lovely cathedral is mainly Gothic with an 18th-century neoclassical facade. Between 1536 and 1564 Protestant John Calvin preached both here – see his seat in the north aisle – and in the Gothic **Auditoire de Calvin** (Cour St-Pierre; admission free; ⏱10am-noon & 2-4pm Mon-Sat) neighbouring the cathedral. In summer free **organ and carillon concerts** (www.concerts-cathedrale.com; ⏱5pm & 6pm Sat Jun-Sep) fill the cathedral with soul.

Don't leave the cathedral without buying a ticket for the **cathedral towers** (adult/child Sfr4/2). Seventy-six steps twist up to the cathedral attic – a fascinating insight into its architectural construction – from where you can hike another 40 steps up the northern or southern towers for a magnificent lake panorama or bell tower and old WWII observation post respectively.

MUSÉE INTERNATIONAL
DE LA RÉFORME   History Museum
(www.musee-reforme.ch; Rue du Cloître 4; adult/child Sfr13/6; ⏱10am-5pm Tue-Sun) To the side of the cathedral sits this thoroughly modern museum inside a lovely 18th-century mansion. It focuses on the Reformation, with state-of-the-art exhibits and audiovisuals bringing to life everything from the earliest printed bibles to the emergence of Geneva as 'Protestant Rome' in the 16th century, and from John Calvin to Protestantism in the 21st century. History buffs will love it. A combined ticket covering museum, cathedral and archaeological site costs Sfr18 for adults and Sfr10 for children.

MUSÉE D'ART ET
D'HISTOIRE   Art Museum
(Rue Charles Galland 2; permanent/temporary collection free/Sfr5; ⏱10am-6pm Tue-Sun) Konrad Witz' *La pêche miraculeuse* (c 1440–44), portraying Christ walking on water on Lake Geneva, is a highlight of Geneva's elegant art and history museum, built between 1903 and 1910.

Plainpalais
Wedged between the Rhône and Arve rivers, this fairly nondescript district is home to the university and a bevy of museums.

MUSÉE D'ART MODERNE
ET CONTEMPORAIN   Art Museum
(MAMCO; www.mamco.ch, in French; Rue des Vieux Grenadiers 10; adult/child Sfr8/free; ⏱noon-6pm Tue-Fri, from 11am Sat & Sun) Set in an industrial 1950s factory, Geneva's museum of modern and contemporary art plays cutting-edge host to young, international and cross-media exhibitions. The museum is free between 6pm and 9pm on the first Wednesday of every month.

Right Bank
Cross the water either aboard a seagull (p74), via Geneva's only road-traffic bridge Pont du Mont-Blanc (notorious for traffic jams) or on foot across pedestrian footbridge Pont de la Machine.

QUAI DU MONT-BLANC   Waterfront
Flowers, statues, outdoor art exhibitions and views of Mont Blanc (on clear days only) abound on this picturesque northern lakeshore promenade which leads past the **Bains des Pâquis** (p69), where Genevans have frolicked in the sun since 1872, to **Parc de la Perle du Lac**, a large park where Romans built ornate thermal baths. Further north, the peacock-studded lawns of **Parc de l'Ariana** ensnare the UN and the pretty **Jardin Botanique** (Botanical Garden; admission free; ⏱8am-7.30pm).

PALAIS DES NATIONS   Historic Building
(www.unog.ch; Ave de la Paix 14; adult/child Sfr12/7; ⏱10am-noon & 2-4pm Mon-Fri Sep-Mar, 10am-noon & 2-4pm daily Apr-Jun, 10am-5pm daily Jul & Aug) Home to the UN since 1966,

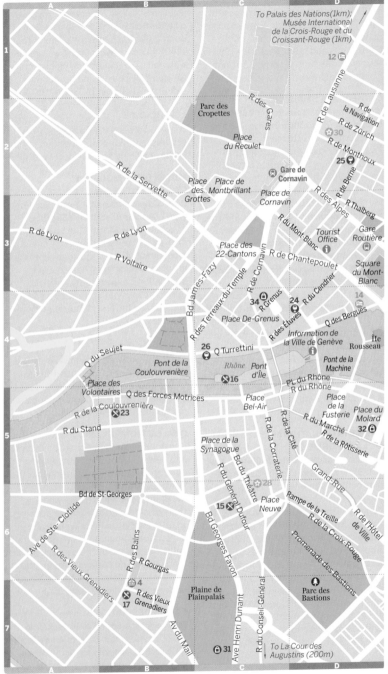

To Palais des Nations(1km);
Musée International
de la Crois-Rouge et du
Croissant-Rouge (1km)

12

R de Lausanne

R de
la Navigation

R de Zürich

30

R de Monthoux

25

R de Berne

R Thalberg

Parc des
Cropettes

R des Gares

Place
du Reculet

Gare de
Cornavin

R de la Servette

Place
des
Grottes

Place de
Montbrillant

Place de
Cornavin

R des Alpes

R de Lyon

R de Lyon

R Voltaire

Place des
22-Cantons

R de Chantepoulet

R du Mont-Blanc

Tourist
Office

Gare
Routière

Square
du Mont-
Blanc

Bd James-Fazy

R des Terreaux-du-Temple

R de Cornavin

34

R Grenus

24

R des Etuves

R du Cendrier

Place De-Grenus

14

Q des Bergues

Information de
la Ville de Genève

Île
Rousseau

26

Q Turrettini

Q du Seujet

Pont de la
Coulouvrenière

Rhône

Pont
d'Île

16

Pont de la
Machine

Place des
Volontaires

Q des Forces Motrices

PL du Rhône

R du Rhône

R de la Coulouvrenière

23

Place
Bel-Air

Place
de la
Fusterie

Place du
Molard

32

R du Stand

R de la Cité

R de la Corraterie

R du Marché

R de la Rôtisserie

Place de la
Synagogue

Bd du Théâtre

Grand-Rue

Bd de St-Georges

R du Général Dufour

28

Rampe de la Treille

R de la Croix-Rouge

R de l'Hôtel
de Ville

15

Place
Neuve

Ave de Ste-Clotilde

R des Vieux Grenadiers

R des Bains

R Gourgas

Bd Georges Favon

Promenade des Bastions

4

R des Vieux
Grenadiers

17

Plaine de
Plainpalais

Parc des
Bastions

Ave du Mail

Ave Henri Dunant

R du Conseil-Général

31

To La Cour des
Augustins (200m)

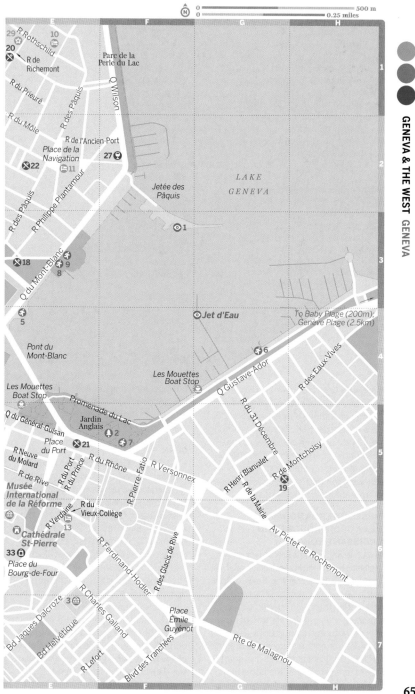

0   500 m
0   0.25 miles

R Rothschild
29
10
20
R de Richemont
R du Prieuré
R du Môle
R des Pâquis
Parc de la Perle du Lac
Q Wilson
R de l'Ancien-Port
Place de la Navigation
22
11
27

Jetée des Pâquis

LAKE GENEVA

R des Pâquis
R Philippe Plantamour
R du Mont-Blanc
18
9
8
5

Pont du Mont-Blanc

Jet d'Eau

6

To Baby Plage (200m);
Genève Plage (2.5km)

Les Mouettes Boat Stop

Q du Général-Guisan
Les Mouettes Boat Stop
Promenade du Lac
Jardin Anglais
2
Place du Port
21
R du Rhône
R Neuve du Molard
R du Port
R du Prince
R de Rive
7
R Versonnex
R Pierre-Fatio
Q Gustave-Ador
R du 31 Décembre
R des Eaux-Vives
R de Montchoisy
R Henri Blanvalet
R de la Mairie
19

Musée International de la Réforme
13
R du Vieux-Collège
R Verdaine
Av Pictet de Rochemont

Cathédrale St-Pierre
33
Place du Bourg-de-Four
R Ferdinand-Hodler
R des Glacis de Rive

3
R Charles Galland
Bd Jacques Dalcroze
Bd Helvétique
Place Émile Guyénot
R Léfort
Blvd des Tranchées
Rte de Malagnou

Geneva

the Palais des Nations was built between 1929 and 1936 to house the now-defunct League of Nations. Admission (bring ID card or passport) includes an hour-long tour of the building and entry to the surrounding park where a grey monument sprouts, coated with heat-resistant titanium donated by the USSR to commemorate the conquest of space.

MUSÉE INTERNATIONAL DE LA CROIX-ROUGE ET DU CROISSANT-ROUGE Museum
(www.micr.org; Ave de la Paix 17; temporary exhibition free, permanent exhibition adult/child Sfr10/free; ⊙10am-5pm Wed-Mon) Compelling multimedia exhibits at Geneva's fascinating International Red Cross & Red Crescent Museum trawl through atrocities perpetuated by humanity. The long litany of war and nastiness, documented in films, photos, sculptures and soundtracks, are set against the noble aims of the organisation created by Geneva

businessmen and philanthropists Henri Dunant and Henri Dufour in 1864. Take bus 8 from Gare de Cornavin to the 'Appia' stop.

CERN Science Laboratory
(☎022 767 76 76; http://outreach.web.cern. ch; admission free; ⊙guided tours in English 10.30am Mon-Sat year-round, 3.30pm Mon, Tue, Thu & Fri mid-Jun–mid-Sep) Founded in 1954, the European Organisation for Nuclear Research, 8km west of Geneva near Meyrin, is a laboratory for research into particle physics. It accelerates electrons and positrons down a 27km circular tube (the Large Hadron Collider, the world's biggest machine) and the resulting collisions create new forms of matter.

Two fascinating permanent exhibitions shed light on the ground-breaking work done by the centre: The dazzling **Universe of Particles** (admission free; ⊙10am-5pm Mon-Sat), housed inside a 27m-tall and 40m-diameter globe intended to symbolise planet Earth, is a dazzling interactive voyage into the enigmatic world of particles. **Microcosm (admission free;** ⊙**8.30am-5.30pm Mon-Fri, 9am-5pm Sat)** likewise uses multimedia to help visitors understand through games, experiments and hands-on workshops just how accelerators recreate the Big Bang among other things.

From the train station take tram 18 to its terminus in front of CERN (Sfr3, 40 minutes).

 Tours

The one-stop shop for boat, bus and electric-train tours is **Ticket Point (**☎**022 781 04 06; www.ticket-point.ch)** which has all the schedules and sells tickets at its waterfront kiosk on Quai du Mont-Blanc.

CGN   Boat Tour
(☎0848 811 848; www.cgn.ch; Quai du Mont-Blanc) Lake cruises, some aboard beautiful belle époque steamers, by Lake Geneva's main boat operator.

SWISSBOAT   Boat Tour
(www.swissboat.com; Quai du Mont-Blanc 4; ⊙May-Oct) Thematic cruises – castles, nature and so on – around the lake and along the Rhône River.

MINI TRAIN TOURS   Train Tour
(☎022 735 43 00; Jardin d'Anglais; adult/child Sfr8/5; ⊙10.15am-10.15pm) At least hourly departures year-round along the left bank to Parc des Eaux-Vives and back again aboard a solar-powered red train; count on 45 minutes' journey time.

 **Sleeping**

Plug into the complete list at www.geneva -hotel.ch. Rates in Geneva's predominantly business, midrange and top-end hotels are substantially higher Monday to Thursday.

When checking in, be sure to get your free Public Transport Card, which offers unlimited bus travel for the duration of your stay.

CERN, Geneva

GEMMA DAY / ALAMY © ARCHITECTS: T. BÜCHI AND H. DESSIMOZ

LYNDON M / GETTY IMAGES ©

Don't Miss Jet d'Eau

If you're landing by plane, this fountain is the first dramatic glimpse you get of Geneva. The 140m-tall lakeside fountain shoots up water with incredible force – 200km/h, 1360 horsepower – to create the sky-high plume, which is kissed by a rainbow on sunny days. At any one time, 7 tonnes of water is in the air, much of which sprays spectators on the pier beneath. Two or three times a year, it is illuminated pink, blue or some other vivid colour to mark a humanitarian occasion (World Suicide Prevention Day, Breast Cancer Awareness Month, World AIDS Day etc).

THINGS YOU NEED TO KNOW

Quai Gustave-Ador

HÔTEL BEL'ESPERANCE   Hotel $
(☎ 022 818 37 37; www.hotel-bel-esperance.ch; Rue de la Vallée 1; s/d/tr/q from Sfr105/160/195/235; @ 🛜) This two-star hotel is a two-second flit to the Old Town and offers extraordinary value for a pricey city like Geneva. Rooms are quiet and cared for, and those on the 1st floor share a kitchen. Ride the lift to the 5th floor to flop in a chair on its wonderful flower-filled rooftop terrace.

EDELWEISS   Hotel $$
(☎ 022 544 51 51; www.manotel.com; Place de la Navigation 2; d/tr from Sfr160/210; ❄ @ 🛜)

Plunge yourself into the heart of the Swiss Alps with this Heidi-style hideout, very much the Swiss Alps *en ville* with its fireplace, wildflower-painted pine bedheads and big, cuddly St Bernard lolling over the banister. Its chalet-styled restaurant is a key address among Genevans for traditional cheese fondue.

LA COUR DES AUGUSTINS   Boutique Hotel $$
(☎ 022 322 21 00; www.lacourdesaugustins.com; Rue Jean-Violette 15; s/d from Sfr189/248; P ❄ @ 🛜) 'Boutique gallery design hotel' is how this slick, contemporary space in

Carouge markets itself. Disguised by a 19th-century facade, its crisp white interior screams cutting edge. Before leaving, invest in a designer lamp or household art object from the hotel boutique.

HÔTEL AUTEUIL Design Hotel $$
(☏022 544 22 22; www.manotel.com; Rue de Lausanne 33; d from Sfr320; P ✱ @ 🛜) The star of this crisp, design-driven hotel near the station is its enviable collection of B&W photos of 1950s film stars in Geneva. Borrow the book from reception to find out precisely who's who and where.

HÔTEL DES BERGUES Historic Hotel $$$
(☏022 908 70 00; www.bergueshotel.com; Quai des Bergues 33; d from Sfr620; P ✱ @ 🛜) Geneva's oldest hotel continues to live up to its magnificent heritage. Chandelier-lit moulded ceilings, grandiose flower arrangements, original oil paintings in heavy gold frames and diamonds glittering behind glass is what this lakeside neoclassical gem from 1834 is all about. But how can a suite cost Sfr12,500 a night?

AUBERGE DE JEUNESSE Hostel $
(☏022 732 62 60; www.yh-geneva.ch; Rue Rothschild 28-30; dm Sfr29, d/q with bathroom or toilet Sfr95/135; @ 🛜) At this well-equipped, Hostelling International–affiliated apartment block rates include breakfast and bunk-bed dorms max out at 12 beds. Non HI-card holders pay Sfr6 more a night.

 Eating

Geneva flaunts ethnic cuisines galore. If it's local and traditional you're after, dip into a cheese fondue or platter of pan-fried *filets de perche* (perch fillets). But beware: not all those cooked up are fresh from the lake. Many come frozen from Eastern Europe, so it's imperative to pick the right place to sample this simple Lake Geneva speciality.

Pâquis

There's a tasty line-up of more-affordable restaurants on Place de la Navigation. For Asian-cuisine lovers without a fortune

to blow, try a quick-eat joint on Rue de Fribourg, Rue de Neuchâtel, Rue de Berne or the northern end of Rue des Alpes.

LE COMPTOIR Fusion $
(☏022 731 32 37; www.lolabar.ch; Rue de Richemont 7-9; mains Sfr15-30; ⏲lunch & dinner Tue-Fri, dinner Sat) To savour the real vibe of this U-shaped space, come here at dusk or later when night lights twinkle on sideboards and the Counter's retro decor really comes into its own. We love the faux sheepskins and crystal in the faintly kitsch Lola Bar lounge! The cuisine is a tasty mix of sushi, curries and wok-cooked dishes.

COTTAGE CAFÉ Mediterranean $
(☏022 731 60 16; www.cottagecafe.ch; Rue Adhémar-Fabri 7; tapas Sfr9-15; ⏲7.15am-10pm Mon-Sat) Hovering right on the fringe of Pâquis near the waterfront, this quaint little cottage sits plum in a park guarded

Geneva for Children

Predictably, the lake is an endless source of family entertainment: feed the ducks and swans; rent a pedalo, speedboat or sleek sailing boat from **Les Corsaires** (☏022 735 43 00; www.lescorsaires.ch; Quai Gustave-Ador 33; ⏲10.30am-8pm); fly down the water slide at 1930s lakeside swimming pool complex **Genève Plage** (www.geneve-plage.ch; Port Noir; adult/child Sfr7/3.50; ⏲10am-8pm mid-May–mid-Sep); or dive head-first into the pools at historic and hip **Bains des Pâquis** (www.bains-des-paquis.ch, in French; Quai du Mont-Blanc 30; ⏲9am-8pm mid-Apr–mid-Sep).

Other amusing options include an electric-train tour, the Tarzan-inspired tree park with rubber tyre swings at lakeside **Baby Plage** (Quai Gustave-Ador), and the well-equipped playgrounds for toddlers in lakeside **Parc de la Perle du Lac** (Rue de Lausanne).

MATTHIAS LÜFKENS ©

Don't Miss **Brasserie des Halles de l'Île**

Oh, how the menu lives up to its setting at this unique address on an island in the Rhône. At home in Geneva's old market hall, Brasserie des Halles de l'Île is an industrial-style venue that cooks up an entertaining cocktail of after-work aperitifs with music, after-dark DJs and a fabulous seasonal fare of fresh veggies and regional products (look for the Appellation d'Origine Contrôllée products flagged on the menu) cooked 101 ways. In early summer try the *frappé de petits pois glacé à la menthe* (cold pea and mint soup) and spring lamb. Get here early to snag the best seat in the house: a tiny terrace hanging over the water. Otherwise go for a seat in the courtyard or cavernous main hall.

THINGS YOU NEED TO KNOW

022 311 08 88; www.brasseriedeshallesdelile.ch; Place de l'Île 1; mains Sfr20-50, brunch Sfr25; lunch & dinner

by two stone lions and a mausoleum (Geneva's Brunswick Monument no less). On clear sunny days, views of Mont Blanc from its garden are swoon-worthy, while lunching or lounging inside is akin to hanging out in your grandma's book-lined living room. From 6pm the wine-bar menu with lots of tapas kicks in.

LES 5 PORTES   Bistro $
(022 731 84 38; Rue de Zürich 5; mains Sfr15-20; 6pm-2am Mon, from 9am Tue-Fri, from 5pm Sat, from 11am Sun) The Five Doors – with

indeed five doors – is a fashionable Pâquis port of call that successfully embraces the whole gamut of moods and moments – eating and drinking. Its Sunday brunch is a particularly buzzing affair.

Vieille Ville

Eateries crowd Place du Bourg-de-Four, Geneva's oldest square, in the lovely Old Town. Otherwise, head down the hill towards the river and Place du Molard, packed with tables and chairs for much of the year.

Rive & Eaux-vives

L'ADRESSE
Modern $$

(☎ 022 736 32 32; www.ladresse.ch; Rue du 31 Décembre 32; mains Sfr25-35; ⊙lunch & dinner Tue-Sat) Something of an urban loft with a fabulous rooftop terrace, it is all hip at The Address, a hybrid fashion/lifestyle boutique and contemporary bistro at home in renovated artists' workshops. *The* Genevan address for lunch (great value Sfr18 lunch), brunch or Saturday slunch, a cross between tea and dinner (ie a casual evening 'meal' of cold and warm nibbles, both sweet and savoury, shared between friends over a drink or three around 5pm).

L'ENTRECÔTE
Steakhouse $$

(☎ 022 310 60 04; www.relaisentrecote.fr; Rue du Rhône 49; steak & chips Sfr46; ⊙lunch & dinner) Key vocabulary to know before entering this timeless classic where everyone eats the same dish is *à point* (medium), *bien cuit* (well done) and *saignant* (rare). Indeed the place doesn't bother with menus. Sit down, say how you like your steak cooked and wait for it arrive – two handsome servings of it (!) pre-empted by a green salad and accompanied by perfectly crisp, skinny fries. Should you have room at the end of it all, the desserts are justly raved about.

Plainpalais

OMNIBUS
European $$

(☎ 022 321 44 45; www.omnibus-cafe.ch; Rue de la Coulouvrenière 23; mains Sfr30-45; ⊙11.30am-midnight Mon-Fri, from 6pm Sat) Don't be fooled or deterred by the graffiti-plastered facade of this Rhône-side, industrial-inspired bar, cafe and restaurant. Inside a maze of retro, romantic and eclectic rooms seduces on first sight. Particularly popular is the back room (reservations essential) with carpet wall hangings and lots of lace.

AU GRÜTLI
International $$

(☎ 022 328 98 68; www.cafedugrutli.ch; Rue du Général Dufour 16; mains Sfr25-40; ⊙8am-midnight Mon-Thu, to 1am Fri, 4pm-1am Sat, to 11pm Sun) As much cafe as cutting-edge restaurant, this industrial-styled eating space with mezzanine seating is razor sharp. Indonesian lamb, moussaka, scallops pan-fried with ginger and citrus fruits or Provençal-inspired chicken are among its many international flavours.

CAFÉ DES BAINS
Modern European $$

(☎ 022 321 57 98; www.cafedesbains.com; Rue des Bains 26; mains Sfr25-50; ⊙lunch Mon-Fri, dinner Tue-Sat) No brand labels, beautiful objects and an eye for design are trademarks of this fusion restaurant opposite the contemporary-art museum where Genevan beauties flock. Several dishes woo vegetarians.

 **Drinking**

Summer ushers in dozens of scenic spots around the city where you can lounge in the sun over a mint tea or mojito – Place du Bourg-de-Four in the Old Town and Carouge are strewn with seasonal cafe terraces.

On the water's edge try left-bank kiosk **Paillote** (Quai du Mont-Blanc 30; ⊙to midnight) or right-bank **Le Paradis** (www.terrasse-paradis.ch; Quai Turrettini; ⊙9am-9pm) with its Rhône-side striped deckchairs.

MARIUS
Wine Bar

(Place des Augustins 9; ⊙5.30pm-1.30am Mon-Fri) This doll's house-sized *bar à vin* – an old butcher's shop hence the tiles and ceramic – is a great little spot in Plainpalais to discover both regional and natural wines. Pair your chosen vintage with a cold meat, cheese or antipasti platter for the perfect gourmet experience.

LE CHEVAL BLANC
Bar

(www.lechevalblanc.ch; Place de l'Octroi 15; ⊙11.30am-late Tue-Sat, from 10.30am Sun; 🛜) The White Horse is a real Carouge favourite. Quaff cocktails and tapas – some of Geneva's best – at the pink neon-lit bar upstairs, then head downstairs to its club and concert space, **Le Box** (www.lebox.ch).

BAR DU NORD
Bar

(www.bardunord.ch; Rue Ancienne 66; ⊙5pm-2am Thu & Fri, from 9am Sat) One of Carouge's oldest drinking holes, this trendy young bar

is stuffed with Bauhaus-inspired furniture, the best whisky selection in town and a small courtyard terrace out back. The best nights are Thursdays and Fridays with good music (lots of it electro) and DJs.

LA BRETELLE
Bar

(Rue des Étuves 17; ⏱6pm-2am) Little has changed since the 1970s when this legendary bar opened. The Strap is just the place to tune in to a good old accordion-accompanied French chanson.

 **Entertainment**

LE PALAIS MASCOTTE
Cabaret Bar

(📞022 741 33 33; www.palaismascotte.ch; Rue de Berne 43; ⏱6pm-5am Mon-Sat) Closed for years before it reopened as a cabaret bar much-loved by the over 30-somethings, this mythical Pâquis address buzzes with atmosphere. Dine on the top floor, enjoy cabaret on the ground floor and take in concerts followed by '90s dance music

in the basement nightclub, **Zazou Club** (⏱11pm-5am Fri & Sat).

GRAND THÉÂTRE DE GENÈVE
Opera

(www.geneveopera.ch; Bd du Théâtre 11) The city's lovely theatre hosts ballet too.

MILK KLUB
Nightclub

(www.milk-klub.ch; Rue de Monthoux 60; ⏱10pm-5am Thu, from 11pm Fri & Sat) The latest club to hit Pâquis pounds out techno, house and loadsa live sets.

K-36
Gay & Lesbian

(www.k36.ch; Rue de Richemont 9; ⏱10pm-5am Thu-Sat) Crazy techno, house, soul and deep techno are the mixed sounds DJs spin at this tiny nocturnal hangout in Pâquis.

🛍 **Shopping**

Designer shopping is wedged between Rue du Rhône and Rue de Rive. **Globus** (Rue du Rhône 50) and **Manor** (Rue de Cornavin) are the main department stores. Grand-

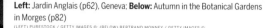

Left: Jardin Anglais (p62), Geneva; **Below:** Autumn in the Botanical Gardens in Morges (p82)

(LEFT) PURESTOCK / GETTY IMAGES ©; (BELOW) BERTRAND MONNEY / GETTY IMAGES ©

Rue in the Old Town and Carouge boasts artsy boutiques, or try Geneva's twice-weekly **flea market** (Plaine de Plainpalais; ⊙Wed & Sat).

MAISON DES COULEURS FINES Arts & Crafts
(www.carandache.ch; Place du Bourg-de-Four 8; ⊙2-6.30pm Mon, 10am-6.30pm Tue-Fri, to 5pm Sat) Beautifully designed boutique packed with a rainbow of pencils, pastels, paints and crayons crafted by Swiss colour maker Caran d'Aché in Geneva since 1915.

ℹ Information

Tourist Information

Information de la Ville de Genève (☎022 311 99 70; www.ville-ge.ch; Pont de la Machine; ⊙noon-6pm Mon, from 9am Tue-Fri, 10am-5pm Sat) City information point; ticketing desk for cultural events.

Tourist Office (☎022 909 70 00; www.geneve-tourisme.ch; Rue du Mont-Blanc 18; ⊙10am-6pm Mon, from 9am Tue-Sat, 10am-4pm Sun)

ℹ Getting There & Away

Air

Aéroport International de Genève (☎0900 571 500; www.gva.ch) 4km from the town centre.

Boat

CGN (Compagnie Générale de Navigation; ☎0848 811 848; www.cgn.ch) runs steamers from Jardin Anglais and Pâquis to other villages on Lake Geneva, including Lausanne (Sfr60, 3½ hours). Those aged six to 16 pay half-price and kids under six years sail for free. A one-day Carte Journalière CGN pass (Sfr60) allows unlimited boat travel. Eurail and Swiss travel passes are also valid.

Train

Trains to/from Annecy, Chamonix and other destinations in neighbouring France use Gare des Eaux-Vives (Av de la Gare des Eaux-Vives). More-or-less-hourly connections run from Geneva's

73

If You Like...
Watches

If seeing ads and shops everywhere for Switzerland's famous watches has whet your appetite, consider these timely attractions:

1 PATEK PHILIPPE MUSEUM

(www.patekmuseum.com; Rue des Vieux Grenadiers 7, Geneva; adult/child Sfr10/free; ⊙2-6pm Tue-Fri, from 10am Sat) A treasure trove of precision art, this elegant museum by one of Switzerland's leading luxury watchmakers displays exquisite timepieces and enamels from the 16th century to the present. The Patek Philippe collection includes pocket watches from the master watchmaker's inception in 1839.

2 LA CITÉ DU TEMPS

(www.citedutemps.com; Pont de la Machine 1, Geneva; admission free; ⊙9am-6pm) This 19th-century industrial building on Lake Geneva is the striking home to **La Collection Swatch**, the world's largest collection of the funky Swiss Swatch watches. The amusing collection includes the world's thinnest plastic varieties, and watches for James Bond.

central train station Gare de Cornavin (Place de Cornavin) to most Swiss towns:

Geneva Airport (Sfr2.20, six minutes)

Lausanne (Sfr21, 30 minutes)

Bern (Sfr47, 1¾ hours)

Zürich (Sfr82, 2¾ hours)

ℹ Getting Around

Bicycle

Genève Roule (www.geneveroule.ch; 4hr free, then per hr Sfr2) Jetée des Pâquis (Jetée des Pâquis; ⊙9am-7pm May-Oct); Place de Montbrillant (Place de Montbrillant 17; ⊙8am-9pm May-Oct); Place du Rhône (Place du Rhône; ⊙9am-7pm May-Oct) Bike hire requiring proof of ID and Sfr20 cash deposit.

Boat

Yellow shuttle boats called Les Mouettes ('Seagulls') cross the lake every 10 minutes between 7.30am and 6pm. Public-transport tickets from by machines at boat bays are valid.

Car & Motorcycle

Much of the Old Town is off limits to cars and street parking elsewhere can be hard to snag; try public car parks Parking du Mont Blanc (Quai du Général-Guisan; per 25 min Sfr1) or Parking Plaine de Plainpalais (Av du Mail; per 30 min Sfr1). Before leaving the car park, validate your parking ticket in an orange TPG machine to get one hour's free travel for two people on city buses, trams and boats.

Public Transport

Tickets for buses, trolley buses and trams run by TPG (www.tpg.ch) are sold at dispensers at stops and through the TPG office (Place de la Gare; ⊙7am-7pm Mon-Fri, to 6pm Sat) inside the main train station. A one-hour ticket for multiple rides in the city costs Sfr3 and a ticket valid for three stops in 30 minutes is Sfr2.

LAUSANNE

POP 128,200 / ELEV 495M

This hilly city (pronounced loh-san), Switzerland's fifth largest, enjoys a blessed lakeside location. The medieval centre is dominated by a grand Gothic cathedral and, among the museums, its unusual Art Brut collection stands out. Throughout the year Lausanne's citizens are treated to a busy arts calendar, while the lake drums up a plethora of activities on and out of the water. Strolling the lakeshore in picturesque Ouchy (once a lakeside village in its own right, long since enveloped by the city) is a pure pleasure, as is a meander day or night around Flon, an area of formerly derelict warehouses rejuvenated as a hip urban centre with a cinema complex, art galleries and trendy shops, and restaurants and bars galore.

Sights & Activities

Downhill by the water in **Ouchy**, Lake Geneva (Lac Léman) is the source of many a sporting opportunity, including sailing, windsurfing, waterskiing and swimming; the tourist office has details. Seasonal stands in front of Château d'Ouchy rent pedalos and kayaks, and cycling and rollerblading are big on the silky-smooth waterfront promenades.

PLACE DE LA PALUD   Square

In the heart of the Vieille Ville (Old Town), this 9th-century medieval market square – pretty as a picture – was originally bogland. For five centuries it has been home to the city government, now housed in the 17th-century **Hôtel de Ville** (town hall). A fountain pierces one end of the square, presided over by a brightly painted column topped by the allegorical figure of Justice, clutching scales and dressed in blue. What you see is a copy – the 1585 original is in the **Musée Historique de Lausanne**.

From the eastern end of the square, bear left along Rue Mercière to pick up **Escaliers du Marché**, a timber-canopied staircase with tiled roof that hikes up the hill to Rue Pierre Viret and beyond to the cathedral.

MUSÉE OLYMPIQUE   Museum

(Olympic Museum; www.museum.olympic.org; Quai d'Ouchy 1) Lausanne's Musée Olympique is easily the city's most lavish, and a real must for sports buffs (and kids). Under renovation until late 2013, its usual home is a gorgeous building atop a tiered landscaped garden in the Parc Olympique. Inside, there is a fabulous rooftop restaurant with champion lake views and a state-of-the-art museum recounting the Olympic story from its inception to present-day through video, archival film and other multimedia. While renovation work is carried out (from April 2012 until late 2013), a fraction of the museum collection can be viewed in a belle époque CGN paddle steamer moored in front of the museum and park.

MUSÉE HISTORIQUE DE LAUSANNE   History Museum

(Place de la Cathédrale 4; adult/child Sfr8/free, 1st Sat of month free; ⏱11am-6pm Tue-Thu, to 5pm Fri-Sun) Until the 15th century, the

Lausanne's Vieille Ville (Old Town)

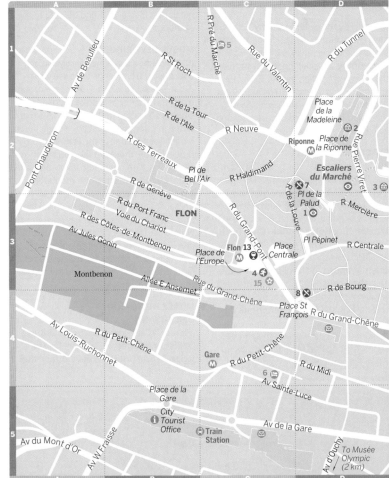

city's bishops resided in this lovely manor across from the cathedral (after which it became a jail, then a court, then a hospital). Since 1918 it has devoted itself to evoking Lausanne's heritage through paintings, drawing, stamps, musical instruments, silverware and so on. Don't miss the film featuring Lausanne in 1638.

MUSÉE DE L'ART BRUT Art Museum
(www.artbrut.ch; Av des Bergières 11-13; adult/child Sfr10/free; 1st Sat of month free; ⏱11am-6pm Tue-Sun) *Brut* means crude or rough,

and that's what you get in this extraordinary gallery, put together by French artist Jean Dubuffet in the 1970s in what was a late-18th-century country mansion. Exhibits offer a striking variety and, at times, surprising technical capacity and an often inspirational view of the world. View sculptures made out of broken plates and discarded rags, faces made out of shells, sculptures in wood, paintings, sketches and much more. Take bus 2 or 3 to the Beaulieu stop.

works by landscape painter Louis Ducros (1748–1810).

Tours

CGN
Boat Tour

(☎ 0848 811 848; www.cgn.ch) Lake cruises, some aboard beautiful belle époque steamers, by Lake Geneva's main boat operator.

LES BALADEURS
Bicycle Tour

(www.lesbaladeurs.ch; Place de l'Europe 1b; free; ⏰ Jun-Sep) Bring your own bike or borrow one for free from bike-tour organisers Lausanne Roule (p81). Cycling tours are themed and cater to all levels.

GUIDES D'ACCUEIL MDA
Walking Tour

(☎ 021 320 12 61; www.lausanne.ch/visites; adult/child Sfr10/free; ⏰ 10am & 2.30pm Mon-Sat May-Sep) Walking tours of the Old Town, departing from in front of the Hôtel de Ville on Place de la Palud. They run themed tours for up to five people on demand.

Sleeping

In return for the Sfr2.50 tourist tax added to your hotel bill, you get a Lausanne Transport Card, which gives you unlimited use of public transport for the duration of your stay; pick it up when you check in to your accommodation.

HÔTEL BEAU-RIVAGE
PALACE
Historic Hotel $$$

(☎ 021 613 33 33; www.beau-rivage-palace.ch; Place du Port 17-19; d from Sfr550; P ✳ @ 🛜 ⛱) Easily the most-stunningly located hotel in town and one of only two five-star options, this luxury lakeside address is suitably sumptuous. A beautifully maintained early 19th-century mansion set in immaculate grounds, it tempts with magnificent lake and Alp views, a spa, two bars and a trio of upmarket terrace restaurants.

MUSÉE CANTONAL DES
BEAUX ARTS
Art Museum

(www.mcba.ch; Place de la Riponne 6; adult/child Sfr10/free, 1st Sat of month free; ⏰ 11am-6pm Tue-Thu, to 5pm Fri-Sun) Palais de Rumine, the neo-Renaissance pile (1904) where the Treaty of Lausanne finalising the break-up of the Ottoman Empire after WWI was signed in 1923, safeguards the city's fine-arts museum. Works by Swiss and foreign artists, ranging from Ancient Egyptian art to Cubism, are displayed, but the core of the collection is made up of

Lausanne

HÔTEL DU MARCHÉ　　　Hotel $

(☎021 647 99 00; www.hoteldumarche
-lausanne.ch; Rue Pré du Marché 42; s/d/tr/q
Sfr114/133/156/179, s/d with shared bathroom
Sfr81/132; P@🛜) For a friendly welcome
at a price that won't break the bank,
check into this address, a five-minute
walk from the Old Town. No-frills rooms
are clean and spacious, and the kettle
with complimentary tea and coffee in
each room is a great touch. On sunny
days loll on the tiny tree-shaded terrace
out front.

HÔTEL ELITE　　　Boutique Hotel $$

(☎021 320 23 61; www.elite-lausanne.ch;
Av Sainte Luce 1; s/d/q Sfr155/215/400;
P❄@🛜) The same family has run
this lovely apricot townhouse of a
hotel for three generations. A couple of
sun-loungers and tables dot the pretty
handkerchief-sized garden and inside
at reception it's all fresh flower arrange-
ments and soft background music.
Rooms on the 4th floor look over the lake
and the best have a balcony too.

HÔTEL DU PORT　　　Hotel $

(☎021 612 04 44; www.hotel-du-port.ch; Place
du Port 5; s/d Sfr160/195; 🛜) A perfect loca-
tion in Ouchy, just back from the lake,
makes this a good choice. The better
doubles look out across the lake (Sfr20
extra) and are spacious (about 20 sq me-
tres). Up on the 3rd floor are some lovely
junior suites.

Eating

Lausanne's dining scene is laidback. Its
best addresses are stylish cafe-bars and
bistros that morph, come dusk, into great
places for drinks and tapas.

CAFÉ ST-PIERRE　　Modern European $

(☎021 326 36 36; www.cafesaintpierre.ch; Place
Benjamin Constant 1; mains Sfr20-30, tapas
Sfr6-8.50, brunch Sfr10-23; ⏰7.30am-midnight
Tue & Wed, to 1am Thu, to 2am Fri, 11am-2am Sat,
11am-6pm Sun; 🛜) The very fact that every
table is snapped up by noon while waiters
buzz between tables and the telephone
constantly rings says it all – this hip cafe-
bar rocks! Its interior is retro, trendy and
relaxed, and the cuisine is contemporary
European – quiches, pasta, salad, fish and
so on at lunchtime, creative tapas from
7pm and brunch on weekends. Reserve in
advance.

CAFÉ ROMAND　　　Swiss $

(☎021 312 63 75; Place St François 2; mains
Sfr20-30; ⏰11am-11pm Mon-Sat) Hidden
in an unpromising-looking arcade, this
Lausanne legend dating to 1951 is a wel-
come blast from the past. Everyone from
bankers to punks pours into the broad,
somewhat-sombre dining area littered
with timber tables to gorge on fondue,
cervelle au beurre noir (brains in black
butter), tripe, *pied de porc* (pork trotters)
and other feisty traditional dishes. Simple

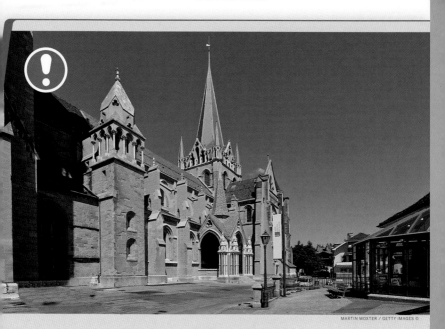

MARTIN MOXTER / GETTY IMAGES ©

Don't Miss **Cathédrale de Notre Dame**

Lausanne's Gothic cathedral, Switzerland's finest, stands proudly at the heart of the Old Town. Raised in the 12th and 13th centuries on the site of earlier, humbler churches, it lacks the lightness of French Gothic buildings but is remarkable nonetheless. Pope Gregory X, in the presence of Rudolph of Habsburg (the Holy Roman Emperor) and an impressive group of European cardinals and bishops, consecrated the church in 1275.

Although touched up in parts in the following centuries (notably the main facade, which was added to the original to protect the interior against ferocious winds), the cathedral remains largely as it was. The most striking element is the elaborate entrance on the south flank of the church (which, unusually for Christian churches, was long the main way in). The painted statuary depicts Christ in splendour, the coronation of the Virgin Mary, the Apostles and other Bible scenes. Free 40-minute guided tours run from July to September.

THINGS YOU NEED TO KNOW

Place de la Cathédrale; ⊘7am-7pm Mon-Fri, 8am-7pm Sat & Sun, to 5.30pm Sep-Mar

---

omelettes (between Sfr11 and Sfr14), sandwiches (Sfr7) and soups ensure all tastes are catered for. The kitchen operates all day, rare for this town.

CAFÉ DE GRANCY   Modern European $
(☏021 616 86 66; www.cafédegrancy.ch; Av du Rond Point 1; mains Sfr20-35, brunch Sfr29; ⊘8am-midnight Mon-Fri, from 10am Sat & Sun; ⏶) Something of an iconic address where

Lausanne's hip and trendy have long hung out, this place just to the south of the train station has floppy lounges in the front and a tempting restaurant out back. The cuisine is creative – think mozzarella and black tomato salad, smoked clams with peaches and an unbeatable value *pâte du jour* (daily pasta dish) served with salad or soup. Wednesday is fondue day, the first Tuesday of the month is

Bridge Bars

When there's a bridge, there's a bar. At least that's how it works in artsy Lausanne where the monumental arches of its bridges shelter the city's most happening summertime bars.

First port of call for that all-essential, after-work drink in the warm evening sun and last port of call before bed is **Les Arches** (www.lesarches.ch; Place de L'Europe; ⊙11am-late Mon-Sat, 1pm-midnight Sun), occupying four arches of Lausanne's magnificent Grand Pont (built between 1839 and 1940) above Place de l'Europe. Mid-evening, the crowd moves to **Bourg Plage** (www.le-bourg.ch; ⊙2pm-midnight), with pool table, table football, palm trees and deckchairs in one old stone arch of Pont Charles Bessières (built between 1908 and 1910); steps lead up to it from Rue Centrale and down to it from opposite MUDAC on Rue Pierre Veret.

always themed and the weekend ushers in brunch.

CAFÉ DE L'HÔTEL DE VILLE   Cafe $
(Place de la Palud 10; salads Sfr13-25; ⊙11.30am-6pm Tue, 9am-11.30pm Wed-Fri, 9am-7pm Sat) Old-fashioned salads are the trademark of this retro cafe à l'ancienne in the Old Town. Ingredients are locally sourced, often organic, and give a nod to the past in the shape of dried figs and grains. Marie's salad with gooey, oven-baked tomme (a type of cheese) is to die for.

L'ÉLÉPHANT BLANC   Modern European $$
(☎021 312 64 89; Rue Cité-Devant 4; mains Sfr25-40; ⊙lunch & dinner Tue-Sat) One of just a handful of restaurants behind the cathedral, the White Elephant is one of Lausanne's finest dines. But what's

staggeringly good value is its lunchtime plat du jour (dish of the day, Sfr18.50) and creative meal-sized salads (between Sfr15 and Sfr25).

🍷 Drinking

Eating venues Café St-Pierre and Café de Grancy are stylish drinking addresses too, packed with a hip crowd year-round.

BLEU LÉZARD   Bar
(www.bleu-lezard.ch; Rue Enning 10; ⊙7am-late Mon-Fri, from 8am Sat, from 9.30am Sun; 🛜) This corner bar and bistro with royal-blue paintwork and wicker chairs to match is an old favourite that never loses its appeal – day or night (or at weekends for brunch). Lunch (mains cost between Sfr25 and Sfr30), including some great veggie options, is served until 3pm and when your feet wanna' jive to a live band, there's the basement music club La Cave.

⭐ Entertainment

Lausanne is among Switzerland's busier night-time cities; look for free listings mag What's Up (www.whatsupmag.ch) in bars.

LE ROMANDIE   Live Music
(www.leromandie.ch; Place de l'Europe 1a; ⊙10pm-4am Tue & Thu-Sat) Lausanne's pre-mier rock club resides in a post-industrial location within the great stone arches of the Grand Pont. Expect live rock, garage and even punk, followed by DJ sounds in a similar vein.

CHORUS   Jazz
(www.chorus.ch; Av Mon Repos 3; ⊙8.30pm-2am Thu-Sat) Top jazz venue.

LE D! CLUB   Music, Club
(www.dclub.ch; Place Centrale; ⊙11pm-5am Wed-Sat) DJs spin house in all its latest sub-forms at this heaving club. Take the stairs down from Rue du Grand Pont and turn right before descending all the way into Place Centrale.

ℹ️ Information

Canton de Vaud Tourist Office (📞021 613 26 26; www.lake-geneva-region.ch; Av d'Ouchy 60; 🕐8am-5.30pm Mon-Fri)

City Tourist Office (📞021 613 73 73; www.lausanne-tourisme.ch) Train Station (Place de la Gare 9; 🕐9am-7pm); Ouchy (Place de la Navigation 4; 🕐9am-7pm Apr-Sep, to 6pm Oct-Mar)

ℹ️ Getting There & Away

Boat

CGN (📞0848 811 848; www.cgn.ch; Quai JP Delamuraz 17) runs passenger boats (no car ferries) from Ouchy to destinations around Lake Geneva. To hop on and off as you please, buy a one-day pass (Sfr60) covering unlimited lake travel.

Train

You can travel by train to and from the following:
Geneva (Sfr28, 30 to 50 minutes, up to six hourly)

Geneva Airport (Sfr25, 50 minutes, up to four hourly).

Bern (Sfr31, 70 minutes, one or two an hour)

ℹ️ Getting Around

Bicycle

Pick up a bike to pedal around town from **Lausanne Roule** (www.lausanneroule.ch; Place de l'Europe 1b; 4/24hr free/Sfr6; 🕐8am-6pm), under the arches of the Grand Pont.

Car & Motorcycle

Parking in central Lausanne is a headache. In blue zones you can park for free (one-hour limit) with a time disk. Most white zones are meter parking.

Public Transport

Buses and trolley buses service most destinations; the m2 Métro line (single trip/day pass Sfr1.90/Sfr8.60) connects the lake (Ouchy) with the train station (Gare) and the Flon district.

AROUND LAUSANNE

Head out of Lausanne, and wine tasting and gastronomy suddenly become key dominators, be it westbound along La Côte (the Coast) or eastbound towards jazz-famed Montreux along a lakeshore pretty enough to be called the Swiss Riviera (p84). For dedicated wine buffs, a tasting pilgrimage to Lavaux's Unesco-protected vineyards is essential.

La Côte

Fantasy castles, imposing palaces and immaculately maintained medieval villages sprinkle the Coast – the luxuriant lakeshore between Lausanne and Geneva where more than half of the Canton de Vaud's wine, mostly white, is produced.

Château on Lake Geneva
INGOLF POMPE / GETTY IMAGES ©

Detour:
Coppet

Midway between Nyon and Geneva, this tightly packed medieval village is a delight to meander through with its lakeside warren of hotels and restaurants bowing at the feet of hilltop, 18th-century **Château de Coppet** (www.coppet.ch; adult/child Sfr8/4; ☺2-6pm Easter-Oct). The rose-coloured stately home belonged to the wily Jacques Necker, Louis XVI's banker and finance minister. The pile, sumptuously furnished in Louis XVI style, became home to Necker's daughter, Madame de Staël, after she was exiled from Paris by Napoleon. In her literary salons here she entertained the likes of Edward Gibbon and Lord Byron.

The train line from Geneva follows the course of the lake here, but arriving by a CGN paddle steamer (try to catch one of the beautifully restored belle époque ones) is definitely the more romantic option.

St Sulpice & Morges

A pleasant walk west of Lausanne, about 6km from Ouchy, brings you to **St Sulpice**, a semi-suburban settlement whose jewel is the Romanesque church of the same name by the lake. A handful of restaurants are well placed to alleviate hunger. Take bus 2 from Place St François and change to bus 30 at Bourdonette.

Some 12km west of Lausanne, the first town of importance is the wine-growing village of **Morges** (www.morges-tourisme.ch). Dominating its bijou port is the squat, four-turreted 13th-century **Château de Morges** (Place du Port; adult/child Sfr10/3; ☺10am-5pm Jul & Aug, 10am-noon & 1.30-5pm Tue-Fri, 1.30-7pm Sat & Sun Mar-Jun & Sep-Nov),

built by Savoy duke Louis in 1286 and home to four military-inspired museums today. Don't miss the 10,000 toy soldiers on parade in the **Musée de la Figurine Historique**.

🍽 Eating

METROPOLIS CAFÉ Bistro, Bar $$
(☎021 803 23 33; Rue de Louis-de-Savoie 20, Morges; mains Sfr20-30; ☺7am-midnight Mon-Wed, to 1am Thu, to 2am Fri & Sat, 9am-midnight Sun; 🛜) Dine beneath turquoise parasols around an age-old stone fountain outside or on vintage flexi-plastic inside at this hybrid eating-drinking space that morphs into a happening bar after dark. Mains cleverly come in two sizes, the daily special (between Sfr17 and Sfr19) is great value and the Sunday brunch is fabulous.

CAFÉ DE BALZAC Cafe $
(www.balzac.ch; Rue de Louis-de-Savoie 37, Morges; mains Sfr20-25, hot chocolate Sfr6.20-7.20; ☺8.15am-6.30pm Tue-Wed & Fri, to 10pm Thu, 9.15am-5pm Sat, from 11am Sun) Lovers of exotic hot chocolate, teas and salads with an Asian twist should make a pilgrimage to this gorgeous old-fashioned cafe, one block back from the lakeside promenade in the heart of the old centre.

Nyon
POP 18,800

Of Roman origin but with a partly Celtic name (the 'on' comes from *dunon,* which means fortified enclosure), Nyon is a pretty lake town pierced at its hilltop-heart by the gleaming white turrets of a fairytale château – a tasty lunch address.

Nyon's castle was started in the 12th century, modified 400 years later and now houses the town's **Musée Historique et des Porcelaines** (History & Porcelain Museum; Place du Château; adult/child Sfr8/free; ☺10am-5pm Tue-Sun) and, in its old stone cellars, the **Caveau des Vignerons** (Place du Château; ☺2-9pm Fri & Sat, 11am-8pm Sun) where you can taste different Nyon wines by local producers. Pay Sfr20 to sample two reds and two whites with a plate of *charcuterie* (cold meats).

🛏 Eating

L'AUBERGE DU CHÂTEAU   Italian $$

(📞022 361 00 32; www.aubergeduchateau.
ch; Place du Château 8, Nyon; mains Sfr30-50;
⏰8am-midnight, closed Sun Oct-Apr) No
restaurant and cafe terrace has such a
stunning view as this. Filling the pretty pe-
destrian square in front of Nyon's pretty
château, tables look out on the Sleeping
Beauty towers and lake beyond. Cuisine
is Italian and creative – *taglierini* with figs,
simple homemade gnocchi and authentic
pizza cooked in a wood-fired oven.

GELATERIA VENEZIA   Ice Cream $

(Rue de Rive 44; ice cream Sfr3-7; ⏰11am-
7pm) Punters pour across the water
from France for it... the extraordinary
Italian-style ice cream, that is, at Nyon's
legendary ice-cream boutique Gelateria
Venezia. The flavours tease tastebuds
with creative combos such as banana
split, After Eight and lots of chocolate
variations. From Nyon's CGN boat jetty on
the lakefront, walk one block inland and
look for the line outside the door.

LA YOGOURTERIE   Desserts $

(Rue de Rive 48; frozen yoghurt Sfr5-7; ⏰1-7pm)
The frozen yoghurt here comes *au naturel*
from the Moléson cheese dairy near
Gruyères before being flavoured
with fruit in Nyon.

Lavaux Wine Region

East of Lausanne, the
mesmerising serried
ranks of lush, pea-green
vineyards that stagger
up the steep terraced
slopes above Lake Ge-
neva form the Lavaux
wine region – suf-
ficiently magnificent
to be a Unesco World
Heritage Site. One-fifth
of the Canton de Vaud's

wine is produced on these steep, gravity-
defying slopes.

Walking between vines and wine
tasting on weekends in local *caveaux*
(wine cellars) are key reasons to explore
the string of 14 villages beaded along this
fertile and wealthy, 40km stretch of shore.
The tourist office in Montreux is the best
place to pick up detailed information and
maps.

Lutry
POP 9300

This captivating medieval village, just
4km east of Lausanne, was founded in the
11th century by French monks. Its central
Église de St Martin et St Clément was
built in the early 13th century, and there's
a modest **château** a short way north.
Stroll along the pretty waterfront and
the slightly twee main street lined with
art galleries, antique stores, the occa-
sional cafe and wine cellar **Caveau des
Vignerons** (Grand Rue 23; ⏰5-9pm Tue-Fri,
11am-2pm & 5-9pm Sat) where you can taste
wine by different local producers. The two
main wine types are Calamin and Dézaley,

Terraced vineyards of the Lavaux
wine region
ANDREAS STRAUSS / GETTY IMAGES ©

Below: Outdoor dining in Place de la Palud (p75), Lausanne;
Right: Lakeside trail near Montreux (p86)

(BELOW) INGOLF POMPE 84 / ALAMY ©; (RIGHT) CKCHIU / SHUTTERSTOCK ©.

there instead before looping back to Cully (4.4km).

and most of the whites (about three-quarters of all production) are made with the Chasselas grape.

Bus 9 links Lutry with Place St François in Lausanne. From Lutry a beautiful 5.5km **walking trail** winds east through vines and the tiny hamlets of **Le Châtelard** and **Aran** to the larger wine-making villages of **Grandvaux** and **Riex**. For staggering vine and lake views, hike up to **La Conversion** (3.8km) above Lutry and continue on the high trail to Grandvaux (4km).

Cully
POP 1800

Lakeside Cully, 5km east of Lutry, is a lovely village for a waterfront meander and early evening mingle with *vignerons* (winegrowers) in its **Caveau des Vignerons** (www.caveau-cully.ch; Place d'Armes 16; ⏲5-9pm Thu-Sun Apr-Oct). Alternatively hike along the well-signposted walking trail uphill to the inland villages of **Riex** and **Epesses**, and have a tipple in a wine cellar

Rivaz to Chardonne

Lavaux Vinorama (☎021 946 31 31; www.lavaux-vinorama.ch; Route du Lac 2; tasting Sfr13-20; ⏲10.30am-8.30pm Mon-Sat, to 7pm Sun, closed Mon & Tue Nov-Jun), a thoroughly modern tasting and discovery centre 5km east of Cully in Rivaz, is the best place to discover the various appellations of the Lavaux vineyards.

SWISS RIVIERA

Stretching east to Villeneuve, the Swiss Riviera rivals its French counterpart as a magnet for the rich and famous. Magnificent belle époque paddle steamers cruise the lake as they did in 1910, treating passengers to a banquet of gourmet views and paparazzi glimpses of otherwise-hidden lakeside properties, while panoramic trains saunter from the shore to Swiss-perfect mountain scenes.

All this barely an hour's drive from Alpine ski spots, in a climate so mild that palm trees and other subtropical flora flourish.

Vevey
POP 18,600

Lakeside Vevey exudes a certain understated swankiness with its tiny but perfect Old Town, lakeside central square and promenades, stylish dining, unusual museums and treasure trove of little boutiques made for post-lunch browsing. Don't miss Charlie Chaplin, signature 'little tramp' cane in hand, posing on the waterfront.

 Sights

ALIMENTARIUM Museum
(☎ 021 924 41 11; www.alimentarium.ch; Quai Perdonnet; adult/child Sfr12/free, audioguide Sfr6; ⊙10am-5pm Tue-Fri, to 6pm Sat & Sun) Nestlé's headquarters have been in Vevey since 1814, hence its presence in the form of this museum dedicated to nutrition and all things edible, past and present. Boring it is not. Its displays are clearly meant to entertain as well as inform, starting with the gigantic silver fork that sticks out of the water in front of the lakeside mansion (great picnic spot thanks to the handful of wooden chairs screwed into the rocks here on the lakeshore). End with a healthy lunch in the **museum restaurant** (lunch Sfr18; ⊙noon-1.30pm Tue-Sun mid-Jul–mid-Sep).

 **Eating & Drinking**

LE LITTÉRAIRE Cafe $
(www.cafe-litteraire.ch; Quai Perdonnet 33; ⊙9am-9pm; 🛜) Take the local town library, add a trendy cafe with ceiling-to-floor windows facing the lake and an idyllic summertime terrace, and you get this much-loved local favourite. Check the blackboard outside for the good-value *plat du jour* (Sfr19.90).

Scenic Trips

The panorama of Lavaux vineyards staggering down to the lake is particularly fine from the back of a boat. CGN's **Fabuleux Vignobles de Lavaux** (Fabulous Lavaux Vineyards) cruise departs from Lausanne twice daily (five times daily between mid-June and mid-September), with stops in Lutry, Cully, Vevey, Chillon and Montreux. A Lausanne–Montreux adult return ticket costs Sfr42.20.

Another fun and easy way to lose yourself in green vines and blue lake views is aboard the **Lavaux Express** (www.lavauxexpress.ch; adult/child Sfr13/5; ☺Tue-Sun Apr-Oct), a tractor-pulled tourist train that chugs through Lavaux' vineyards and villages. Pick from two routes: Lutry CGN boat pier up to the wine-growing villages of Aran and Grandvaux (one hour return trip), or Cully pier to Riex, Espesses and Dézaley (1¼ hours).

LE MAZOT Swiss $$
(☎021 921 78 22; Rue du Conseil 7; mains Sfr20-40; ☺lunch & dinner Mon-Tue & Thu-Sat, dinner Sun) In the heart of the Old Town, this tiny little restaurant with quintessential striped canopy and flower-box pavement terrace is an institution of classic local cooking.

LE CHÂTEAU Swiss $$$
(☎021 921 12 10; www.denismartin.ch; Rue du Château 2; tasting menu Sfr350; ☺dinner Tue-Sun, closed 3wks Jul-Aug & 2wks Dec-Jan) Charismatic and engaging, chef Denis Martin is one of the country's biggest names in Swiss contemporary cooking. His tasting menu – think two Michelin stars – is a thrilling succession of 25-odd different bite-sized taste sensations, served in a traditional 17th-century mansion a block from the lake.

🔒 Shopping

Shopaholics, this is heaven! The tiny but perfect maze of boutique-riddled, Old Town streets that fan out east of central square Grande Place are pure joy to meander. Don't miss the one-off pieces of jewellery, ceramics, bags and frilly parasols – all of which exude a real old-world elegance – at **Ozange** (Rue du Conseil 23), the quirky knick-knacks for the home at **Balthazar** (Rue du Lac 32) and the extraordinary electro-mechanical sculptures by Vevey's resident British goldsmith Charles Morgan at **Galerie d'Art Morgan** (Rue du Théâtre 9).

ℹ️ Information

Tourist Office (☎084 886 84 84; www.montreux-vevey.com; Grande Place; ☺9am-6pm Mon-Fri, 9am-1pm Sat & Sun May-Sep, 9am-noon & 1-5.30pm Mon-Fri, 9am-noon Sat & Sun Oct-Apr)

ℹ️ Getting There & Around

Vevey is linked by train to Lausanne (Sfr4.90, 15 to 25 minutes) and Montreux (Sfr3.30, five to 10 minutes).

Or indulge in a scenic lakeside cycle from Lausanne (19km) or Montreux (6.5km): **Altmann Sports** (☎021 921 96 77; Rue de la Madeleine 22) in Vevey rents bicycles.

Montreux
POP 23,000

In the 19th century, writers, artists and musicians (Lord Byron and the Shelleys among them) flocked to this pleasing lakeside resort, and it has remained a magnet ever since. Peaceful walks along a lakeshore beaded with 19th-century hotels, a mild microclimate, a hilltop Old Town, the famous jazz fest and a fabulous 13th-century fortress are its main drawcards.

Sights

FREDDIE MERCURY STATUE Monument
(Place du Marché) Year round, fresh flowers smother the feet of this 3m-tall statue of Freddie Mercury, 'lover of life, singer of

RICHARD TAYLOR / 4CORNERS ©

Don't Miss Château de Chillon

From the waterfront in Montreux, the fairytale **Chemin Fleuri** (Flower Path) – a silky smooth promenade framed by flowerbeds positively tropical in colour and vivacity – snakes dreamily along the lake for 4km to the magnificent stone hulk of the Château de Chillon.

Occupying a stunning position on Lake Geneva, this oval-shaped 13th-century fortress is a maze of courtyards, towers and halls filled with arms, period furniture and artwork. The landward side is heavily fortified but lakeside it presents a gentler face. Chillon was largely built by the House of Savoy and taken over by Bern's governors after Vaud fell to Bern. Don't miss the medieval frescos in the **Chapelle St Georges** and the spooky Gothic **dungeons**.

The fortress gained fame in 1816 when Byron wrote *The Prisoner of Chillon*, a poem about François Bonivard, thrown into the dungeon for his seditious ideas and freed by Bernese forces in 1536. Byron carved his name into the pillar to which Bonivard was supposedly chained. Painters William Turner and Gustave Courbet subsequently immortalised the castle's silhouette on canvas, and Jean-Jacques Rousseau, Alexandre Dumas and Mary Shelley all wrote about it.

It takes about 45 minutes to walk from Montreux to Chillon, or take trolley bus 1. CGN boats and steamers – a wonderful way to arrive – call at Château de Chillon from Lausanne (adult return Sfr33, 1¾ hours), Vevey (adult return Sfr21.60, 50 minutes) and Montreux (adult return Sfr16, 15 minutes).

THINGS YOU NEED TO KNOW

www.chillon.ch; Av de Chillon 21; adult/child Sfr12/6; ☺9am-7pm Apr-Sep, 9.30am-6pm Mar & Oct, 10am-5pm Nov-Feb

Detour:
Aigle

An absolute must for anyone with a passion for wine or turreted castles, Aigle (population 8160), at the southeast end of Lake Geneva, is the capital of the Chablais wine-producing region in southeast Vaud. Grapes grown on the vines carpeting the gentle slopes here make some of Switzerland's best whites.

Two thousand years of wine-making is explored in the compelling **Musée de la Vigne et du Vin** (www.museeduvin.ch; adult/child Sfr11/6; 11am-6pm Jul-Aug, Tue-Sun Apr-Jun & Sep-Oct), a thoroughly modern and interactive wine museum inside Aigle's fairytale château. The six hands-on digital experiments – indulge in your own Chasselas grape harvest, make wine etc – in the 'lab' are particularly fun.

Afterwards, cross the castle courtyard to the 13th-century **Maison de la Dîme** and peek at whatever temporary exhibition is on upstairs (entry included in the wine-museum ticket price). Then lunch in the lovely **La Pinte du Paradis** (024 466 18 44; www.lapinteduparadis.com; Place du Château d'Aigle 2; mains Sfr25-45; lunch & dinner Tue-Sat Apr-Oct). It's got a great-value lunchtime Sfr20 *menu* – eaten between rustic wood and suspended spoons inside or on the terrace with vineyard and Alps views.

There are several other equally atmospheric places to lunch in the narrow old-world lanes on the approach from Aigle's new town to the old, château-crowned part of Aigle known as the Quartier du Cloître.

Regular trains link Lausanne (Sfr7.60, 30 minutes) with Aigle via Montreux. Pick up wheels at **Rent a Bike** (051 224 60 04; www.rentabike.ch; per day Sfr33) at Aigle train station.

songs', in front of Montreux' old covered market on the waterfront. From 1979 until his premature death in 1991, the lead vocalist came to Montreux with rock band Queen to record hit after hit at the Mountain Studios in Montreux Casino.

 **Festivals & Events**

MONTREUX JAZZ Music
(www.montreuxjazz.com) Montreux' best-known fest, established in 1967, lasts two weeks in July. Free concerts take place daily, but tickets cost anything from Sfr75 to Sfr240 for bigger-name gigs. Music is not just jazz; The Strokes, Sting, Arcade Fire, BB King, Paul Simon and Deep Purple (with their big comeback gig in 2011) have all played here.

 **Sleeping & Eating**

TRALALA HÔTEL Design Hotel $$
(021 963 49 73; www.tralalahotel.ch; Rue du Temple 2; d Sfr130-280; P@) A boutique hotel designed around Montreux' extraordinary musical heritage just had to open – and it has, perched up high from the lake in the old part of Montreux. Rooms come in three sizes – S ('Small & Sexy'), L or XL – and each pays homage to a different artist, giving guests the chance to sleep with Aretha Franklin, David Bowie and 33 other famous artists.

HÔTEL MASSON Historic Hotel $$$
(021 966 00 44; www.hotelmasson.ch; Rue Bonivard 5, Montreux-Veytaux; s/d/tr/q Sfr200/270/360/410; P) In 1829, this vintner's mansion was converted into a hotel. The old charm has remained intact

and the hotel, set in magnificent grounds, is on the Swiss Heritage list of the country's most-beautiful hotels. It lies back in the hills southeast of Montreux, best reached by taxi.

LA ROUVENAZ   Hotel $

(☎ 021 963 27 36; www.montreux.ch/rouvenaz -hotel; Rue du Marché 1; s/d Sfr130/190; @) A stylish family-run spot with its own tasty restaurant downstairs and wine bar next door – you cannot get any closer to the lake or the heart of the action. Its six rooms are simple, but pleasant; most have at least a lake glimpse.

CAFÉ DU GRÜTLI   Swiss $

(☎ 021 963 42 65; Rue du Grand Chêne 8; mains Sfr10-25; ⏰ 8am-3pm Tue, to midnight Thu-Mon) No Riviera glam at this address, rather a handful of locals who lunch here every day on hearty meat dishes, fondues, omelettes and perfectly crispy rösti. And yes, the hike up the hill to this banana-yellow village cafe, around for at least a century, definitely warrants dessert.

ℹ Information

Tourist office (☎ 084 886 84 84; www. montreux-vevey.com; Rue du Théâtre 5; ⏰ 9am-6pm Mon-Fri, 9.30am-5pm Sat & Sun)

ℹ Getting There & Away

From Lausanne, some three trains an hour (Sfr11.40, 20 to 35 minutes) serve Montreux. Montreux is also on the scenic Golden Pass route to the Bernese Oberland. For CGN boats, see p73.

Bern, Jura & Mittelland

Easily one of the most charming capitals on the planet, Bern's 15th-century Old Town is fairytale-like with its terraced stone buildings, covered arcades, clock towers and cobbled streets. When Swiss politicians had to pick a capital it leapt out as the unthreatening choice: Geneva was too French, Zürich too German. Bern was just right.

Tucked up against the French and German borders in the northwest corner of the country, businesslike Basel straddles the majestic Rhine. The town is home to top-flight art galleries and boasts an enchanting Old Town.

A far cry from the staggering Alpine scenes more readily associated with Switzerland, a gentle corner in the west remains a 'secret'. From the evocative medieval towns of Fribourg and Neuchâtel to gorgeous medieval villages such as Gruyères and St Ursanne, it proffers sights and 'scapes off the tourist track.

Bern's Bärenpark (p106)

ANDY CHRISTIANI / GETTY IMAGES ©

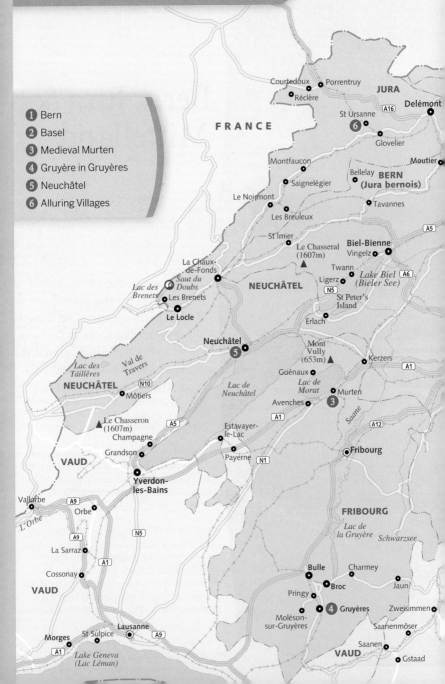

Bern, Jura & Mittelland

20 km
12 miles

1 Bern
2 Basel
3 Medieval Murten
4 Gruyère in Gruyères
5 Neuchâtel
6 Alluring Villages

Courtedoux
Porrentruy
Réclère
JURA
A16
Delémont
St Ursanne
6
Glovelier
FRANCE
Moutier
Montfaucon
Belleau
BERN
(Jura bernois)
Saignelégier
Tavannes
Le Noirmont
Les Breuleux
St Imier
A5
Le Chasseral
(1607m)
Biel-Bienne
La Chaux-
de-Fonds
Vingelz
Saut du
Doubs
Twann
Lac des
Brenets
Les Brenets
NEUCHÂTEL
Ligerz
Lake Biel
(Bieler See)
A6
N5
St Peter's
Island
Le Locle
Erlach
Neuchâtel
5
Mont
Vully
(653m)
Kerzers
A1
Lac des
Táillères
Val de
Travers
Guénaux
Lac de
Morat
Murten
3
NEUCHÂTEL
N10
Môtiers
Lac de
Neuchâtel
Avenches
Saane
A12
Le Chasseron
(1607m)
A5
Estavayer-
le-Lac
A1
Fribourg
Champagne
Payerne
N1
Grandson
VAUD
Yverdon-
les-Bains
FRIBOURG
Vallorbe
A9
Orbe
Lac de
la Gruyère
Schwarzsee
L'Orbe
A9
N5
La Sarraz
Bulle
Charmey
Cossonay
A1
Broc
Jaun
VAUD
Pringy
Zweisimmen
Moléson-
sur-Gruyères
4
Gruyères
Morges
St Sulpice
Lausanne
A9
Saanenmöser
Saanen
Lake Geneva
(Lac Léman)
VAUD
Gstaad

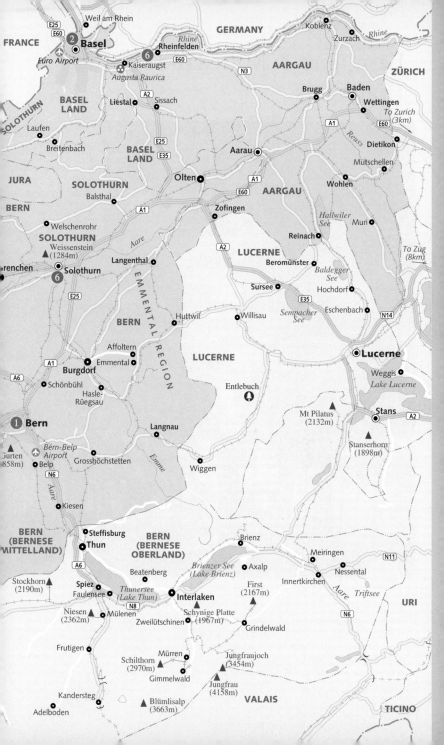

Bern, Jura & Mittelland's Highlights

1

Bern

Oddly overlooked by many, Switzerland's capital of Bern (p102) is a fantasyland of medieval buildings spilling down to the sinuous River Aare. You can get lost for days in 6km of covered arcades that mix modern commercial flair with the sort of deeply held conservatism you'd expect. Above: Zytglogge (clock tower; p105); Bottom right: Gurten

Need to Know

BEST TIME TO VISIT Try spring or autumn when Bern enjoys a timeless bustle. **TOP TIP** You can't feed the bears. **For further coverage, see p102**.

Bern Don't Miss List

CHRISTINE LAUTERBURG, SINGER

1 MATTE

Matte is a lovely quarter near the River Aare with old houses and a lot of clubs and bars. We like to start at one and keep wandering, visiting many. It's pretty by day and very fun by night, and the river is right alongside.

2 REITHALLE

Everyone thinks Switzerland is so tidy and orderly but they haven't seen the **Reithalle** (www.reitschule.ch). It was built in 1897 as a riding school, so it has a huge indoor space. Later it was a squat and you can still find its wild past. Local people love it. Here you can see many concerts, theatre, other performances, film and pretty much anything that's experimental. It's not far from the main train station.

3 BREITENRAIN

Breitenrain is a quiet quarter with French flair and a real feel for the culture. It's on the east side of the river and it's fun to wander its quiet streets and visit one of the tempting restaurants.

4 MARZILIBAD

In summer we all take a dip in this **open-air swimming pool** (www.aaremarzili.ch; ⊘May-Sep) right beside the Aare River. We work on our tans and play on the huge lawns, foosball tables and other sports. You have to be a really strong swimmer to go in the river itself, so the pool is perfect – and it's free!

5 GURTEN

From Gurten, a hilly neighbourhood near Bern, you can see the whole city. It's a pretty place to walk and it's easy to get to. Catch a tram from the main station (direction: Wabern), exit at Gurtenbahn and walk on the top. There's also a little train that goes up the hill. Have dinner in the nice restaurant and then have a good stroll back down.

Basel

Greater Europe never feels closer to Switzerland than it does in Basel (p107), where France and Germany are a short toss of raclette away. International companies make their headquarters here and help support some excellent museums, including one of the nation's mos compelling, the Beyeler Foundation, which mixes media in both engaging and challenging ways. For more traditional pleasures, the Old Town is a gem.

Medieval Murten

Like your best childhood fantasy, tiny Murten (p112) is an ancient walled town that seems almost toy-sized in scale. Ye it's the real deal: for various reasons, th locals never yanked down their defensive perimeter like most other Europea towns. The result is that you can dash back six centuries while exploring wat towers, battlements and more. Go ahead, boil some oil.

Gruyère in Gruyères

The folks over in the Emmental region might object to us saying this, but Gruyères (p114) is the nearly name-sake town for what could be the best Swiss cheese. And what a name-sake it is! A beautiful downtown of ancient buildings tumbles down to its old streets where wheels echo on the cobblestones. Cheese factories and bistros serving fondue abound, and overlooking it all is a classic castle.

Neuchâtel

For some, Neuchâtel (p116) will conjure up images of eminently spreadable cheese. You might even fantasise about toasting a bagel. But for many, this tidy place with a classically walkable Old Town is all about the lake of the same name, which cuts a long swathe of lovely blue across the gently rolling countryside. You can get boats to various little towns dotting the shore. Old Town (p116)

Alluring Villages

The west of Switzerland doesn't have the postcard-worthy Alps but that doesn't mean that it's lacking in charms. Rather, there are treasures waiting for anyone willing to take the time to find them. This less-visited region is a land of many forests hiding fantastic little towns (p117). Solothurn, St Ursanne and Rheinfelden are all easily reached as day trips by train from Bern and Basel. Solothurn (p117)

Bern, Jura & Mittelland's Best...

Historic Spots

○ **Murten** (p112) A perfectly preserved jewel-box of an old walled town.

○ **Bern's Old Town** (p111) A warren of medieval covered arcades and old streets that tumble down towards the river.

○ **Château de Gruyères** (p115) A turreted beauty dating to the 15th century. Don't miss the dungeon.

○ **Basel's Old Town** (p111) Get lost on narrow 16th-century lanes.

Local Foods

○ **La Maison du Gruyère** (p114) Traditional factory for the namesake cheese.

○ **Fromagerie d'Alpage de Moléson** (p114) An even more old-fashioned Gruyère cheese dairy.

○ **Cailler** (p114) Another famous Swiss name offers extensive tours of the chocolate factory.

○ **Villars** (p114) One of the greatest names in Swiss chocolates has a company store and cafe with the goods at great prices.

Museums

○ **Fondation Beyeler** (p107) Brilliant and wide-ranging private collection, one of the country's best.

○ **Augusta Raurica** (p110) Remains of a large Roman town near Basel with an excellent museum.

○ **Puppenhausmuseum** (p108) Who can't love Basel's museum filled with teddy bears?

○ **Zentrum Paul Klee** (p102) Eye-catching museum with thousands of stunning works by the prodigious artist.

Outdoor Spots

○ **Bärenpark** (p106) Bern's great attraction has several bears living in relative natural splendour.

○ **Sentier des Fromageries** (p114) A beautiful trail amid the clanging cow bells of the dairy farms around Gruyères. See where the cheese comes from.

○ **Neuchâtel** (p116) The town sits on the shores of its namesake lake, Switzerland's largest and noted for clear, fresh water.

Need to Know

○ **Two months before** Start the diet as you'll be inundated with amazing chocolate and amazing cheese. Need we say more?

○ **One month before** Give up on the diet and vow to start one *after* your trip. You don't want to skip on delicacies like Gruyère-filled fondue.

RESOURCES

○ **Schweizer Mittelland Tourismus** (www.smit.ch) The tourist office for the region around Bern.

○ **Pays de Fribourg** (www. pays-de-fribourg.ch) Provides info on Fribourg and the surrounding region.

○ **La Gruyère** (www. gruyere.com) Everything you want to know about the delicious, hard, nutty cheese.

○ **Lonely Planet** (www. lonelyplanet.com/ switzerland/bern) The low-down on the capital.

GETTING AROUND

○ **Train** Frequent trains in all directions make getting around this part

of Switzerland as easy as it is to tear off the wrapper on your chocolate bar. Bern is an excellent hub.

○ **Car** As always, a car will let you get off the beaten path and make visiting outlying attractions – like cheese and chocolate factories – that much easier.

BE FOREWARNED

○ **Summer** Basel is often the warmest part of Switzerland in summer and gets almost sweaty on May days. Everybody heads out to cafes. Elsewhere the mild weather makes a visit ideal as you can hike around the verdant countryside, especially Gruyères and Neuchâtel.

○ **Winter** Don't expect downhill skiing in this region but the Swiss are good at adopting the German love of Christmas markets, which can be found on central squares everywhere. Bern in particular has late-fall and winter-time festivals starting with the legendary Onion Market on the fourth Monday in November.

Cycling on the shores of Neuchâtel Lake (p116);
ve: Monet's *Le bassin aux nymphéas* (the Water-Lily Pond) at Basel's Fondation Beyeler (p107)

EFT) PRISMA BILDAGENTUR AG / ALAMY ©; (ABOVE) HEMIS / ALAMY ©

Bern, Jura & Mittelland Itineraries

Some of Switzerland's best Old Towns are in this region (think Bern and Murten to start) along with some of the best local foods (think chocolate and cheese). These two tours give you a chance to savour both.

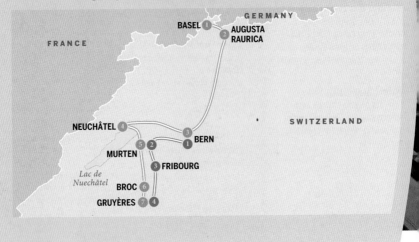

3 DAYS

BERN TO GRUYÈRES
History & Cheese

Start, naturally enough, in Switzerland's capital, the surprisingly urbane and enticing **(1) Bern**. Wander the **Old Town** and check out the namesake bears in the **Bärenpark**. Retrace the steps of Albert Einstein and visit the **Einstein Haus** where he showed a few hints of future fame while working as a clerk.

A quick train ride and you are in **(2) Murten**. Europe used to be filled with these tiny medieval towns surrounded by evocative defensive walls, but no longer. Murten is a rare surviving example and you can spend half a day happily exploring its stone walls.

Stop in **(3) Fribourg** and listen for French spoken on one side of town and German on the other. While its wall is long gone, its 12th-century **Old Town** survives and is good for strolling. Be sure to climb the 74m-tower on **Cathédrale de St Nicolas de Myre** for views of the region.

Finally, pretty train rides will take you through the rolling green hills of the dairy farms around **(4) Gruyères**. The cute town and splendid castle would be reason enough to visit but it's the cheese that is the real star. Visit a **cheesemaker** to see how it's done (and taste of course). Afterwards, walk it off on **beautiful hiking paths**.

BASEL TO GRUYÈRES

A Swiss Taste

(1) Basel combines old world allure with modern flash. Take in the sweep of the Rhine River and visit museums like the **Fondation Beyeler**, which has an incredible art collection. Afterwards have a fine meal at any of the many restaurants which take their inspiration from across Europe.

Take a train or drive to **(2) Augusta Raurica**, which preserves the ruins of a large Roman town that originated more than 2000 years ago. From here move on to **(3) Bern**, which is worth a day or more of your time. Admire the ancient **Zytglogge**, an ancient iconic clock tower, and then explore the centuries-old streets. Don't

miss museums including the **Zentrum Paul Klee**, which exhibits many of the Cubist works by the master.

Train it to **(4) Neuchâtel**, which sits on the beautiful shores of its vast lake. Go for a stroll and try the local soft cheese. Wander along the old walls of **(5) Murten**. Climb the steps a few extra times as you want to be hungry: first at **(6) Broc**, where you can enjoy the famous **Cailler chocolate factory** and second at **(7) Gruyères**, which makes one of the world's most-popular cheeses, a key ingredient of luscious Swiss fondue.

Cailler chocolate factory (p114), Broc

DAVID CHIA / ALAMY ©

Discover Bern, Jura & Mittelland

At a Glance

○ **Bern** (p102) The Swiss capital is worthy of the honour thanks to its beautiful old architecture and parks.

○ **Basel** (p107) Museums and an old quarter good for exploring.

○ **Murten** (p112) Medieval town with a perfectly preserved wall.

○ **Gruyères** (p114) Almost as tasty as its namesake cheese.

BERN

POP 123,500 / ELEV 540M

Wandering its picture-postcard Old Town, with arcaded stone streets and a provincial, laid-back air, it is hard to believe that Bern (Berne in English and French) is the capital of Switzerland – but it is, plus a Unesco World Heritage Site to boot.

Indeed, on the city's long, cobbled streets, lined with 15th-century terraced buildings and fantastical folk figures frolicking on fountains since the 16th century, you feel as if you're in some kind of dizzying architectural canyon.

◎ Sights

ZENTRUM PAUL KLEE   Art Museum
(www.zpk.org; Monument in Fruchtland 3; adult/child Sfr22/10, audioguides Sfr5; ◯10am-5pm Tue-Sun) Bern's answer to the Guggenheim, the architecturally bold Paul Klee Centre is an eye-catching 150m-long building filled with popular modern art. Renzo Piano's curvaceous building swoops up and down like waves to create a trio of 'hills' in the agricultural landscape east of town.

The middle hill houses the main exhibition space, showcasing 4000 rotating works from Paul Klee's prodigious and often-playful career. In the basement of another 'hill' is the fun-packed **Kindermuseum Creaviva** (◯10am-5pm Tue-Sun), an inspired children's museum.

Take bus 12 from Bubenbergplatz to Zentrum Paul Klee (Sfr4). By car the museum is right next to the Bern-Ostring exit of the A6.

Zentrum Paul Klee, Bern
IZZET KERIBAR / GETTY IMAGES ©

Bern

Rosengarten
Aargauerstalden
Klösterlistutz
Grosser Muristalden
Murist
Semlarstr
Alpenstr

Unterdorfbrücke
Läuferplatz
Bärenpark
Gerbengässe

Altenbergstr
Brumgasshalde
Postgasse
Rathausgasse
Krampgasse
Junkerngasse
Mühlenplatz
Matte
Schiffläube
Aare
Alpenstr
Jungfraustr
Dufourstr

Kornhausbrücke
Berner
Münster
Münster
Plattform
Budenberg
Lusienstr
Thunstr
Mottastr
Helvetiastr

Alterbergrain
Uferweg
Münstergasse
Münsterplatz
Münstergasse
Herrengasse
Badgasse
Aarstr
Bernastr
Helvetiaplatz

Kunstmuseum
Hodlerstr
Schüttestr
Nägeligasse
Hotelgasse
Theaterpl
Casinoplatz

Bollwerk
Speichergasse
Aarbergergasse
Waisenhausplatz
Zeughausgasse
Schmiedenplatz
Kornhausplatz
Marktgasse
Amthausgasse
Kochergasse
Kirchenfeldbrücke
Dalmaziquai
Dalmazibrücke

OLD TOWN
Neuengasse
Bärenplatz
Spitalgasse
Schauplatzgasse
Bundesgasse
Bundesplatz
Stadt Bern
Drahtseilbahn
Marzili Funicular
Bundesterrasse
Münzrain
Weihergasse
Marzilistr
Brückenstr

Bahnhofplatz
Hauptbahnhof
Bubenbergplatz
Bogenschutzen
Raimatstr
Sulgeneckstr

Schanzenstr
Sidlistr
Falkenplatz
Schanzenstr
Schanzenstr
Monbijoust
Sulgeneckstr

500 m
0.25 miles

Bern

BERNER MÜNSTER   Church
(www.bernermuenster.ch; audioguide Sfr5, tower admission adult/child Sfr5/2; ⊙10am-5pm Tue-Sat, 11.30am-5pm Sun Easter-Nov, noon-4pm Tue-Fri, to 5pm Sat, 11.30am-4pm Sun rest of year, tower closes 30 min earlier) The high point of the 15th-century Gothic cathedral is its lofty spire. At 100m, it's Switzerland's tallest, and those with enough energy to climb the dizzying 344-step spiral staircase are rewarded with vertiginous views of the Bernese Alps on a clear day. Coming down, take a breather by the **Upper Bells** (1356), rung at 11am, noon and 3pm daily.

KUNSTMUSEUM   Art Museum
(www.kunstmuseumbern.ch; Hodlerstrasse 8-12; adult/child permanent collection Sfr7/5, temporary exhibitions from Sfr18; ⊙10am-9pm Tue, 10am-5pm Wed-Sun) The thousands of works at the Museum of Fine Arts represent Switzerland's oldest permanent collection and include examples by Italian artists such as Fra Angelico, Swiss artists like Ferdinand Hodler and Giovanni Giacometti, and heavy hitters like Picasso and Cézanne.

EINSTEIN HAUS   Museum
(www.einstein-bern.ch; Kramgasse 49; adult/child Sfr6/free; ⊙10am-5pm daily Apr-Dec, closed Sun Feb & Mar, closed Jan) The world's most famous scientist developed his special theory of relativity in Bern in 1905. Find out more at the small museum inside the humble apartment where Einstein lived with his young family between 1903 and 1905 while working in the Bern patent office.

🛏 Sleeping

The tourist office makes hotel reservations (free) and has information on 'three nights for the price of two' deals, in which many hotels in town participate.

HOTEL LANDHAUS   Hotel $
(☎031 348 03 05; www.landhausbern.ch, in German; Altenbergstrasse 4; dm without/with pillow & quilt Sfr33/38, d without/with bathroom from Sfr120/160, breakfast Sfr8; P@🛜) In a pretty part of town, fronted by the river and Old Town spires, this boho hotel is well run and has character in spades. Its buzzing ground-floor cafe and terrace attracts a cheery crowd and rooms are both spruce and stylish.

HOTEL SCHWEIZERHOF   Luxury Hotel $$$
(☎031 326 80 80; www.schweizerhof-bern. ch; Bahnhofplatz 11; s/d from Sfr450/550; P❄@🛜) The latest player on the remodelled five-star circuit, the Schweizerhof boasts a lavish refurbishment and excellent amenities and service. A hop, skip and a jump from the train station, it's geared for both business and pleasure.

HOTEL GOLDENER SCHLÜSSEL   Hotel $$
(☎031 311 02 16; www.goldener-schluessel.ch; Rathausgasse 72; s/d/tr from Sfr140/180/240; 🛜) Going strong for 500 years, this hotel had a facelift in 2008 and boasts comfy updated rooms and an atmospheric restaurant with great sausage dishes.

HOTEL BELLE EPOQUE

Boutique Hotel **$$**

(✆031 311 43 36; www.belle-epoque.ch; Gerechtigkeitsgasse 18; s/d from Sfr170/240; 🛜) A romantic Old Town hotel with opulent art-nouveau furnishings, the Belle Epoque's design ethos sees TVs tucked away into steamer-trunk-style cupboards so as not to spoil the look. It's a small operation, with a popular cafe, so don't be surprised by a few minutes' wait at reception, watched over by a rather disconcerting mannequin. Wi-fi costs Sfr12 per day.

 Eating

For a munch between meals, nothing beats the *brezels* (pretzels) smothered in salt crystals or sunflower, pumpkin or sesame seeds from kiosks at the train station, or a bag of piping-hot chestnuts.

ALTES TRAMDEPOT

International **$$**

(Bärenpark; mains Sfr19.50-42; ⏱10am-12.30am daily, from 11am winter) You might think that its location, right by the Bear Park, would make this place a tourist trap, but even locals recommend this cavernous microbrewery out the back of the attractive tourist-office building. Swiss specialities compete against wok-cooked stir-fries for your affection and the microbrews go down a treat.

VERDI

Italian **$$**

(✆031 312 63 68; Gerechtigkeitsgasse 7; pasta & risotto Sfr23-35, mains Sfr32-49) Verdi goes all-out to make an impression and it pays off. With a menu full of dishes from Emilia-Romagna, a solid all-Italian wine list and the kind of attention to decor detail that makes you feel as though you're in an opera, you'll be swept off your feet.

KORNHAUSKELLER

Mediterranean **$$$**

(✆031 327 72 72; Kornhausplatz 18; mains Sfr28-48; ⏱lunch & dinner Mon-Sat, dinner Sun, bar 6pm-1am Mon-Wed, to 2am Thu-Sat, to 12.30am Sun) Fine dining takes place beneath vaulted frescoed arches at Bern's surprisingly ornate former granary, now a stunning cellar restaurant serving Mediterranean cuisine. Beautiful people sip cocktails alongside historic stained-glass windows on the mezzanine, and in its neighbouring

Old Town

Bern's flag-festooned medieval centre is an attraction in its own right, with 6km of covered arcades, cellar shops and bars descending from the streets. After a devastating fire in 1405, the wooden city was rebuilt in today's distinctive grey-green sandstone.

A focal point is Bern's **Zytglogge** (clock tower), once part of the city's western gate (1191–1256). It's reminiscent of the Astronomical Clock in Prague's old town square, in that crowds congregate to watch its revolving figures twirl at four minutes before the hour, after which the actual chimes begin.

The clock tower supposedly helped Albert Einstein hone his theory of relativity, developed while working as a patent clerk in Bern. The great scientist surmised, while travelling on a tram away from the tower, that if the tram were going at the speed of light, the clock tower would remain on the same time, while his own watch would continue to tick – proving time was relative.

Other Bern landmarks are its 11 decorative **fountains** (1545), which depict historic and folkloric characters. Most are along Marktgasse as it becomes Kramgasse and Gerechtigkeitsgasse, but the most famous lies in Kornhausplatz: the **Kindlifresserbrunnen** (Ogre Fountain) of a giant snacking on children!

TAMBAKO / GETTY IMAGES ©

Don't Miss **Bärenpark**

A popular folk etymology is that Bern got its name from the bear (*Bär* in German), when the city's founder, Berthold V, duke of Zähringen, snagged one here on a hunting spree. To the dismay of some, there was still a 3.5m-deep cramped bear pit in the city until 2009, when it was (thankfully) replaced by a spacious 6000-sq-metre open-air riverside park dotted with trees and terraces, in which a number of bears roam (although they still have access to the old pit). With any luck, you'll catch sight of Finn, Björk, Mischa, Mascha, Ursina or Berna as they frolic, swim, eat and poop in the woods, as nature (almost) intended.

THINGS YOU NEED TO KNOW
www.baerenpark-bern.ch; eastern end of the Nydeggbrücke

cafe, punters lunch in the sun on the busy pavement terrace.

DU NORD International $$
(www.dunord-bern.ch; Lorrainestrasse 2; mains Sfr22.50-42.50; ⏰8am-11.30pm Mon-Thu, to 12.30am Fri) A short walk across the bridge from the Old Town, this gay-friendly space, with an international kitchen and a bar that buzzes with Bern's hippest, is one of the city's neatest addresses. Find it crowned by a pale pink, fairytale turret in the leafy Lorraine quarter.

 **Drinking**

Bern has a healthy drinking scene. Several spaces, such as Kornhauskeller and Altes Tramdepot, are as much drinking as dining spots.

CAFÉ DES PYRÉNÉES Cafe
(Kornhausplatz 17; ⏰Mon-Sat) With its mix of wine-quaffing lefties, generation-of-68ers and beer-loving students, this lovely Bohemian joint feels like a Parisian cafe-bar. It serves toasted snacks. Service can be

hit and miss, but the atmosphere makes up for it.

VOLVER
Bar

(Rathausplatz 8; ☺Tue-Sat) With cool decor and a small selection of tapas, Volver is a hip spot for cocktails and coffees, from morning to midnight.

🛍 Shopping

Mooching around the Old Town boutiques, many tucked below the street in bunker-style cellars or above in covered arcades, is delightful. Allow extra time for quaint Gerechtigkeitsgasse and Postgasse with their myriad galleries, antiquarian bookshops, small shops specialising in funky homewares and nifty boutiques.

ℹ Information

Tourist Information

Bern Tourismus (www.berninfo.com) train station (☏031 328 12 12; Bahnhofplatz; ☺9am-8.30pm Jun-Sep, to 6.30pm Mon-Sat, 10am-5pm Sun Oct-May); bear park (☺9am-6pm Jun-Sep, 10am-4pm Mar-May & Oct, 11am-4pm Nov-Feb) City tours, free hotel bookings, internet access, multilingual staff.

ℹ Getting There & Away

Train

By rail, there are services at least hourly to most major Swiss destinations, including Geneva (Sfr47, two hours), Basel (Sfr38, one hour), Interlaken Ost (Sfr13, one hour) and Zürich (Sfr47, one hour).

ℹ Getting Around

Bicycle

Borrow a bike from one of the three kiosks of Bernrollt (www.bernrollt.ch; 1st 4hr free, then Sfr1 per hr; ☺7.30am-9.30pm May-Oct), located at the train station, on Zeughausgasse and just off Bubenbergplatz on Hirschengraben.

Bus, Tram & Funicular

Get around on foot or hop on a bus or tram run by Bern Mobil (www.bernmobil.ch, in German; Bubenbergplatz 17; ☺8am-6pm Mon-Fri). Tickets, available from the Bern Mobil office or ticket machines at stops, cost Sfr2.20 for journeys up to six stops (valid 30 minutes) or Sfr4 for a single journey within zones 1 and 2 (valid one hour).

The Stadt Bern-Drahtseilbahn Marzili funicular (one way Sfr1.20; ☺6.15am-9pm) runs from behind the parliament building downhill to the riverside Marzili quarter.

BASEL

POP 166,200 / ELEV 273M

Basel is the closest Switzerland comes to having a seaport; the Rhine is navigable for decent-sized ships from this point until it reaches the North Sea in Holland. Basel's year-round attractions, including the engaging Old Town, are mostly concentrated in Grossbasel (Greater Basel) on the south bank of the Rhine.

 Sights

Opening hours are given for high season (April through October); hours are usually shorter at other times of the year. For more on the city's 30-plus museums and galleries, grab the relevant tourist-office booklet or check out www.museenbasel.ch.

FONDATION BEYELER
Art Museum

(www.fondationbeyeler.ch; Baselstrasse 101, Riehen; adult/child Sfr25/6; ☺10am-6pm Mon-Tue & Thu-Sun, 10am-8pm Wed) Of all the private Swiss collections made public, that of the former art dealers Hildy and Ernst Beyeler is the most astounding. In the Beyeler Foundation collection, sculptures by Miró and Max Ernst are juxtaposed against tribal figures from Oceania. Take tram 6 to Riehen from Barfüsserplatz or Marktplatz.

MÜNSTER
Cathedral

(www.muensterbasel.ch; Münsterplatz; ☺10am-5pm Mon-Fri, to 4pm Sat, 11.30am-5pm Sun) This 13th-century cathedral is a mix of Gothic exteriors and Romanesque interiors and

Basel

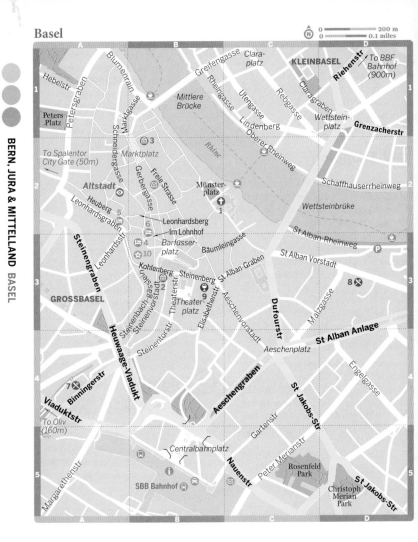

0 ———— 200 m
0 ———— 0.1 miles

Hebelstr
Petersgraben
Peters Platz
Blumenrain
Schneidergasse
Marktgasse
Greifengasse
Clara-platz
Rheingasse
Utengasse
Lindenberg
Oberer Rheinweg
Rebgasse
Claragraben
KLEINBASEL
Riehenstr
To BBF Bahnhof (900m)
Wettstein-platz
Grenzacherstr
Mittlere Brücke
Rhine
To Spalentor City Gate (50m)
Marktplatz
Gerbergasse
Freie Strasse
Münster-platz
Schaffhauserrheinweg
Wettsteinbrüke
Altstadt
Heuberg
Leonhardsgraben
Leonhardstr
Leonhardsberg
Im Lohnhof
Barfüsser-platz
Bäumleingasse
St Alban Vorstadt
St Alban-Rheinweg
Steinengraben
Kohlenberg
Steinenberg
Steinenbachgässlein
Steinenvorstadt
Theater-platz
Elisabethenstr
St Alban-Graben
Aeschenvorstadt
Dufourstr
Malzgasse
GROSSBASEL
Steinentorstr
St Alban Anlage
Aeschenplatz
Engelgasse
Binningerstr
Heuwaage-Viadukt
Aeschengraben
St Jakobs-Str
Viaduktstr
To Oliv (160m)
Gartenstr
Peter Merianstr
Centralbahnplatz
Nauenstr
Rosenfeld Park
St Jakobs-Str
Margarethenstr
SBB Bahnhof
Christoph Merian Park

was largely rebuilt after an earthquake in 1356. The tomb of the Renaissance humanist Erasmus of Rotterdam (1466–1536), who lived in Basel, lies in the cathedral's northern aisle. In the crypt are remnants of the cathedral's 9th-century predecessor. You can climb the soaring Gothic towers (Sfr4) in groups of two or more.

PUPPENHAUSMUSEUM   Museum
(www.puppenhausmuseum.ch; Steinenvorstadt 1; adult/child Sfr7/free; ⏰10am-6pm) Basel's Doll House Museum attracts teddy-bear fans from all over the place. Indeed, the museum claims to have the world's biggest collection of teddy bears and a total of 6000 objects displayed over four floors. There are doll houses galore too, many extraordinarily detailed and on a scale of 1:12.

 **Sleeping**

Book ahead if coming for a convention or trade fair. When you check in, remember to ask for your mobility ticket, which entitles you to free use of public transport.

AU VIOLON   Hotel $$
(☎061 269 87 11; www.au-violon.com; Im Lohnhof 4; s Sfr123-185, d Sfr146-208; ☜) The doors are one of the few hints that quaint, atmospheric Au Violon was a prison from 1835 to 1995. Most of the rooms are two cells rolled into one and either look onto a delightful cobblestone courtyard or have views of the Münster. Sitting on a leafy hilltop, it also has a well-respected restaurant.

DER TEUFELHOF   Hotel $$$
(☎061 261 10 10; www.teufelhof.com; Leonhardsgraben 49; s/d in Galeriehotel from Sfr151/251, r in Kunsthotel Sfr180-748; ℗) 'The Devil's Court' fuses two hotels into one. The Kunsthotel's nine rooms have varying colour schemes, parquet floors and crisp white bedding. The larger Galeriehotel annexe, a former convent, is more about stylish everyday design, but the rooms vary considerably in size and atmosphere. An excellent restaurant caps it all off.

HOTEL STADTHOF   Hotel $
(☎061 261 87 11; www.stadthof.ch; Gerbergasse 84; s/d Sfr80/130) You'll need to book ahead at this spartan but decent central hotel. Set above a pizzeria on an Old Town square, the nine rooms are squeaky clean (with shared loo and shower) and the owners of this centuries-old building are very friendly.

 Eating

Basel's culinary culture benefits from the city's location bang up against the French and German borders and its long history of immigration, especially from southern Europe.

ST ALBAN STÜBLI   Swiss, European $$$
(☎061 272 54 15; www.st-alban-stuebli.ch; St Alban Vorstadt 74; mains Sfr40-55; ☽lunch & dinner Mon-Fri) Set in a quiet street, it looks like a typical cosy tavern but is an exquisite haven for gourmet cooking, local and French.

ACQUA   Italian $$
(☎061 564 66 66; www.acquabasilea.ch; Binningerstrasse 14; mains Sfr18-45; ☽lunch & dinner Tue-Fri, dinner Sat) For a special experience, head to these converted waterworks beside a quiet stream. The atmosphere is glam post- industrial. The food is Tuscan, and Basel's beautiful people drink in the attached lounge bar.

OLIV   Mediterranean $$
(☎061 283 03 03; www.restaurantoliv.ch; Bachlettenstrasse 1; mains Sfr30-42; ☽lunch & dinner Tue-Fri, dinner Sat) Trendy Oliv leans towards fresh and varied Mediterranean cooking. It offers a set lunch for between Sfr25 and Sfr32, and in summer there's a pleasing little outdoor dining area.

Drinking & Entertainment

Steinenvorstadt and Barfüsserplatz teem with teens and 20-somethings on the weekends. A more interesting area is Kleinbasel, around Rheingasse and Utengasse. There is a slight air of grunge,

Detour:
Augusta Raurica

By the Rhine, these **Roman ruins** (☏ 061 816 22 22; www.augustaraurica. ch; admission free; ⏰ 10am-5pm) are Switzerland's largest. They're the last remnants of a colony founded in 43 BC, the population of which grew to 20,000 by the 2nd century AD. Today, restored features include an open-air theatre and several temples.

There's also a **Römermuseum** (Roman Museum; Giebenacherstrasse 17; adult/reduced Sfr7/5; ⏰ 1-5pm Mon, from 10am Tue-Sun) in Kaiseraugst, which features an authentic Roman house among its exhibits.

The train from Basel to Kaiseraugst takes 11 minutes (Sfr5.30); it's then a 10-minute walk to the site.

quite a few watering holes and something of a red-light zone to lend it an edge.

CAMPARI BAR Bar
(☏ 061 272 83 83; www.restaurant-kunsthalle. ch; Steinenberg 7; ⏰ 8am-late) A soothing spot for an upscale cocktail moment. Especially in warmer weather, the terrace is perfect for a sip, natter and a listen to the water play of the Tinguely Fountain.

BIRD'S EYE JAZZ CLUB Jazz
(☏ 061 263 33 41; www.birdseye.ch; Kohlenberg 20; ⏰ 8-11.30pm Tue-Sat Sep-May, Wed-Sat Jun-Aug) This is among Europe's top jazz dens, attracting local and headline foreign acts. Concerts start most evenings at 8.30pm.

ⓘ Information

Tourist Information

Basel Tourismus (☏ 061 268 68 68; www.basel. com) SBB Bahnhof (Bahnhof; ⏰ 8.30am-6pm Mon-Fri, 9am-5pm Sat, to 3pm Sun & holidays);

Stadtcasino **(Steinenberg 14; ⏰ 9am-6.30pm Mon-Fri, to 5pm Sat, 10am-3pm Sun & holidays)**

ⓘ Getting There & Away

Air

EuroAirport (☏ 061 325 31 11; www.euroairport. com) serves Basel (as well as Mulhouse in France and Freiburg in Germany). Located 5km north in France, it has flights to and from a host of European cities.

Train

Basel has two main train stations: the Swiss/French train station SBB Bahnhof, in the city's south, and the German train station BBF (Badischer) Bahnhof, in the north.

Two trains an hour run from SBB Bahnhof via Olten to Geneva (Sfr70, 2¾ hours). As many as seven, mostly direct, leave every hour for Zürich (Sfr31, 55 minutes to 1¼ hours).

ⓘ Getting Around

Buses run every 20 to 30 minutes from 5am to around 11.30pm between the airport and SBB Bahnhof (Sfr3.80, 20 minutes). The trip by **taxi** (☏ 061 325 27 00, 061 444 44 44) costs around Sfr40.

If you're not staying in a hotel in town, tickets for buses and trams cost Sfr2, Sf3.20 and Sfr8.50 for up to four stops, the central zone and a day pass respectively.

CANTON DE FRIBOURG

Canton de Fribourg (population 273,200) tots up 1671 sq km on the drawing board. Pre-Alpine foothills rise grandly around its cold craggy feet; Gruyéres with its sprinkling of small mountain resorts pierces its heart; and Fribourg heads the canton up north, where pretty lakeside villages slumber between vineyards and fruit orchards.

Fribourg
POP 34,500 / ELEV 629M

Nowhere is Switzerland's language divide felt more keenly than in Fribourg (Freiburg) or 'Free Town', a medieval city where inhabitants on the west bank of

PJRTRAVEL / ALAMY ©

Don't Miss **Altstadt**

The medieval Old Town in the heart of Basel is a delight. Start in Marktplatz, which is dominated by the astonishingly vivid red facade of the 16th-century **Rathaus** (town hall). A walk about 400m west of Marktplatz through the former artisans' district along Spalenberg leads uphill to the 600-year-old **Spalentor** city gate, one of only three to survive the walls' demolition in 1866.

The narrow lanes that riddle the hillside between Marktplatz and the Spalentor form the most captivating part of old Basel. Lined by impeccably maintained centuries-old houses, lanes like Spalenberg, Heuberg and Leonhardsberg are worth a gentle stroll.

Rathaus facade

the Sarine River speak French, and those on the east bank of the Sanne speak German.

 Sights

OLD TOWN   Neighbourhood
The 12th-century Old Town was laid out in simple fashion, with Grand-Rue as the main street and parallel Rue des Chanoines/Rue des Bouchers devoted to markets, church and civic buildings. The bridges here – quaint stone Pont du Milieu and cobbled, roof-covered Pont du Berne – proffer great views.

Fribourg's famous Tilleul de Morat (Morat Linden Tree) stands in front of the Renaissance town hall (Grand-Rue).

**CATHÉDRALE DE
ST NICOLAS DE MYRE**   Church
(www.cathedrale-fribourg.ch, in French; Rue des Chanoines 3; ☺9am-6pm Mon-Fri, to 4pm Sat, 2-5pm Sun) Before entering this brooding 13th-century Gothic cathedral, contemplate the main portal with its 15th-century sculptured portrayal of the Last Judgment.

A 368-step hike up the cathedral's 74m-tall **tower** (adult/child Sfr3.50/1; ☺10am-noon & 2-5pm Mon-Fri, 10am-4pm Sat, 2-5pm Sun Apr-Oct) affords wonderful views.

111

 Eating

CAFÉ DES ARCADES Cafe $

(www.cafedesarcades.ch, in French; Rue des Ormeaux 1; mains Sfr16-25; ☺7am-11.30pm Mon-Thu, 7am-midnight Fri, 8am-midnight Sat, 10am-10pm Sun) Alive and kicking since 1861, when the light's just so, this place will transport you to another time. An authentic address for breakfast, brunch or lunch.

CAFÉ DU GOTHARD Bistro $$

(Rue du Pont Muré 16; fondue mains Sfr23.50-28; ☺9am-11.30pm Tue-Fri, 8am-11.30pm Sat & Sun) Tinguely's favourite eating haunt is a kitsch mix of 19th-century furnish-ings, Niki de Saint Phalle drawings and nostalgia-tinged bric-a-brac. Take your pick from the day's specials chalked on blackboards and revel in this legendary bistro.

ℹ Information

Tourist Information

Tourist office (☎026 350 11 11; www.fribourg tourism.ch; Av de la Gare 1; ☺9am-6pm Mon-Fri, to 3pm Sat May-Sep, to 6pm Mon-Fri, to 12.30pm Sat Oct-Apr)

ℹ Getting There & Away

Trains travel hourly to/from Neuchâtel (Sfr20.20, 55 minutes), and more frequently to Geneva (Sfr39, 1½ hours) and Bern (Sfr13.20, 20 minutes). Regular trains run to Lausanne (Sfr23, 45 to 55 minutes).

Murten

POP 6100 / ELEV 450M

This German-speaking medieval village on the eastern shore of Murten See (Lac de Morat) isn't called Murten (Morat) – derived from the Celtic word *moriduno* meaning 'fortress on the lake' – for nothing.

In May 1476 the Burgundy duke Charles the Bold set off from Lausanne to besiege Murten – only to have 8000 of his men butchered or drowned in the lake during the Battle of Murten. The fortifications that thwarted the duke (who escaped) create a quaint little lakeside town well worth a visit.

 Sights

Murten is a cobblestone three-street town crammed with arcaded houses. A string of hotel-restaurants culminating in a 13th-century castle (closed to visitors) line **Rathausgasse**; shops and eateries stud parallel **Hauptgasse**, capped by the medieval **Berntor city gate** at its eastern end; while parallel Deutsche Kirchgasse and its western continuation, Schulgasse, hug the city ramparts.

Scale the wooden **Aufstieg auf die Ringmauer** (rampart stairs) behind the **Deutsche Kirche** (German Church; Deutsche Kirchgasse) to reach the covered walkway traversing part of the sturdy medieval walls. It's magical at sunset, but any time is a good time.

 **Sleeping & Eating**

HOTEL MURTENHOF & KRONE Hotel $$
(026 672 90 30; www.murten hof.ch; Rathausgasse 1-5; s Sfr120-165, d Sfr160-240; P) The Murtenhof, in a 16th-century patrician's house, mixes old and less-old to create a spacious space to eat and sleep. Its terrace restaurant (mains Sfr21 to Sfr25) cooks up dreamy lake views and fairly traditional cuisine.

ⓘ Getting There & Around

From the train station (Bahnhofstrasse), 300m south of the city walls, hourly trains run to/from Fribourg (Sfr11, 30 minutes), Bern (Sfr13.20, 35

113

If You Like...
Chocolate

If you like chocolate (and who doesn't?), you'll love visits to some of Switzerland's most famous chocolate brands:

1 CAILLER
(www.cailler.ch; Rue Jules Bellet 7, Broc; adult/child Sfr10/free; ⊙10am-6pm Apr-Oct, to 5pm Nov-Mar) In business since 1825, Cailler has modern facilities these days, and offers anecdotes, samples, demonstrations and a sensory overload (no doubt exacerbated by the chance to buy factory seconds a mere 80m up the road). The factory is 2km north of Gruyères, in Broc.

2 VILLARS
(Rte de la Fonderie 2, Fribourg; ⊙cafe-shop 8.30am-5.30pm Mon-Fri, 9am-noon Sat) Buy slabs of Swiss chocolate made from Alpine-rich Gruyère milk and child-friendly *têtes au choco* (chocolate-covered marshmallow heads) in the factory's cafe-shop.

minutes) via Kerzers (Sfr4.50, nine minutes) and Neuchâtel (Sfr12.20, 25 minutes).

Murten train station rents **bicycles** (per day Sfr33; ⊙9am-4pm).

Navigation Lacs de Neuchâtel et Morat runs seasonal boats to/from Neuchâtel; see p117.

Gruyères
POP 1800 / ELEV 830M

Cheese and featherweight meringues drowned in thick cream are what this dreamy village is all about. Named after the emblematic *gru* (crane) brandished by the medieval Counts of Gruyères, it is a riot of 15th- to 17th-century houses tumbling down a hillock. Its heart is cobbled, a castle is its crowning glory and hard AOC Gruyère (the village is Gruyéres but the 's' is dropped for the cheese) has been made for centuries in its surrounding Alpine pastures.

◎ Sights & Activities

SENTIER DES FROMAGERIES   Walking
Cheese is still produced in a couple of traditional mountain chalets along the Sentier des Fromageries, a trail that takes walkers through green Gruyères pastures. Ask at the Maison du Gruyère for the brochure outlining the two-hour walk (7km to 8km).

LA MAISON DU GRUYÈRE   Dairy
(www.lamaisondugruyere.ch; adult/child Sfr7/3; ⊙9am-7pm Apr-Sep, to 6pm Oct-Mar) The secret behind Gruyère cheese is revealed here in Pringy, 1.5km from Gruyères. Cheesemaking takes place three to four times daily between 9am and 11am and 12.30pm to 2.30pm.

FROMAGERIE D'ALPAGE DE MOLÉSON   Dairy
(www.fromagerie-alpage.ch, in French; adult/child Sfr5/2; ⊙cheesemaking display 10am, restaurant 9am-7pm early May-end Sep) At this 17th-century Alpine chalet, 5km southwest of Gruyères in Moléson-sur-Gruyères (elevation 1100m), cheese is made a couple of times a day in summer using old-fashioned methods. Both dairies sell cheese and serve fondue.

🛏 Sleeping & Eating

Cheese fondue is the natural star of every menu, irrespective of season (locals only eat fondue in winter); *moitié-moitié* is a mix of Gruyère and soft local Vacherin.

LA FERME DU BOURGOZ   Farmstay $
(☎079 252 74 51; www.lafermedubourgoz.ch, in French; Chemin du Bourgoz 14; r per person, incl breakfast Sfr45; 🅿) You'll sleep well thanks to the authentic cheese dreams that a stay at the Murith family's cheesemaking home encourages. Simple, cosy rooms and unbeatable farm-fresh breakfasts, plus chunks of homemade Gruyère for sale.

GLENN VAN DER KNIJFF / GETTY IMAGES ©

Don't Miss **Château de Gruyères**

This bewitching turreted castle was home to 19 different Counts of Gruyères, who controlled the Sarine Valley from the 11th to 16th centuries, and was rebuilt after a fire in 1493. Inside, you can view period furniture, tapestries and modern 'fantasy art'. Don't miss the short footpath that weaves its way around the castle.

THINGS YOU NEED TO KNOW

www.chateau-gruyeres.ch; adult/child Sfr9.50/3; ⊗9am-6pm Apr-Oct, 10am-4.30pm Nov-Feb

---

CHALET DE GRUYÈRES Swiss $$
(www.chalet-gruyeres.ch, in French; Rue du Château 53; fondues & raclettes from Sfr29.50; ⊗lunch & dinner daily) A quintessential Gruyères address, this cosy wooden chalet strung with cow bells oozes Alpine charm – and fodder (fondue, raclette, grilled meats).

Information

Tourist office (☎0848 424 424; www.la -gruyere.ch; Rue du Bourg 1; ⊗10.30am-noon & 1-4.30pm Sep-Jun, 9.30am-5.30pm Jul & Aug)

Getting There & Around

Gruyères can be reached by hourly bus or train (Sfr15.40, 43 minutes to one hour) from Fribourg to Bulle, where you need to hop on another hourly bus or train (Sfr4.50, 15 to 20 minutes). Gruyères is a 10-minute walk uphill from its train station.

CANTON DE NEUCHÂTEL

The focus of this heavily forested 800 sq km canton (population 171,700), north-west of its Fribourg counterpart, is Lac de Neuchâtel – the largest lake entirely

MARTIN BOND / ALAMY ©

within Switzerland. Canton capital Neuchâtel sits plumb on its northern shore and the gentle Jura Mountains rise to the north and west.

Neuchâtel

POP 32,800 / ELEV 430M

Its Old Town sandstone elegance, the airy Gallic nonchalance of its cafe life and the gay lakeside air that imbues the shoreline of its lake makes Neuchâtel disarmingly charming.

Sights

OLD TOWN Neighbourhood
The attractive Old Town streets are lined by fine, shuttered 18th-century mansions and studded with fanciful gold-leaf fountains topped by anything from a banner-wielding knight, **Fontaine du Banneret** (Rue Fleury), to a maiden representing Justice, **Fontaine de la Justice** (Rue de l'Hôpital); see a copy on the street and the original in the Musée d'Art et d'Histoire.

Heading uphill along Rue du Château, walk through the medieval city gate to view the **Tour des Prisons** (Rue Jehanne

de Hochberg 5; admission Sfr2; ⊘8am-6pm Apr-Sep). Scale it for views over the town below and its lake and Alpine backdrop. Inside the largely Gothic Église Collégiale a mix of Romanesque elements (notably the triple apse) looms large.

CHÂTEAU Castle
(☑032 889 40 03; ⊘guided tours hourly 10am-noon & 2-4pm Mon-Fri, 2-4pm Sat & Sun Apr-Sep) Behind the church is the 15th-century castle with a pretty courtyard made for meandering. Excellent summertime guided tours (45 minutes) allow you to poke your nose around the castle's innards.

Eating

Local specialities include tripe and *tomme neuchâteloise chaude* (baked goat's-cheese starter). Rue des Moulins and nearby Rue des Chavannes in the commune are the places to imbibe.

HÔTEL DUPEYROU French $$$
(☑032 725 11 83; www.dupeyrou.ch, in French; Av Du Peyrou 1; mains Sfr52-56, menus from Sfr95; ⊘lunch & dinner Tue-Sat) DuPeyrou presides like a mini-Versailles over mani-

cured gardens. Built between 1765 and 1770, it regales with gastronomic dining in an 18th-century ambience. Come autumn, its game dishes are not to be missed.

CHAUFFAGE COMPRIS Bar

(www.chaufaggecompris.ch; Rue des Moulins 37; ⏰11am-late Mon-Sat) Despite its name – Heating Included – this retro bar with a decorative tiled entrance is one cool place to loiter, be it for morning coffee, evening aperitif, night-owl drink or easy snacks.

ℹ️ Getting There & Away

Boat

Navigation Lacs de Neuchâtel et Morat (✆032 729 96 00; www.navig.ch; Port de la Ville) runs boats late April to mid-October to/from Murten (Sfr24, 1¾ hours) and Biel (Bienne; Sfr36, 2½ hours).

Train

From the **train station** (Av de la Gare), a 10-minute walk northeast of the Old Town, hourly trains run to/from Geneva (Sfr39, 1¼ to 1½ hours), Bern (Sfr18.60, 30 to 50 minutes), Basel (Sfr36, 1½ hours) and other destinations.

♥ If You Like...
Cute Towns

If you like Murten (p112), you'll love these other cute old towns:

1 SOLOTHURN
This enchanting little town with a mellow cobblestone centre has one very big cathedral: the imposing, 66m-tall facade of St Ursus. Fountains, churches and city gates bolster Solothurn's claim to be Switzerland's most beautiful baroque town. There are two trains per hour to Bern.

2 ST URSANNE
The Jura's most enchanting village is medieval St Ursanne with its 12th-century Église Collégiale, a grand Gothic church. Ancient houses, the 16th-century town gates, a lovely stone bridge and a bevy of eating options on miniature central square, Place Roger Schaffter, tumble down towards the Doubs River. The train station is 1km east of the centre.

3 RHEINFELDEN
Rheinfelden, 24km east of Basel, has a pretty Old Town. Several medieval city gates, defensive towers and parts of the old walls still stand. It's a short train ride from Basel.

Bernese Oberland & Central Switzerland

Start in Interlaken and end up on top of the world: it's the reason to come to Switzerland. Whether you're hiking a trail with a jaw-dropping view that never quite seems real, carving virgin powder on a crisp winter's morning, or riding some improbable combination of railways and cable cars, the Swiss Alps don't get more beautiful than this. And we're talking big, in-your-face, stop-dead-in-your-tracks beauty. Nowhere are the resorts more chocolate box, the peaks higher, the glaciers grander. Fittingly watched over by Mönch (Monk) and Jungfrau (Virgin), the Bernese Oberland sends spirits soaring to heaven.

Meanwhile the dreamy city of Lucerne has old-world charm, a buoyant cultural scene and a stunning setting on the lake that bears its name. Ringing the town are fabled peaks like Mt Pilatus and Mt Rigi just waiting for you to ascend.

Alpine meadow and valley
DAVID C TOMLINSON / GETTY IMAGES ©

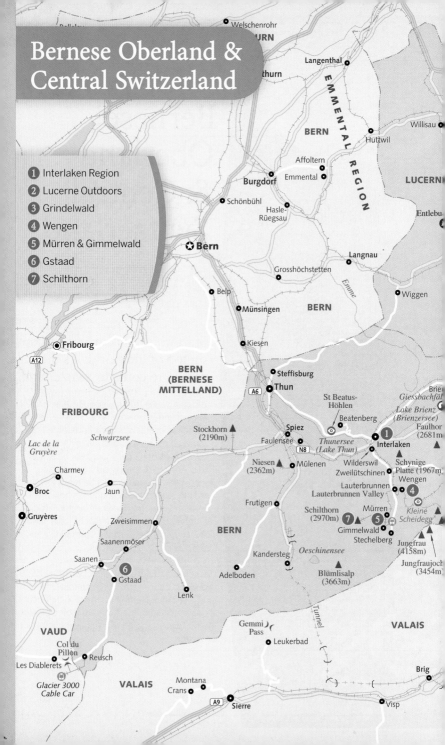

Bernese Oberland & Central Switzerland

Welschenrohr
Langenthal
EMMENTAL REGION
BERN
Huttwil
Willisau
Affoltern
Emmental
LUCERNE
Burgdorf
Schönbühl
Hasle-Rüegsau
Entlebu
☆ Bern
Belp
Münsingen
Kiesen
Langnau
Grosshöchstetten
Emme
Wiggen
BERN
Fribourg
A12
BERN (BERNESE MITTELLAND)
Steffisburg
A6
Thun
St Beatus-Höhlen
Beatenberg
Brie
Giessbachfä
FRIBOURG
Schwarzsee
Stockhorn (2190m)
Spiez
Faulensee
N8
Lake Brienz (Brienzersee)
Faulhor (2681m)
Lac de la Gruyère
Thunersee (Lake Thun)
Interlaken 1
Charmey
Niesen (2362m)
Mülenen
Wilderswil
Zweilütschinen
Schynige Platte (1967m)
Broc
Jaun
Lauterbrunnen
Lauterbrunnen Valley
Wengen 4
Gruyères
Zweisimmen
Frutigen
Schilthorn (2970m)
7
Mürren
5
Kleine Scheidegg
Saanenmöser
BERN
Gimmelwald
Stechelberg
Jungfrau (4158m)
Saanen
Kandersteg
Oeschinensee
Jungfraujoch (3454m)
6 Gstaad
Lenk
Adelboden
Blümlisalp (3663m)
VAUD
Gemmi Pass
Tunnel
VALAIS
Col du Pillon
Reusch
Leukerbad
Les Diablerets
Glacier 3000 Cable Car
VALAIS
Montana
Crans
A9
Sierre
Brig
Visp

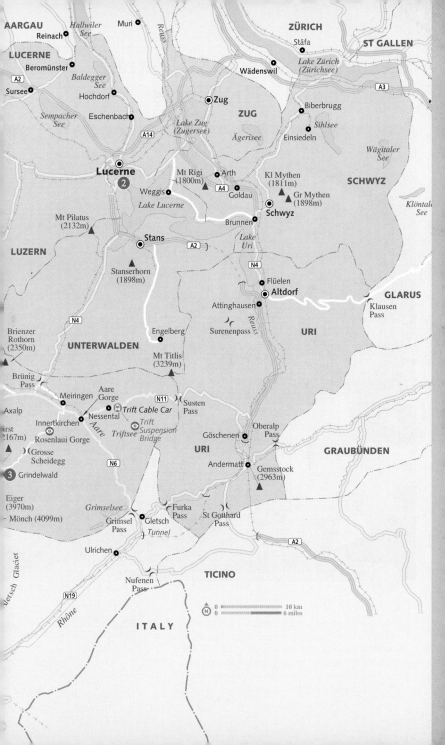

Bernese Oberland & Central Switzerland's Highlights

Interlaken Region

Just arriving on the train in this charming outpost (p132) is a reward, with its views of the surrounding lakes. But those Alps looming large are Interlaken's raison d'être. This is the gateway to the Jungfrau region, one of the most beautiful places on the planet. Above: Interlaken (p132); Top right: Staubbach Falls (p144); Bottom right: Schloss Spiez (p137)

Need to Know

BEST TIME TO VISIT
If you ski, come in winter. Otherwise, come May to October for outdoor rambles.
TOP TIP Budget lots for trains and cable cars. **For further coverage, see p132.**

Interlaken Region Don't Miss List

KURT AEBERHARD, GUIDE AND
LONGTIME RESIDENT

1 WATERFALLS

Take the Alpine train through the glacier-carved valley to Lauterbrunnen. Be impressed by the **Staubbach Falls** (p144), the highest waterfall in the Swiss Alps, and walk behind the falls. Continue travelling by a short bus ride to the spectacular **Trümmelbach** waterfalls (p144). Travel back to Interlaken by train, then take a **paddle steamer** (www.bls.ch) to **Giessbach** and you'll see more waterfalls on the way.

2 HIKING ON THE ETERNAL ICE

Three cogwheel trains transport you in about two hours from **Interlaken** (p132; 567m) to **Lauterbrunnen** (p144; 800m) to **Kleine Scheidegg** (p142; 2060m) to **Jungfraujoch** (p142; 3454m). From here, hike for one hour to the heart of the Swiss Alps, the **Mönchsjoch** hut at around 3700m. Bring warm clothes, sunglasses and good shoes, and be prepared for a great walk.

3 FIVE CASTLE VISIT

From Interlaken take a **paddle steamer** (www.bls.ch) to **Thun** (p148). Along the way you'll see five castles, some dating back to the 15th century. Stop off at **Oberhofen** and/or **Spiez castles** (p137): you can climb their watch towers for good views. Back down at the lakeside, enjoy the beach and admire the swans.

4 IN AND ABOVE THE CAVE

At **Beatus Caves** (www.beatushoehlen.ch) a fascinating underground world opens with lakes, wild water flows and impressive stalagmites; every few steps there's another surprise. Take a bus for a few minutes and change to a funicular to **Beatenberg**. Now catch a cable car to the **Niederhorn**, a great viewpoint nearly 2000m high; you'll see the turquoise waters of **Lake Thun** and the Alps behind. An easy one-hour walk brings you 100m higher to the **Gemmenalphorn**. Here you are surrounded by mountain flowers, ibexes and cows. It's an Alpine dream.

Lucerne Outdoors

Cute as all hell is one description for Lucerne (p155) you're unlikely to challenge. And as you wander its Old Town you'll keep finding yet another reason to stay outside, exploring its bridges, plazas and promenades. Before long you'll find yourself drawn along the aqua lake and to the surrounding peaks. Below: Lucerne's Männliturm and Wachturm (p157); Top right: Mt Pilatus (p161)

Need to Know

BEST TIME TO VISIT From April to November you can explore the region without too many layers. TOP TIP When in doubt, just walk anywhere. For further coverage, see p155.

2

 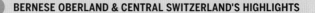

Lucerne Outdoors Don't Miss List

RENÉ WELTI, GUIDE AND FOUNDER OF ECHO TRAILS

1 WALK THE MUSEGG WALL
As you walk along this 14th-century Lucerne **fortification** (p157) and go up the self-guided historic towers you are rewarded with the best views of town, the lake and the mountains.

2 DO THE PILATUS MOUNTAIN
Pilatus (p161; 2100m) is Lucerne's home mountain. It features friendly dragon playgrounds for kids, rope parks, dragon-cave walks, a secure Alpine flower path and Swiss Alps as far as you can see. Hear your own echo, enjoy delicious food and even luxurious accommodation, all accessible with public transport: the world's steepest cogwheel railway, aerial trams, gondolas and boats.

3 SWIM LAKE LUCERNE
Cool off at the many Lake Lucerne **swimming facilities** and savour Alpine scenery while you swim in crystal-clear waters that start in the Gotthard Pass and flow down the Ruess river. (**Tribschen**, the lakeside swimming facility run by the city of Lucerne, is my favourite.)

4 HIKE THE SWISS PATH
If you want to understand how Switzerland was founded, walk and hike segments of the 35km scenic **Swiss Path**, built to celebrate Switzerland's 700-Year Anniversary in 1991. It circles Lake Uri and begins at the Rütli, the meadow in the town of Seelisberg where Switzerland was born. It's 35km east of Lucerne. Take the Tell bus from the Lucerne train station to Altdorf (runs Mondays to Saturdays) and a local bus to the Swiss trailhead.

5 E-BIKE TO KUESNACHT
Hop on a Swiss-built Flyer electric bike (ask at the tourist office) and ride from Lucerne through villages and farms on signposted paths. It's spectacular and easy. (And you can do this by regular bike too.) About 15km east along the lake, **Kuesnacht's Hohle Gasse** (www.hohlegasse.ch/hp/index_engl.html) offers displays on Switzerland's national hero William Tell.

125

Grindelwald

Smaller than Interlaken but also cuter, Grindelwald (p138) is the forward outpost to the Jung frau Alps. It has a wide range of adventure-sports companies and tour outfits, and is well-linked to any vista that captures your fancy. Red flowers spill out of window boxes and the chalet-style lodgings have the requisite woodsy quality and the views along with it: glaciers and iconic peaks may keep you transfixed for days.

Wengen

Arrayed along a shelf of land on the side of a mountain, Wengen (p145) is serious Alps. Completely car-free, you access th village by train or, if feeling fleet of foot, by a sinuous track from Lauterbrunner in the valley below. In winter you can sk out the door of your hotel; in summer you can walk in any direction and enjoy a panoply of meadows, babbling brooks and jaw-dropping views.

GLENN VAN DER KNIJFF / GETTY IMAGES ©

Mürren & Gimmelwald

Just reaching these two mountainside villages is fun. Cable cars and oddball trains combine to get you up from the valley below but also lift you out of your regular existence and elevate you to something far better. Mürren (p147) is the slightly more mainstream of the pair, while a short cow path away, Gimmelwald (p147) is a timeless vision of rural Switzerland. Mürren (p147)

HIROSHI HIGUCHI / GETTY IMAGES ©

DOUG PEARSON / AWL ©

Gstaad

Another one of those familiar Swiss resort names that conjures images of wealth and exclusivity, Gstaad (p152) is first simply a great place to hit the snow; second it's a place that boasts its own contingent of paparazzi all winter long. There are myriad ski and board runs and you can always find a stretch somewhere along the 250km of slopes where the crowds are a distant memory.

Starring Schilthorn

Forever linked to 007, even if no one can remember which movie (1969's *On Her Majesty's Secret Service*), Schilthorn (p148) rectifies the one problem with surmounting beautiful Jungfraujoch: once on top, you can't see it. From Schilthorn, you can see Jungfraujoch and seemingly every other Alp ever made. The series of cable cars needed to reach the summit are part of the adventure and you can skip some for exhilarating walks.

Bernese Oberland & Central Switzerland's Best...

Mountain Peaks

○ **Jungfraujoch** (p142) Top of the heap for summit visits. The views go on and on.

○ **Schilthorn** (p148) You'll recognise it from an old Bond movie; the ride up is pure fun.

○ **Mt Titlis** (p162) Views of the Eiger, Mönch, Jungfrau and more.

○ **Mt Pilatus** (p161) The capper on a circle trip from Lucerne by boat, train and cable car.

Hikes

○ **Grindelwald** (p138) Trails fan out across the Alps in all directions. Go for an hour or a week.

○ **Kleine Scheidegg** (p142) More Alpine trails: up, down and all around.

○ **Lauterbrunnen** (p144) Glaciers melt and the water crashes down in waterfalls you can hike to through beautiful forests.

○ **Mürren** (p147) Meadows of wildflowers and impossibly beautiful vistas await.

Skiing

○ **Jungfrau Region** (p149) More than 200km of prepared runs and 44 (and counting) ski lifts in one of the world's best settings spread over several gorgeous Alpine towns.

○ **Gstaad** (p152) A chic and celebrity-filled setting with more than 250km of ski runs.

○ **Kandersteg** (p150) More than 50km of cross-country ski trails in a beautiful river valley.

Need to Know

Nightlife

○ **Interlaken** (p132) Daredevil adventurers, ski bums and vista-seeking visitors combine for year-round fun.

○ **Lucerne** (p155) The cultured region has chic bars, remarkable concerts – and the odd distant cowbell.

○ **Gstaad** (p152) Famed for highbrow food and drink, a place where half the people are used to seeing their names in bold type.

○ **Mürren** (p147) Although not known for its nightlife, Mürren has a front-row seat on the Alps. Sit outside and watch dusk and moonlight play colours across their granite faces.

ADVANCE PLANNING

○ **Two months before** Sort out your accommodation in the major ski areas if travelling from mid-December to March; do the same for the Jungfrau region and Lucerne from June to September.

○ **One month before** Book adventure sports activities with operators for any time from May to September. The same goes for extreme winter sports in winter. If driving to car-free Wengen and Mürren, book the Interlaken train-station garage.

RESOURCES

○ **Swiss Panorama** (www.swisspanorama.com) See conditions at top peaks across the Alps.

○ **Lucerne Hotels** (www.luzern-hotels.ch) Good local source for lodging in a popular city.

○ **Gstaad** (www.gstaad.ch) All the glitz, even during a blizzard.

GETTING AROUND

○ **Trains** From regular to rack, railways add to the fun of exploring the region.

○ **Cable Cars** Where the rails end, cables arc up to the peaks, usually with gravity-defying views on the way.

○ **Boats** From Lucerne, you can get boats to towns with links to the summits.

○ **Walking** Hoofing it between Alpine spots is the reason for many a trip.

BE FOREWARNED

○ **Seasons** Many businesses in the Alps close in April and from mid-October to mid-December.

○ **Weather** Whether it's skiing, hiking or making an expensive summit journey, check the weather right up until the last minute and have a Plan B ready if nature isn't ready for you.

○ **Passes** A Swiss or Eurail Pass alone will take you only so far into the Jungfrau region. See p287 for more information.

Bernese Oberland & Central Switzerland Itineraries

Everyone loves Lucerne and the first itinerary bases you there to explore the town, its lake and some of the surrounding peaks. The second itinerary takes you to the heart of the Alps and the most jaw-dropping sights.

LUCERNE ①
Lake Lucerne
MT PILATUS (2132M) ③
SWITZERLAND
MT TITLIS (3239M) ②
Brienzersee (Lake Brienz)
Thunersee (Lake Thun)
INTERLAKEN ①
WENGEN ⑥ ⑤ **GRINDELWALD** ②
LAUTERBRUNNEN
SCHILTHORN (2970M) ⑥ ⑦ **KLEINE SCHEIDEGG** ③
MÜRREN
JUNGFRAUJOCH (3454M) ④

3 DAYS

LUCERNE TO LUCERNE
Lucerne Glories

Is there a more genteel city in Switzerland than **(1) Lucerne**? Start by walking over one of its iconic wooden bridges. Then wander through the tidy streets to **Lake Lucerne**, which laps right up to the heart of the city. Follow the north shore east at the pace of one of the white swans and enjoy views that include snow-clad Alps across the ice-blue waters. After a visit to the **Verkehrshaus**, a fabulous museum dedicated to the country's incredibly diverse transportation, stop by **Sammlung Rosengart** to revel in the beauty of painters from the Impressionists onwards. After a night of music at a concert or lounge, set off in the morning for **(2) Mt**

Titlis, one of the most breathtaking Swiss peaks. A train to **Engelberg** is followed by a series of four cable cars to the top (including one that spins). Here you'll find a fantasyland of glaciers and jagged peaks. Look southwest to see the backsides of the fabled Jungfrau peak and its mates.

Back in Lucerne for another day, board a **lake steamer** to start a fun-filled journey that includes a **cog railway** (a train that uses gears to climb) and puts you atop the comparatively modest **(3) Mt Pilatus**, where all of Lucerne and its lake stretch out before you.

INTERLAKEN TO SCHILTHORN

Best of the Alps

5 DAYS

Look across the calming waters of **Lakes Thun** and **Brienz** from the ideally located **(1) Interlaken** as a sort of sensory respite from what's to come (although you'll want no respite from the bubbling nightlife). Catch the train to **(2) Grindelwald** and plan your assault on the Alps, which loom almost overhead. Get a morning train up the hill to **(3) Kleine Scheidegg**, a barren crossroads 2000m up. Change to the legendary train through the mountain to **(4) Jungfraujoch**, which at 3454m is one of the most famous high spots on the planet; glacier-clad peaks spread out before you.

Back in Kleine Scheidegg, take the winding hiking path down the mountain to **(5) Wengen**, a cliffside village with Alps in all directions. Spend a night or two and wander the **myriad trails**. Take a train to **(6) Lauterbrunnen** and see glacier-fed **waterfalls**. Now head up another mountain by cable car to **Grütschalp**, where you change to a mountain train to **(7) Mürren**, for another angle on the earth's most beautiful pageant. Finally take cable cars to **(8) Schilthorn** where, on a clear day, you can see everywhere you've just been.

Wengen (p145)

Discover Bernese Oberland & Central Switzerland

INTERLAKEN

POP 5400 / ELEV 570M

Once Interlaken made the Victorians swoon with mountain vistas from the chandelier-lit confines of grand hotels; today it makes daredevils scream with adrenalin-loaded adventures. Straddling the glittering Lakes Thun and Brienz and dazzled by the pearly whites of the Eiger, Mönch and Jungfrau, the scenery here is mind-blowing. Particularly, some say, if you're abseiling waterfalls, thrashing white water or gliding soundlessly above 4000m peaks.

Though the streets are filled with enough yodelling kitsch to make Heidi cringe, Interlaken still makes a terrific base for exploring the Bernese Oberland.

 Sights

Cross the turquoise Aare River for a mooch around Interlaken's compact and quiet old quarter, Unterseen.

TOURIST MUSEUM Museum
(Obere Gasse 26; adult/child Sfr5/2; ☉2-5pm Tue-Sun May-Oct) This low-key museum sits on a cobbled, fountain-dotted square in Unterseen. The permanent exhibition presents a romp through tourism in the region with costumes, carriages and other curios.

HEIMWEHFLUH Mountain
(www.heimwehfluh.ch, in German; funicular adult/child return Sfr14/7, toboggan Sfr6; ☉10am-5pm mid-Apr–late Oct) When the sun's out, take the nostalgic funicular up to family-friendly Heimwehfluh for long views across Interlaken. Kids love the bob run down the hill.

Interlaken
ELPIS IOANNIDIS / SHUTTERSTOCK ©

Interlaken

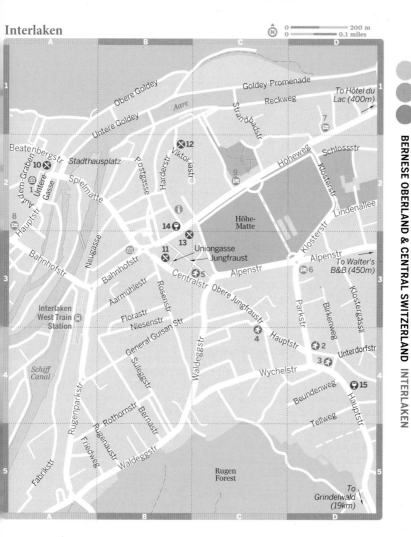

🏃 Activities

Tempted to hurl yourself off a bridge, down a cliff or along a raging river? You're in the right place. Switzerland is the world's second-biggest adventure-sports centre and Interlaken is its busiest hub.

Almost every heart-stopping pursuit you can think of is offered here. You can white-water raft on the Lütschine, Simme and Saane Rivers, go canyoning in the Saxetet, Grimsel or Chli Schliere

gorges, and canyon jump at the Gletscherschlucht near Grindelwald. If that doesn't grab you, there's paragliding, glacier bungee jumping, skydiving, ice climbing, hydrospeeding and, phew, much more.

Sample prices are around Sfr110 for rafting or canyoning, Sfr120 for hydrospeeding, Sfr130 for bungee or canyon jumping, Sfr160 for tandem paragliding, Sfr180 for ice climbing, Sfr225 for hang-gliding, and Sfr430 for

Interlaken

Sights
1 Tourist Museum ... A2

Activities, Courses & Tours
2 Alpinraft ... D4
3 Outdoor Interlaken ... D4
4 Swissraft ... C4
5 Vertical Sport ... C3

Sleeping
6 Backpackers Villa Sonnenhof ... D3
Gasthof Hirschen ... (see 2)
7 Hotel Royal St Georges ... D1
8 Post Hardermannli ... A2
9 Victoria-Jungfrau Grand Hotel & Spa ... C2

Eating
10 Benacus ... A2
11 Blueberry's ... B3
La Terrasse ... (see 9)
12 Pizzeria Horn ... B2
13 Schuh ... B3

Drinking
14 Buddy's Pub ... B2
15 Metro Bar ... D4

skydiving. A half-day mountain-bike tour will set you back around Sfr25.

Most excursions are without incident, but there's always a small risk and it's wise to ask about safety records and procedures.

The major operators able to arrange most sports from May to September include the following. Advance bookings are essential.

ALPINRAFT Adventure Sports
(033 823 41 00; www.alpinraft.com; Hauptstrasse 7; 8am-6.30pm)

OUTDOOR INTERLAKEN Adventure Sports
(033 826 77 19; www.outdoor-interlaken.ch; Hauptstrasse 15; 8am-6pm)

SWISSRAFT Adventure Sports
(081 911 52 50; www.swissraft.ch; Obere Jungfraustrasse 72)

Sleeping

Ask your hotel for the useful Guest Card for free bus transport plus discounts on attractions and sports facilities. Call ahead during the low season, as some places close.

VICTORIA-JUNGFRAU GRAND HOTEL & SPA Historic Hotel $$$
(033 828 28 28; www.victoria-jungfrau.ch; Höheweg 41; s/d from Sfr560/680, d with Jungfrau views from Sfr780; P @) The reverent hush and impeccable service here evoke an era when only royalty and the seriously wealthy travelled. A perfect melding of well-preserved Victorian features and modern luxury make this Interlaken's answer to Raffles – with plum views of Jungfrau to boot.

BACKPACKERS VILLA SONNENHOF Hostel $
(033 826 71 71; www.villa.ch; Alpenstrasse 16; dm Sfr39-45, s Sfr69-79, tw Sfr118-138; P @) Sonnenhof is a slick combination of ultramodern chalet and elegant art nouveau villa. Dorms are immaculate, and some have balconies with Jungfrau views. There's also a relaxed lounge, a well-equipped kitchen and a leafy garden for kicking back and enjoying the Jungfrau views. Kids are amused in the playroom.

HÔTEL DU LAC Historic Hotel $$
(033 822 29 22; www.dulac-interlaken.ch; Höheweg 225; s/d Sfr160/280; @) Smiley old-fashioned service and a riverfront location near Interlaken Ost make this 19th-century hotel a solid choice. It has been in the same family for generations and, despite the mishmash of styles, has kept enough belle époque glory to remain charming.

WALTER'S B&B B&B $
(033 822 76 88; www.walters.ch; Oelestrasse 35; s/d/tr/q Sfr50/66/99/112; P) Walter is a real star with his quick smile, culinary

skills and invaluable tips. Sure, the rooms are a blast from the 1970s, but they are super-clean and you'd be hard pushed to find better value in Interlaken. Breakfast (Sfr7) is copious, and the fondue dinner a bargain at Sfr19 per person.

POST HARDERMANNLI   Hotel $$
(☎ 033 822 89 19; www.post-hardermannli.ch; Hauptstrasse 18; s Sfr90-105, d 135-175; P) An affable Swiss-Kiwi couple, Andreas and Kim, run this ornate, flower-bedecked chalet. Rooms are simple yet comfy, decorated with pine and pastels. Cheaper rooms forgo balconies and Jungfrau views. Home-grown farm produce is served at breakfast.

HOTEL ROYAL ST GEORGES   Historic Hotel $$
(☎ 033 822 75 75; www.royal-stgeorges.ch; Höheweg 139; s Sfr130-200, d Sfr190-300) High-ceilinged spaces decorated with wrought iron, marble and chandeliers transport you back to the more graceful era of art nouveau. Choose between antique-strewn historic rooms and clean-lined, contemporary rooms. There's a small spa and a first-rate restaurant.

GASTHOF HIRSCHEN   Hotel $$
(☎ 033 822 15 45; www.hirschen-interlaken.ch, in German; Hauptstrasse 11; s/d Sfr110/180; P 🛜) With its dark-wood, geranium-clad facade and low ceilings, this heritage-listed, 17th-century chalet has plenty of old-world charm. Rooms are 'rustic modern', with parquet floors, downy duvets, bathroom pods and wi-fi. The restaurant (mains Sfr20 to Sfr35) rustles up local favourites.

Eating

BENACUS   Fusion $$
(☎ 033 821 20 20; www.benacus.ch; Stadthaus-platz; mains Sfr26-50; 🕑 lunch & dinner Tue-Fri, dinner Sat) Super-cool Benacus is a breath of urban air with its glass walls, wine-red sofas, lounge music and street-facing terrace. The TV show *Funky Kitchen Club* is filmed here. The menu stars creative flavours like perch filets with guacamole and Simmentaler veal with creamy basil mash.

BLUEBERRY'S   Cafe $
(Centralstrasse 7; snacks Sfr5-10; 🕑 9am-9pm Mon-Fri, 10am-9pm Sat, noon-8pm Sun) Every

Interlaken's clock tower in spring

IZZET KERIBAR / GETTY IMAGES ©

If You Like...
Extreme Activities

If you like high adventure like the plethora of activities you'll find in Interlaken (p132), consider some of these outfits that can help you find pulse-pounding experiences across the Alps:

1 PARAGLIDING JUNGFRAU
(☎079 779 90 00; www.paragliding-jungfrau.ch; Grindelwald) Call ahead to organise your jump from First at a height of 2150m (from Sfr170) or above the Staubbach Falls (Sfr160).

2 DORIS HIKE
(☎033 855 42 40; www.doris-hike.ch; Lauterbrunnen) Doris' informative guided hikes include glacier, waterfall and high-alpine options. Call ahead for times and prices.

3 SWISS ADVENTURES
(☎033 748 41 64; www.swissadventures.ch; Alpinzentrum, Gstaad) Organises guided climbs (Sfr99) and *via ferrate* (Sfr125), rafting (Sfr99), canyoning (Sfr125) and, in winter, igloo building (Sfr98) and snowshoe trekking (Sfr98).

4 VERTICAL SPORT
(http://verticalsport.ch; Jungfraustrasse 44, Interlaken; ⏱9am-noon & 1.30-6pm Mon-Fri, 9am-4pm Sat) This rock-climbing store sells and rents out top-quality climbing gear and is run by expert mountaineers who can give sound advice.

bit as zingy as its name suggests, this lime-walled cafe churns out fresh-pressed juices (try watermelon or apple-mint), appetising wraps and bagels, and spot-on blueberry smoothies.

LA TERRASSE   Fusion $$$
(☎033 828 28 28; Höheweg 41; mains Sfr54-68, tasting menus Sfr115-145; ⏱dinner Tue-Sat) La Terrasse is a high-class vision of marble, chandeliers and gleaming silverware. Thanks to chef Lukas Stalder, the food is as exquisite as the setting. The sommelier will help you choose fine wines to go with innovative dishes.

PIZZERIA HORN   Pizzeria $$
(☎033 822 92 92; Hardererstrasse 35; pizzas Sfr14-22, mains Sfr23.50-42; ⏱dinner Wed-Sun) Exposed brick, chunky tables and photos of Don Camillo set the scene at this inviting pizzeria. Find a cosy nook to feast on antipasti and delicious wood-oven pizza. There's alfresco dining on the garden terrace in summer.

SCHUH   Cafe $
(☎033 822 94 41; Höheweg 56; lunch menu Sfr19.50; ⏱9am-midnight) A Viennese-style coffee house famous for its pastries, pralines and park-facing terrace. The menu covers all the bases, from rösti to yellow curry.

 Drinking

METRO BAR   Bar, Club
(www.metrobar-interlaken.com; Hauptstrasse 23; ⏱9pm-2.30am) With its crazy themed parties and cheap booze, the bar/club at Balmer's is the liveliest haunt for revved-up 20-something travellers. DJs pump out house tunes as the night wears on.

BUDDY'S PUB   Pub
(☎033 822 76 12; Höheweg 33) Pull up a stool, order a draft Rugenbräu or a 'sex on the mountain' (for want of a beach) cocktail and enjoy a natter with the locals. Switzerland's first pub is loud, smoky and convivial.

ℹ Information

Tourist office (☎033 826 53 00; www.interlaken tourism.ch; Höheweg 37; ⏱8am-7pm Mon-Fri, 8am-5pm Sat, 10am-noon & 5-7pm Sun Jul-Aug, 8am-noon & 1.30-6pm Mon-Fri, 9am-noon Sat rest of year) Halfway between the stations. There's a hotel booking board outside.

ℹ Getting There & Away

Interlaken has two train stations: Interlaken West and Interlaken Ost; each has bike rental, money-changing facilities and a landing stage for boats on Lake Thun and Lake Brienz.

Trains to Lucerne (Sfr56, two hours), Brig via Spiez (Sfr42, one hour) and Montreux via Bern or Visp (Sfr58 to Sfr67, 2½ to three hours) depart frequently from Interlaken Ost train station.

The only way south for vehicles without a big detour round the mountains is to take the car-carrying train from Kandersteg, south of Spiez.

ⓘ Getting Around

You can easily get around Interlaken on foot, but taxis, buses and even horse-drawn carriages (around Sfr40) are found at each train station.

AROUND INTERLAKEN
Schynige Platte

The must-do day trip from Interlaken is Schynige Platte, a 1967m plateau where the **Alpengarten** (admission free; ⊗8.30am-6.30pm) nurtures 600 types of Alpine blooms, including snowbells, arnica, gentian and edelweiss. The biggest draw up here, however, is the hiking. The **Panoramaweg** is an easy two-hour circuit. If you're here in July or August, don't miss the **moonlight hikes** that follow the same route.

You reach the plateau on a late-19th-century **cog-wheel train** (www.schynigeplatte.ch, www.jungfraubahn.ch; one way/return Sfr35/60; ⊗closed late Oct–late May) from Wilderswil. Trains run up to Schynige Platte at approximately 40- to 50-minute intervals until around 5pm.

JUNGFRAU REGION

If the Bernese Oberland is Switzerland's Alpine heart, the Jungfrau region is where yours will skip a beat. Presided over by glacier-encrusted monoliths Eiger, Mönch and Jungfrau (Ogre, Monk and Virgin), the scenery is positively uplifting. Hundreds of kilometres of walking trails allow you to capture the landscape from many angles, but it never looks less than astonishing.

The 'big three' peaks have an enduring place in mountaineering legend, particularly the 3970m Eiger, whose fearsome north wall has claimed many lives and remained unconquered until

Detour:
Spiez

Hunched around a horseshoe-shaped bay, with a medieval castle rising above emerald vineyards, the oft-overlooked town of Spiez makes a great escape. The vibe is low-key but the setting magical, with views to conical Niesen (2362m) and a fjord-like slither of the lake. Its vines yield crisp, lemony riesling and Sylvaner white wines.

The turreted medieval **Schloss Spiez** (www.schloss-spiez.ch; Schlossstrasse 16; adult/child Sfr10/2; ⊗2-5pm Mon, 10am-5pm Tue-Sun Easter-Jun, mid-Sep–mid-Oct, 10am-6pm Jul–mid-Sep) is filled with oil paintings of its former masters, the influential von Bubenburg and von Erlach families. But it's the view that will grab you, whether from the lofty tower (which also sports 13th-century graffiti) or the banqueting hall.

From Interlaken West, trains run very frequently to Spiez (Sfr9.80, 20 minutes). By boat it's Sfr19 from Thun and Sfr25 from Interlaken West.

1938. Reaching great heights is easier today; it takes just hours to whizz up by train to Jungfraujoch (3454m), the highest station in Europe.

Staying in resorts entitles you to a Gästekarte (Guest Card), good for discounts throughout the entire region.

ⓘ Getting There & Around

Hourly trains depart for the region from Interlaken Ost station. Sit in the front half of the train for Lauterbrunnen or the back half for Grindelwald. The two sections of the train split up where the two valleys diverge at Zweilütschinen. The rail tracks loop around and meet up again at Kleine

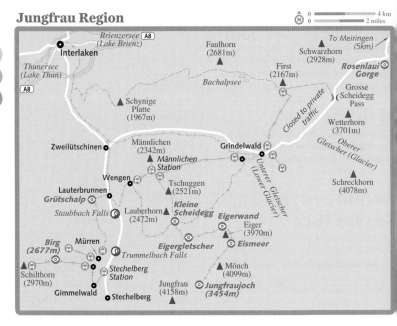

Scheidegg at the base of the Eiger, from where the route goes up and back to Jungfraujoch.

The Swiss Half-Fare Card is valid within the entire region. See p139 for details on good-value travel passes such as the Berner Oberland Regional Pass and the six-day Jungfraubahnen Pass.

Without a money-saving pass, sample fares include the following: Interlaken Ost to Grindelwald Sfr10.40; Grindelwald to Kleine Scheidegg Sfr32; Kleine Scheidegg to Jungfraujoch Sfr112 (return); Kleine Scheidegg to Wengen Sfr24; Wengen to Lauterbrunnen Sfr6.40; and Lauterbrunnen to Interlaken Ost Sfr7.20.

Many of the cable cars close for servicing in late April and late October.

Grindelwald

POP 3900 / ELEV 1034M

Grindelwald's sublime natural assets are film-set stuff – the chiselled features of the Eiger north face, the glinting tongues of Oberer and Unterer Glaciers and the crown-like peak of Wetterhorn will make you stare, swoon and lunge for your camera. Skiers and hikers cottoned onto its charms in the late 19th century, which makes it one of Switzerland's oldest resorts. And it has lost none of its appeal over the decades, with geranium-studded Alpine chalets and verdant pastures set against an Oscar-worthy backdrop.

 Sights

OBERER GLETSCHER   Viewpoint
(adult/child Sfr6/3; ☉9am-6pm mid-May–Oct)
The shimmering, slowly melting Oberer Gletscher is a 1½-hour hike east from the village, or catch a bus to Hotel-Restaurant Wetterhorn. Walk 10 minutes from the bus stop, then clamber up 890 wooden steps to reach a terrace offering dramatic views. A vertiginous hanging bridge spans the gorge.

Activities

Summer Activities

Grindelwald is outstanding hiking territory, veined with trails that command arresting views to massive north faces, crevassed glaciers and snow-capped peaks. One of the most-stunning day hikes is the 15km Kleine Scheidegg walk from Grindelwald to Wengen.

GRINDELWALD
SPORTS Adventure Sports
(033 854 12 80; www.grindelwaldsports.ch; Dorfstrasse 110; 8am-noon & 1.30-6pm, closed Sat & Sun in low season) In the tourist office, this outfit arranges mountain climbing, ski and snowboard instruction, canyon jumping and glacier bungee jumping at the Gletscherschlucht.

Winter Activities

Stretching from Oberjoch at 2486m right down to the village, the region of First presents a fine mix of cruisy red and challenging black ski runs. From Kleine Scheidegg or Männlichen there are long, easy runs back to Grindelwald, with the Eiger demanding all the attention.

🛏 Sleeping

Grindelwald brims with characterful B&Bs and holiday chalets. Pick up a list at the tourist office, or log onto www.wir -grindelwalder.ch for a wide selection of holiday apartments.

Nearly everywhere closes in April and from mid-October to mid-December. Local buses, tourist-office guided walks and entry to the sports centre are free with the Guest Card.

GLETSCHERGARTEN Hotel $$
(033 853 17 21; www.hotel-gletschergarten.ch; Dorfstrasse; s Sfr120-150, d Sfr230-300; P @) The sweet Breitenstein family make you feel at home in their rustic timber chalet, brimming with heirlooms from landscape paintings to snapshots of Elsbeth's grandfather who had 12 children (those were the days...). Decked out in pine and flowery fabrics, the rooms have balconies facing Unterer Gletscher at the front and Wetterhorn (best for sunset) at the back.

HOTEL BODMI Hotel $$
(033 853 12 20; www.bodmi.ch; Terrassenweg; s/d/apt Sfr200/294/392; P @) Wake up to memorable Eiger views and creamy goats' cheese – courtesy of the resident herd – at this postcard-perfect chalet. Surrounded by meadows, the hotel sits above First cable car station and is a great base for summer hiking and winter skiing. Unwind in the spa or in the restaurant (mains Sfr25 to Sfr45), which dishes up market-fresh Alpine fare.

HOTEL TSCHUGGEN Hotel $$
(033 853 17 81; www.tschuggen-grindelwald. ch; Dorfstrasse 134; s Sfr70-95, d Sfr160-190; P 🛜) Monika and Robert extend a warm welcome at this dark-wood chalet in the centre of town. The light, simple rooms are spotlessly clean; opt for a south-facing double for terrific Eiger views.

NATURFREUNDEHAUS Hostel $
(033 853 13 33; www.naturfreundehaeuser.ch; Terrassenweg 18; dm Sfr32-37, d Sfr74-84, break-fast Sfr10; P @ 🛜 ♿) Vreni and Heinz are your welcoming hosts at this wood chalet, picturesquely perched above the village.

Discount Travel Passes

You can save francs with **Berner Oberland Regional Pass** (www.regiopass-berner oberland.ch; May-Oct). The seven-day pass (Sfr233) gives you three days' unlimited free travel and four days' discounted travel in the region, while the 15-day pass (Sfr290) offers five days' unlimited free travel and 10 days' discounted travel. Children pay half price.

A good alternative is the **Jungfraubahnen Pass** (www.jungfrau.ch; May-Oct), which provides six days of unlimited travel throughout the region for Sfr210 (Sfr160 with Swiss Pass, Swiss Card or Half-Fare Card), though you still have to pay Sfr55 from Eigergletscher (just past Kleine Scheidegg) to Jungfraujoch.

Grindelwald

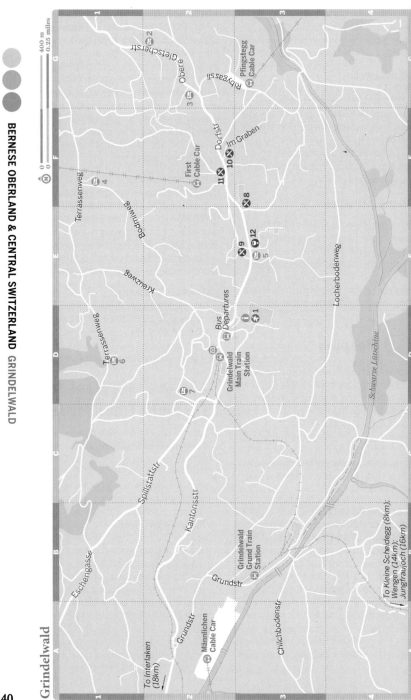

400 m
0.25 miles

Grindelwald

Creaking floors lead to cute pine-panelled rooms with checked curtains, including a shoebox single that's apparently Switzerland's smallest. The garden has wonderful views to the Eiger and Wetterhorn.

ROMANTIK HOTEL SCHWEIZERHOF   Historic Hotel $$$
(☏ 033 854 58 58; www.hotel-schweizerhof.com; Dorfstrasse; s/d/ste with half-board Sfr295/510/640; P @) The grand dame of Grindelwald, this plush art nouveau hotel has stylish rooms with gleaming slate-floored bathrooms. The spa is a big draw, with massage jets, treatment rooms, a teeth-chattering ice grotto and a pool with wide-screen mountain vistas. The restaurant (mains Sfr26 to Sfr44) uses home-grown vegetables and herbs.

ALPENBLICK   Hotel $$
(☏ 033 853 11 05; www.alpenblick.info; Obere Gletscherstrasse; dm Sfr40-45, d Sfr140-180; P) In a quiet corner of town, 10 minutes' stroll from the centre, Alpenblick is a great budget find, with squeaky-clean, pine-filled rooms. Basement dorms are jazzed up with bright duvets. There's an American-style diner (mains Sfr15 to Sfr19) and a terrace with glacier views.

Eating

Bars, restaurants, bakeries and supermarkets line central Dorfstrasse.

ONKEL TOM'S HÜTTE   Pizzeria $$
(☏ 033 853 52 39; Im Graben 4; pizzas Sfr13-33; ⏰ 6pm-midnight Thu, noon-midnight Fri-Tue)

Tables are at a premium in this incredibly cosy barn-style chalet. Yummy pizzas are prepared fresh in three sizes to suit any appetite.

MEMORY   Swiss $$
(☏ 033 854 31 31; mains Sfr21-30; Dorfstrasse; ⏰ 11.30am-10.30pm) Always packed, the Eiger Hotel's unpretentious restaurant rolls out tasty Swiss grub like rösti, raclette and fondue. Try to bag a table on the street-facing terrace.

C & M   Fusion $$
(☏ 033 853 07 10; mains Sfr23-36; ⏰ 8.30am-11pm Wed-Mon) Just as appetising as the menu are the stupendous views to Unterer Gletscher from this gallery-style cafe's sunny terrace.

PIZZERIA DA SALVI   Pizzeria $
(☏ 033 853 89 89; Dorfstrasse 189; pizza Sfr17-23;) This cheerful Italian in Hotel Steinbock rolls out delicious wood-fired pizza. There are 110 different kinds of grappa on the menu.

Drinking

ESPRESSO BAR   Bar
(Dorfstrasse 136; ⏰ 2pm-1am) Full to the gills in winter, the misleadingly named Espresso Bar in the Hotel Spinne draws a boisterous beer-guzzling crowd. It also harbours kitschy Mexican-themed **Mescalero** (⏰ Mon-Sat winter, Wed, Fri & Sat summer) with a DJ and occasional live music.

ℹ Information

The **tourist office** (☏ 033 854 12 12; www. grindelwald.ch; Dorfstrasse 110; ⏱ 8am-noon & 1.30-6pm Mon-Fri, 9am-noon & 1.30-5pm Sat & Sun) in the Sportzentrum hands out brochures and maps. There's an accommodation board with a phone outside.

ℹ Getting There & Around

See p142 for train information.

Around Grindelwald
Kleine Scheidegg

The Eiger, Mönch and Jungfrau soar almost 2000m above you at Kleine Scheidegg (2061m), where restaurants huddle around the train station. Most people only stay for a few minutes while changing trains for Jungfraujoch, but it's worth lingering to appreciate the dazzling views, including those to the fang-shaped peak of Silberhorn.

Kleine Scheidegg is a terrific base for hiking. There are short, undemanding trails, one hour apiece, to Eigergletscher, down to Wengernalp, and up the Lauberhorn behind the village. These areas become intermediate ski runs from December to April. Alternatively, you can walk the spectacular 6km **Eiger Trail** from Eigergletscher to Alpiglen (two hours) for close-ups of the mountain's fearsome north face.

Jungfraujoch

Sure, everyone else wants to see Jungfraujoch (3454m) and yes, tickets are expensive, but don't let that stop you. It's a once-in-a-lifetime trip that you need to experience first-hand. And there's a reason why two million people a year visit Europe's highest train station. The icy wilderness of swirling glaciers and 4000m turrets that unfolds at the top is staggeringly beautiful.

The last stage of the train journey from Kleine Scheidegg burrows through the

Left: Kleine Scheidegg, with the Eiger looming in the background; **Below:** Hikers in Lauterbrunnen (p144)

(LEFT) DENNIS K. JOHNSON / GETTY IMAGES ©; (BELOW) ANDY CHRISTIANI / GETTY IMAGES ©

heart of the Eiger before arriving at the sci-fi Sphinx meteorological station. Opened in 1912, the tunnel took 3000 men 16 years to drill.

Good weather is essential for this journey; check on www.jungfrau.ch or call ☎033 828 79 31. Don't forget to take warm clothing, sunglasses and sunscreen, as there's snow and glare up here all year.

Outside there are views of the moraine-streaked 23km tongue of the **Aletsch Glacier**, the longest glacier in the European Alps and a Unesco World Heritage Site. The views across rippling peaks stretch as far as the Black Forest in Germany on cloudless days.

When you tire (as if!) of the view, you can zip across the frozen plateau on a flying fox (adult/child Sfr20/15), dash downhill on a sled or snow disc (adult/child Sfr15/10), or enjoy a bit of tame skiing or boarding (adult/child Sfr35/25) at the **Snow Fun Park**. A day pass covering all activities costs Sfr45 for adults and Sfr25 for children.

From Interlaken Ost, the journey time is 2½ hours each way and the return fare is Sfr186.20. The last train back sets off at 5.45pm in summer and 4.45pm in winter. However, from May through to October there's a cheaper Good Morning Ticket costing Sfr140 if you take the first train (which departs at 6.35am from Interlaken Ost) and leave the summit by noon.

Getting these early trains is easier if your starting place is deeper in the region. Stay overnight at Kleine Scheidegg to take advantage of the excursion-fare train at 8am. From here, a return Good Morning Ticket is Sfr90.

Even the ordinary return ticket to Jungfraujoch is valid for one month, so you can use that ticket to form the backbone of your trip, venturing as far as Grindelwald and stopping for a few

143

ANDY CHRISTIANI / GETTY IMAGES ©

Don't Miss **Waterfalls**

Especially in the early-morning light, it's easy to see how the vaporous, 297m-high **Staubbach Falls** captivated prominent writers with its threads of spray floating down the cliffside. What appears to be ultra-fine mist from a distance, however, becomes a torrent when you walk behind the falls. Be prepared to get wet.

The glacier falls of **Trümmelbachfälle** are more of a bang-crash spectacle. Inside the mountain, up to 20,000L of water per second corkscrews through ravines and potholes shaped by the swirling waters. The 10 falls drain from 24 sq km of Alpine glaciers and snow deposits. A 10-minute bus ride (Sfr3.40) from the Lauterbrunnen train station takes you to the falls. Staubbach Falls

THINGS YOU NEED TO KNOW

Staubbach Falls (☉8am-8pm Jun-Oct); **Trümmelbachfälle** (www.truemmelbachfaelle.ch; adult/child Sfr11/4; ☉9am-5pm Apr-Jun & Sep-Nov, 8.30am-6pm Jul & Aug)

days' hiking, before moving on to Kleine Scheidegg, Jungfraujoch, Wengen and Lauterbrunnen.

Lauterbrunnen
POP 2500 / ELEV 796M

Lauterbrunnen's wispy Staubbach Falls inspired both Goethe and Lord Byron to pen poems to their ethereal beauty. Today the postcard-perfect village, nestled deep in the valley of 72 waterfalls, attracts a less highfalutin crowd. Laid-back and full of chalet-style lodgings, Lauterbrunnen is a great base for nature-lovers wishing to hike or climb.

Hikes heading up into the mountains from the waterfall-laced valley include a 2½-hour uphill trudge to Mürren and a more-gentle 1¾-hour walk to Stechelberg. In winter, you can glide past frozen waterfalls on a well-prepared 12km cross-country trail.

Eating & Drinking

AIRTIME
Cafe $

(www.airtime.ch; snacks & light meals Sfr6-15; ◷9am-7pm; 📶) Inspired by their travels in New Zealand, Daniela and Beni have set up this funky cafe, book exchange, laundry and extreme-sports agency. Munch wraps, sandwiches and homemade cakes.

FLAVOURS
Cafe $

(www.flavours.ch; snacks & light meals Sfr6-14; ◷7.30am-6.30pm) Whether you fancy a slap-up egg-and-bacon breakfast, homemade cakes with locally roasted coffee or a smoothie, Flavours is the go-to place. Housed in the former bakery, it's a grocery store on one side and a sleek cafe on the other. Warm up over hearty soups and savoury quiches.

ⓘ Information

The tourist office (☏033 856 85 68; www. mylauterbrunnen.com; ◷8.30am-noon & 1.30-6pm Jun-Sep, 9am-noon & 1.30-5pm Mon-Fri rest of year) is opposite the train station.

If you're travelling to the car-free resorts of Wengen and Mürren, there's a multistorey car park (☏033 828 71 11; www.jungfraubahn.ch; per day/week Sfr13.50/82) by the station, but it's advisable to book ahead. There is also an open-air car park by the Stechelberg cable-car station, charging Sfr5 for a day.

Wengen
POP 1300 / ELEV 1274M

Photogenically poised on a mountain ledge, Wengen's 'celestial views' have lured Brits here since Edwardian times. The fact you can only reach this chocolate-box village by train gives it romantic appeal. From the bench in front of the church at dusk, the vista takes on watercolour dreaminess, peering over to the misty Staubbach Falls, down to the

Lauterbrunnen Valley and up to glacier-capped giants of the Jungfrau massif. In winter, Wengen morphs into a ski resort with a low-key, family-friendly feel.

Skiing is mostly cruisy blues and reds, though experts can brave exhilarating black runs at Lauberhorn and the aptly named 'Oh God'.

The same area is excellent for hiking in the summer. Some 20km of paths stay open in winter too. The hour-long forest trail down to Lauterbrunnen is a sylvan beauty.

🛏 Sleeping

Expect summer rates to be roughly 30% cheaper than those quoted below.

HOTEL CAPRICE
Boutique Hotel $$$

(☏033 856 06 06; www.caprice-wengen.ch; d Sfr380-540; 📶) If you're looking for design-oriented luxury in the Jungfrau mountains, this boutique gem delivers with discreet service and authentically French cuisine. Don't be fooled by its cute Alpine trappings; inside it exudes Scandinavian

Brunnen (p161)
INTERNATIONAL PHOTOBANK / ALAMY ©

simplicity with chocolate-cream colours, slick rooms and a lounge with an open fire.

HOTEL BERGHAUS Hotel $$
(☎ 033 855 21 51; www.berghaus-wengen.ch; s/d from Sfr135/270) Sidling up to the forest, this family-run chalet is a five-minute toddle from the village centre. Rooms are light, spacious and pin-drop peaceful – ask for a south-facing one for dreamy Jungfrau views. Call ahead and they'll pick you up from the train station.

Eating & Drinking

RESTAURANT SCHÖNEGG Swiss $$$
(☎ 033 855 34 22; mains Sfr39-52; ⏱ lunch & dinner Mon-Sun, dinner only winter) Chef Hubert Mayer serves seasonally inspired dishes like home-smoked salmon with apple horseradish and saddle of venison in port-wine jus. The pine-clad, candlelit dining room is wonderfully cosy in winter and the mountain-facing terrace perfect for summertime dining.

SANTOS Cafe $
(☎ 078 67 97 445; snacks Sfr6-9; ⏱ 10am-midnight, closed Mon in summer) Popular with ravenous skiers coming down from the slopes, this Portuguese TV-and-tiles place is the real deal. Mrs Santos whips up burgers, calamari, sandwiches and divine *pastéis de nata* (custard tarts).

CAFÉ GRUEBI Cafe $
(☎ 033 855 58 55; snacks & mains Sfr7-16; ⏱ 8.30am-6pm Mon-Sat, 1-8pm Sun) Run by a husband-and-wife team, Gruebi offers cheap eats like rösti and goulash. The yummy homemade cakes are baked almost daily by the husband.

CRYSTAL BAR Bar
(Haus Crystal; ⏱ 8am-midnight) Pumping tunes and occasionally hosting gigs, this relaxed bar draws fun-loving après-ski types. It's opposite Männlichen cable car.

ℹ Information

Next to the Männlichen cable car, the tourist office (☎ 033 855 14 14; www.mywengen.ch; ⏱ 9am-6pm Mon-Sat, 9am-noon & 1-6pm Sun, closed Sat & Sun Nov & Mar-Apr) is minutes from the train station, taking a left at Hotel Silberhorn and continuing 100m further on.

Gimmelwald, backed by snow-covered mountains

Mürren

POP 430 / ELEV 1650M

Arriving on a clear evening, as the train from Grütschalp floats along the horizontal ridge towards Mürren, the peaks across the valley feel so close that you could reach out and touch them. And that's when you'll think you've died and gone to Heidi heaven. With its low-slung wooden chalets and spellbinding views of the Eiger, Mönch and Jungfrau, car-free Mürren is storybook Switzerland.

In winter, there are 53km of prepared ski runs nearby, mostly suited to intermediates, and a **ski school** (☏ 033 855 12 47; www.muerren.ch/skischule) charging Sfr50 for a two-hour group lesson. Mürren is famous for its hell-for-leather **Inferno Run** (www.inferno-muerren.ch) down from Schilthorn in late January. Daredevils have been competing in the 16km race since 1928 and today the course attracts 1800 intrepid amateur skiers. It's also the reason for all the devilish souvenirs.

In summer from Mürren, the **Allmendhubel funicular** (one way/return Sfr12/7.40) takes you above Mürren to a panoramic restaurant. From here, you can set out on many walks, including the famous **Northface Trail** (1½ hours), via Schiltalp to the west, leading through wildflower-strewn meadows with views to the glaciers and waterfalls of the Lauterbrunnen Valley and the monstrous Eiger north face – bring binoculars to spy intrepid climbers. There's also a kid-friendly **Adventure Trail** (one hour).

🛏 Sleeping & Eating

In summer, rates are up to 30% cheaper than the high-season winter prices given below.

EIGER GUESTHOUSE   Guesthouse $$
(☏ 033 856 54 60; www.eigerguesthouse. com; d Sfr140-190, q Sfr240; @ �📶) Run by a fun-loving, on-the-ball team, this central pick offers great value. Besides clean, spruced-up rooms (the best have Eiger views), there is a downstairs pub serv-

ing tasty grub and a good selection of draught beers.

HOTEL JUNGFRAU   Historic Hotel $$
(☏ 033 856 64 64; www.hoteljungfrau.ch; s Sfr80-140, d Sfr160-280; ⏷) Set above Mürren and overlooking the nursery slopes, this welcoming family-run hotel dates to 1894. Despite '70s traces, rooms are tastefully decorated in warm hues; south-facing ones have Jungfrau views. Downstairs there's a beamed lounge with an open fire.

HOTEL ALPENRUH   Hotel $$
(☏ 033 856 88 00; www.alpenruh-muerren.ch; s Sfr140-180, d Sfr200-280; ⏷) Lots of loving detail has gone into this much-lauded chalet. Grimacing masks to ward off evil spirits and assorted knick-knacks enliven the place, while the light-flooded rooms feature lots of chunky pine. Guests praise the service, food and unbeatable views to Jungfrau massif.

RESTAURANT LA GROTTE   Swiss $$
(☏ 033 855 18 26; mains Sfr21-35; ◷11am-2pm & 5-9pm) Brimming with cowbells, cauldrons and Alpine props, this kitsch-meets-rustic mock cave of a restaurant is touristy but fun. Fondues and flambées are good bets.

Gimmelwald

POP 110 / ELEV 1370M

If you think Mürren is cute, wait until you see Gimmelwald. This pipsqueak of a village has long been a hideaway for hikers and adventurers tiptoeing away from the crowds. The secret is out, though, and this mountainside village is swiftly becoming known for its drop-dead-gorgeous scenery, rural authenticity and sense of calm.

The surrounding hiking trails include one down from Mürren (30 to 40 minutes). Cable cars are also an option (Mürren or Stechelberg Sfr5.80).

🛏 Sleeping & Eating

ESTHER'S GUEST HOUSE   Guesthouse $$
(☏ 033 855 54 88; www.esthersguesthouse.ch; s/d/tr/q Sfr55/130/150/180, apt Sfr160-230;

) Esther runs this charming B&B with love. Drenched with piny light, the rooms are spotless, while the apartments are ideal for families. The attic room is a favourite with its slanted roof and stargazing window. For an extra Sfr15, you'll be served a delicious breakfast of homemade bread, cheese and yoghurt.

HOTEL MITTAGHORN Guesthouse $
(033 855 16 58; d/tr Sfr86/129, half-board per person Sfr15; Poeschenried 39; @) Staring in wonder at the mountains is the main pursuit at this stunningly situated wooden chalet, run by the irrepressible Walter and his sidekick, Tom. Creaking floors and doors lead to simple, cosy rooms. Dinners are hearty, jovial affairs. It's a 10-minute uphill walk from the cable-car station.

Schilthorn

There's a tremendous 360-degree panorama from the 2970m **Schilthorn** (www.schilthorn.ch). On a clear day, you can see from Titlis around to Mont Blanc, and across to the German Black Forest. Yet some visitors seem more preoccupied with practising their delivery of the line, 'The name's Bond, James Bond', than taking in the 200 or so peaks. That's because a few scenes from *On Her Majesty's Secret Service* were shot here in 1968–69 – as the fairly tacky **Touristorama** below the **Piz Gloria** revolving restaurant will remind you.

From Interlaken, take a Sfr120.80 excursion trip (Half-Fare Card and Swiss Card 50% off, Swiss Pass 65% off) going to Lauterbrunnen, Grütschalp, Mürren, Schilthorn and returning through Stechelberg to Interlaken. A return from Lauterbrunnen (via Grütschalp) and Mürren costs Sfr94.80 as does the return journey via the Stechelberg cable car. A return from Mürren is Sfr74. Ask about discounts for early morning trips.

THE LAKES

Anyone who travels to Interlaken for the first time from Bern will never forget the moment they clap eyes on Thunersee (Lake Thun). As the train loops past pastures and tidy villages on the low southern shore, some people literally gasp at the sight of the Alps rearing above the startlingly turquoise waters.

Bordering Interlaken to the east, Brienzersee (Lake Brienz) has just as many cameras snapping with its unbelievably aquamarine waters and rugged mountain backdrop.

Steamers ply both lakes from late May to mid-September. There are no winter services on Brienzersee, whereas special cruises continue on Thunersee. For more information contact **BLS** (033 334 52 11; www.bls.ch). A day pass valid for both lakes costs Sfr64 from Tuesday to Sunday, Sfr29 on Monday; children pay half-price. Eurail Passes, the Regional Pass and the Swiss Pass are valid on all boats, and InterRail and the Swiss Half-Fare Card get 50% off.

Thun

POP 43,400 / ELEV 559M

Ringed by mountains, hugging the banks of the aquamarine Aare River and topped by a turreted castle, medieval Thun is every inch your storybook Swiss town. History aside, the town is infused with a young spirit, with lively crowds sunning themselves at riverside cafes and one-of-a-kind boutiques filling the unusual arcades.

 **Sights & Activities**

For a magical 360-degree view of Thun, the lake and the glaciated Jungfrau mountains, walk 20 minutes south of the centre to Jakobshübeli viewpoint.

SCHLOSS THUN Castle
(www.schlossthun.ch; adult/child Sfr8/2; 10am-5pm) Sitting on a hilltop and looking proudly back on 900 years of history, Schloss Thun is the castle of your wildest fairytale dreams, crowned by a riot of turrets and affording tremendous views of the lake and Alps. It once belonged to Duke Berchtold V of the powerful Zähringen family. Today it houses a **museum**, showcasing prehistoric and Roman relics,

NORDIC PHOTOS / AWL ©

Don't Miss **Skiing the Jungfrau Region**

Whether you want to slalom wide, sunny slopes at the foot of the Eiger or ski the breathtakingly sheer 16km Inferno run from Schilthorn to Lauterbrunnen, there's a piste that suits in the Jungfrau region. Grindelwald, Männlichen, Mürren and Wengen have access to some 214km of prepared runs and 44 ski lifts. A one-day ski pass for either Grindelwald-Wengen or Mürren-Schilthorn costs Sfr62/31 per adult/child, while a seven-day ski pass for these regions will set you back Sfr291/146. Ski passes for the whole Jungfrau ski region cost Sfr129 for adults and Sfr65 for children for a minimum two days, but switching between ski areas by train can be slow and crowded.

tapestries, majolica and plenty of shining armour.

ALTSTADT   Neighbourhood
It's a pleasure simply to wander Thun's attractive riverfront Old Town, where plazas and lanes are punctuated by 15th- and 16th-century townhouses. A stroll takes in the 300-year-old Untere Schleusenbrücke, a covered wooden bridge that is a mass of pink and purple flowers in summer. Nearby is the split-level, flag-bedecked Obere Hauptgasse, whose arcades hide boutiques and galleries selling everything from handmade jewellery to chocolate and Moroccan babouches (slippers). At the street's northern tip is

cobblestone Rathausplatz, centred on a fountain and framed by arcaded buildings.

Eating & Drinking

FLUSS   Fusion **$$**
(☏ 033 222 01 10; Mühleplatz 9; mains Sfr27-58; ⊙ 11am-12.30am, closed Sun in winter) Right on the banks of the Aare River, this contemporary glass-walled lounge restaurant attracts a young crowd who come for the beautifully prepared sushi, sashimi and herb-infused grill specialities. The olive tree-dotted waterfront deck is perfect for sundowners and people-watching.

KAFFEE UND KUCHEN Cafe $
(Obere Hauptgasse 34; snacks & light meals
Sfr6.50-21; ⏲closed Sun evening & Mon in winter)
This vaulted cellar has an arty vibe and
invites lazy days spent reading, guzzling
coffee and lingering over brunch. The
homemade food – from breakfast rösti to
rich chocolate-chilli cake – is delicious.

ⓘ Information

Tourist office (☏033 225 90 00; www.thun.ch;
Bahnhofplatz; ⏲9am-6.30pm Mon-Fri, to 4pm
Sat, plus to 1pm Sun Jul & Aug)

ⓘ Getting There & Away

Thun is on the main north–south train route from
Frankfurt to Milan and beyond. Frequent trains run
to Interlaken West (Sfr15.20, 30 minutes). Boats
glide across the lake to Interlaken Ost (Sfr39) and
Spiez (Sfr19).

Brienz
POP 3000 / ELEV 566M

Quaint and calm, Brienz peers across
the exquisitely turquoise waters of its
namesake lake to rugged mountains
and thick forests beyond. The deeply
traditional village has a stuck-in-time feel
with its tooting steam train and wood-
carving workshops. In town, mosey down
postcard-perfect Brunngasse, a curving
lane dotted with stout wooden chalets,
each seemingly trying to outdo its neigh-
bour with window displays of vines, kitsch
gnomes and billowing geraniums.

ⓞ Sights & Activities

Kids can splash around in the water
playground on the tree-fringed lake
promenade.

ROTHORN BAHN Railway
(www.brienz-rothorn-bahn.ch; one way/return
Sfr51/80; ⏲hourly 7.30am-4.30pm Jun-late Oct)
This is the only steam-powered cogwheel train still operating in Switzerland,
climbing 2350m, from where you can
set out on hikes or enjoy the long views
over Brienzersee to snow-dusted 4000m
peaks.

**SCHWEIZER HOLZBILDHAUEREI
MUSEUM** Museum
(Hauptstrasse 111; adult/child Sfr5/free; ⏲9am-
6pm May-Sep, 1.30-5.30pm Tue-Sat rest of year,
closed Jan & Nov) Several woodcarvers open
their attached workshops, including Jobin,
which has been in business since 1835. You
can see its intricately carved sculptures,
reliefs and music boxes in this museum.

🛏 Eating

TEA-ROOM HOTEL WALZ Cafe $$
(Hauptstrasse 102; mains Sfr29-35; ⏲7.30am-
10pm daily, 7.30am-6.30pm Thu-Tue winter)
Dirndl-clad waitresses bring hearty
meals and cakes to the table at this old-
fashioned tea room. Try the unfortunate-
sounding but tasty speciality Brienzer
Krapfen: pastries filled with dried pears.

ⓘ Getting There & Away

From Interlaken Ost, Brienz is accessible by train
(Sfr7.80, 20 minutes) or boat (Sfr28, Apr–mid-
Oct). The scenic Brünig Pass (1008m) is the road
route to Lucerne.

WEST BERNESE OBERLAND

At the western side of the Jungfrau are
Simmental and Frutigland, dominated
by two wildly beautiful river valleys, the
Simme and the Kander. Further west
is Saanenland, famous for the ritzy ski
resort of Gstaad.

Kandersteg
POP 1200 / ELEV 1176M

Turn up in Kandersteg wearing anything
but muddy boots and you'll attract a few
odd looks. Hiking is this town's raison
d'être, with 550km of surrounding trails.
An amphitheatre of spiky peaks studded
with glaciers and jewel-coloured lakes
creates a sublime natural backdrop to the
rustic village of dark-timber chalets.

Jagged mountains frame the
impossibly turquoise **Oeschinensee** (www.
oeschinensee.ch). A **cable car** (one way/return

Sfr16/23) takes you to within 20 minutes of the lake by foot. Once there, it takes an hour to hike back down to Kandersteg.

Kandersteg has some first-rate hiking in its wild backyard on the cantonal border with Valais. A superb trek is the high-level **Gemmi Pass** (2314m) to Leukerbad, involving a steep descent. Alternatively, you could walk through flower-strewn pastures in the wildlife-rich Üschenetäli. For more of a challenge, test the 3½-hour *via ferrata* at **Allmenalp**. Equipment can be hired at the valley station for Sfr20.

In winter there are more than 50km of **cross-country ski** trails, including the iced-over Oeschinensee.

Sleeping & Eating

Kandersteg's popularity with hikers means there's lots of cheaper accommodation, but many places close between seasons. Ask for the Guest Card for reductions on activities.

HOTEL ZUR POST   Hotel $
(☎ 033 675 12 58; www.hotel-zur-post.ch; s Sfr55-70, d Sfr100-120) Cheery and central,

these good-value digs offer simple rooms with balconies. Downstairs the restaurant has a menu packed with Swiss staples like fondue and rösti (mains Sfr18 to Sfr35). Sit on the terrace when the sun's out.

HOTEL VICTORIA RITTER   Historic Hotel $$
(☎ 033 675 80 00; www.hotel-victoria.ch; s Sfr130-180, d Sfr220-330; P 🏊 👪) This one-time coach tavern is now an elegant hotel, run by the Platzer family. The Victoria side has traditional 19th-century decor, while the snug wood-panelled rooms in the Ritter are more rustic. There's a fine restaurant, an indoor pool and sauna, a children's club and playground.

RUEDIHUS   Historic Hotel $$
(☎ 033 675 81 81; www.doldenhorn-ruedihus.ch; s/d from Sfr140/270; P) Oozing 250 years of history from every creaking beam, this archetypal Alpine chalet is a stunner. Romantic and warm, the cottage-style rooms feature low ceilings, antique painted furniture and four-poster beds. Home-grown herbs are used to flavour dishes served in the cosy restaurant (mains Sfr34 to Sfr40).

Jungfrau massif from Schynige Platte (p137)

Below: Chalets in chic Gstaad; **Right:** View of the Eiger from Grindelwald (p138)

(BELOW & RIGHT) GLENN VAN DER KNIJFF / GETTY IMAGES ©

While the principal competitive sports are celebrity-spotting and gazing wistfully into Gucci-filled boutiques, others might enjoy the fine hiking and skiing.

ℹ️ Information

The **tourist office** (📞033 675 80 80; www.kandersteg.ch; 🕐8am-noon & 1.30-6pm Mon-Fri, 8.30am-noon & 3-6pm Sat Jun-Sep, 8am-noon & 2-6pm Mon-Fri, 8.30am-noon & 3-6pm Sat Dec-Mar, 8am-noon & 2-5pm Mon-Fri rest of year) can suggest hiking routes and other activities in the area.

ℹ️ Getting There & Away

Kandersteg is at the northern end of the Lötschberg Tunnel, through which trains trundle to Goppenstein (30km from Brig) and onwards to Iselle in Italy. See www.bls.ch/autoverlad for more details.

Gstaad

POP 3600 / ELEV 1100M

Synonymous with the glitterati and fittingly twinned with Cannes, Gstaad appears smaller than its reputation – too little for its designer ski boots, as it were.

 Activities

Winter Activities

Gstaad Mountain Rides' 250km of ski slopes cover a good mix of blues, reds and blacks, and include neighbouring resorts like Saanen, Saanenmöser, St Stephan and Zweisimmen. Beginners can test out the snow on gentle, tree-lined runs at Wispile and Eggli, while more proficient skiers can cruise challenging reds at Les Diablerets. A day ski pass costs Sfr62 for an adult and Sfr31 for a child, and under-nine-year-olds ski free. Snowboarders tackle the curves, bowls and jumps at the ski-cross slope at Riedenberg.

Non skiers and families are in their element in Gstaad, with off-piste fun including ice skating, curling, horse-drawn-trap rides, winter hiking on 30 trails, snowshoeing, airboarding at Saanenmöser and snow golf at Wispile.

Summer Activities

Hiking is the main summer pursuit and the opportunities are boundless, with 300km of marked trails threading through the region. A scenic three-hour hike takes you from Wispile to Launensee, a crystalline Alpine lake, with views of the craggy Wildhorn massif en route. Wispile is the best bet for families, with a dairy trail, a petting zoo and a downhill scooter trail (adult/child Sfr15/8) from its middle station.

 **Sleeping**

The following rates are for winter high season; expect discounts of 30% to 50% in summer. The tourist office has a list of self-catering chalets. Many places close from mid-October to mid-December and from April to mid-June.

HOTEL ALPHORN　　　　　　Hotel $$
(☎ 033 748 45 45; www.gstaad-alphorn.ch; Gsteigstrasse; s/d Sfr137/252; P 🛜) A traditional Swiss chalet with a 21st-century twist, the Alphorn has smart rooms with plenty of warm pine, chunky beds and balconies with country views. Downstairs there's a cosy restaurant (mains Sfr27 to Sfr38), a sauna and a whirlpool big enough for two.

HOTEL CHRISTIANIA　　Guesthouse $$
(☎ 033 744 51 21; www.christiania.ch; Untergstaad 26; s/d Sfr205/355; 🛜) This supercentrally located, family-run chalet stands out for its bright, well-kept rooms and five-star welcome. The Egyptian owner cooks delicious Middle Eastern fare from mezze to couscous in the restaurant (mains Sfr16 to Sfr28).

153

GSTAAD PALACE Luxury Hotel $$$
(☎033 748 50 00; www.palace.ch; Palacestrasse 28; s Sfr470-620, d Sfr720-1020; P ❄ @ ≋) Opulent, exclusive and – in case you happen to be wondering – accessible by helicopter, this hilltop fairytale palace has attracted celebrity royalty like Michael Jackson, Robbie Williams and Liza Minnelli. Lavish quarters, a luxurious spa, several gourmet restaurants and an Olympic-sized pool justify the price tag. Retro disco Green Go is also up here.

Eating & Drinking

If Gstaad's ritzy restaurants aren't for you, head for the mountain chalet restaurants at the summit stations of the cable cars.

MICHEL'S STALLBEIZLI Swiss $
(☎033 744 43 37; www.stallbeizli.ch; Gsteigstrasse 38; mains Sfr20-29; 9.30am-6pm mid-Dec-Mar; 👪) Dining doesn't get more back-to-nature than at this converted barn. In winter, you can feast away on fondue, drink Alpine herbal tea, or munch home-cured meat and cheese, with truly moo-ving views to the cud-chewing cows and goats in the adjacent stable. Kids love it.

WASSERNGRAT Swiss $$
(☎033 744 96 22; mains Sfr20-50; 9.30am-4.30pm Thu-Sun Aug & mid-Dec–Mar) Marvel at views of Les Diablerets glacier and Gstaad from the slope-side perch of Wasserngrat, where a fire crackles in the rustic-chic restaurant and skiers warm up over fondue on the sunny terrace. Top ingredients like truffles and foie gras flavour classic Alpine dishes.

APPLE PIE Cafe $
(Promenade; light meals Sfr10-22; 9am-10pm) Just as nice as its name suggests, Apple Pie has given Gstaad an injection of cool with bubbly young staff and a Boho vibe. The saliva-inducing French menu skips from crêpes to thick onion soup and crisp apple tart.

Information

The tourist office (☎033 748 81 81; www.gstaad.ch; Promenade 41; 8.30am-6.30pm Mon-Fri, 9am-noon & 1.30-5pm Sat & Sun Jul-Aug & Dec-Mar, 8.30am-noon & 1.30-6.30pm Mon-Fri,

Kapellbrücke (Chapel Bridge), Lucerne

10am-noon & 1.30-5pm Sat rest of year) has
stacks of info on the area.

ℹ️ Getting There & Away

Gstaad is on the Golden Pass route between
Montreux (Sfr24, 1½ hours) and Spiez (Sfr25, 1½
hours; change at Zweisimmen). There is an hourly
service to Geneva airport (Sfr52, three hours) via
Montreux.

LUCERNE
POP 59,500 / ELEV 435M

Recipe for a gorgeous Swiss city: take
a cobalt lake ringed by mountains of
myth, add a well-preserved medieval
Altstadt (Old Town) and a reputation for
making beautiful music, then sprinkle
with covered bridges, sunny plazas,
candy-coloured houses and waterfront
promenades. Lucerne is stunning, and
deservedly popular since the likes of
Goethe, Queen Victoria and Wagner
savoured her views in the 19th century.
Legend has it that an angel with a light
showed the first settlers where to build
a chapel in Lucerne, and today it still has
amazing grace.

Though the shops are still crammed
with what Mark Twain so eloquently
described as 'gimcrackery of the souvenir
sort', Lucerne doesn't only dwell on
the past, with a roster of music gigs
keeping the vibe upbeat. Carnival capers
at Fasnacht, balmy summers, golden
autumns – this 'city of lights' shines in
every season.

👁️ Sights

SAMMLUNG ROSENGART   Museum
(Rosengart Collection; www.rosengart.ch;
Pilatusstrasse 10; adult/child Sfr18/10; ⏰10am-
6pm Apr-Oct, 11am-5pm Nov-Mar) Lucerne's
blockbuster cultural attraction occupies
a graceful neoclassical pile. It showcases
the outstanding collection of Angela
Rosengart, a Swiss art dealer and close
friend of Picasso who, in an act of great
civic generosity, made some 200-odd
works available to the public. Alongside

Regional Discounts

If you don't have a Swiss or Eurail
Pass (both of which are valid on lake
journeys), consider purchasing the
regional **Tell-Pass** (www.tell-pass.ch; per
7/15 days Sfr180/246), which is valid
in the Lucerne region from 1 April
until 31 October. Sold at the Lucerne
tourist office and all boat stations,
the Tell-Pass provides free travel for
two or five days, and half-price fares
for the remainder.

The handy **Vierwaldstättersee
Guest Card**, available when you stay
overnight anywhere in the region,
offers benefits, including discounts
on sporting facilities and 10% to
50% off certain cable cars, as well as
reductions on museum admission in
Lucerne and elsewhere.

---

works by the great Spanish master are
paintings and sketches by Cézanne, Klee,
Kandinsky, Miró, Matisse and Monet.
Complementing this collection are some
200 photographs by David Douglas Dun-
can of the last 17 years of Picasso's life
with his family in their home near Cannes.

KAPELLBRÜCKE   Bridge
You haven't really been to Lucerne until
you have strolled the creaky 14th-century
Kapellbrücke (Chapel Bridge), spanning the Reuss river in the Old Town. The
octagonal water tower is original, but its
gabled roof is a modern reconstruction,
rebuilt after a disastrous fire in 1993.
As you cross the bridge, note Heinrich
Wägmann's 17th-century triangular roof
panels, showing important events from
Swiss history and mythology. The icon
is at its most photogenic when bathed in
soft golden light at dusk.

LION MONUMENT   Memorial
(Löwendenkmal; Denkmalstrasse) By far the
most touching of the 19th-century sights
that lured so many British to Lucerne is
the Lion Monument. Lukas Ahorn carved

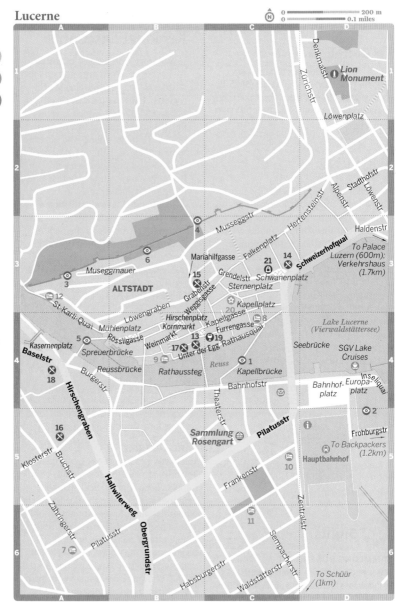

this 10m-long sculpture of a dying lion into the rock face in 1820 to commemorate Swiss soldiers who died defending King Louis XVI during the French Revolution. Mark Twain once called it the 'saddest and most moving piece of rock in the world'.

SPREUERBRÜCKE   Bridge
Further down the river, the Spreuerbrücke (Spreuer Bridge) is darker and smaller

Lucerne

than the Chapel Bridge, but its 1408 structure is entirely original. Lore has it that this was the only bridge where locals were allowed to throw *Spreu* (chaff) into the river in medieval times. Here, the roof panels consist of artist Caspar Meglinger's movie-storyboard-style sequence of paintings, *The Dance of Death,* showing how the plague affected all levels of society.

MUSEGGMAUER   Viewpoint
(City Wall; ◷8am-7pm Apr-Oct) For a bird's-eye view over Lucerne's rooftops to the glittering lake and mountains beyond, wander the medieval ramparts. A walkway is open between the **Schirmerturm** (tower), where you enter, and the **Wachturm**, from where you have to retrace your steps. You can also ascend and descend the **Zytturm** or **Männliturm** (the latter not connected to the ramparts walkway).

VERKEHRSHAUS   Museum
(www.verkehrshaus.ch; Lidostrasse 5; adult/child Sfr28/14, incl cinema Sfr38/24; ◷10am-6pm Apr-Oct, to 5pm Nov-Mar) The fascinating interactive Transport Museum is quite deservedly Switzerland's most popular museum, and is a great kid-pleaser. Alongside space rockets, steam locomotives, flying bicycles and dugout canoes are hands-on activities such as flight

simulators, broadcasting studios and even bikes to ride. Take bus 6, 8 or 24 to the Verkehrshaus stop.

KULTUR UND KONGRESSZENTRUM   Arts Centre
(Arts & Congress Centre; www.kkl-luzern.ch; Europaplatz) French architect Jean Nouvel's waterfront Kultur und Kongresszentrum (KKL) is a postmodern jawdropper in an otherwise historic city. But don't think a strikingly handsome face implies a superficial soul: the main concert hall's acoustics are as close to perfect as humankind has ever known, according to many musicians and conductors who have performed here.

🛏 Sleeping

Most hotels offer winter discounts – sometimes up to one-third off, but you'll be lucky to get a bed (or any kip for that matter) at Fasnacht, so book well ahead.

Altstadt

TOURIST HOTEL   Hotel $
(☎041 410 24 74; www.touristhotel.ch; St-Karli-Quai 12; s/d/tr/q Sfr140/180/220/260; @ ⊛)
Don't be put off by the uninspired name and institutional-green facade of this

central, riverfront cheapie. Dorms are basic, but rooms cheerily modern, with flat-screen TVs. There are also cheaper rooms with shared bathrooms. Private parking costs Sfr15 a day.

HOTEL DES BALANCES Hotel $$$
(☎ 041 418 28 28; www.balances.ch; Weinmarkt 4; s Sfr290-330, d Sfr390-430, ste Sfr530-630; P ⓦ) Behind its elaborately frescoed facade, this hotel flaunts a light and airy design ethos, with ice-white rooms, gilt mirrors and inlaid parquet floors. Suites have river-facing balconies. Parking costs Sfr27 per day.

HOTEL DES ALPES Hotel $$
(☎ 041 417 20 60; www.desalpes-luzern.ch; Furrengasse 3; s/d Sfr160/254; ⓦ) Facing the river and Kapellbrücke, the location is this hotel's biggest draw. The rooms are turn-of-the-21st-century comfy, though light sleepers might find them noisy.

Central Lucerne

THE HOTEL Design Hotel $$$
(☎ 041 226 86 86; www.the-hotel.ch; Sempacherstrasse 14; ste Sfr430-1000; P ❄ ⓦ) This shamelessly hip hotel, bearing the imprint of architect Jean Nouvel, is all streamlined chic, with refined suites featuring stills from movie classics on the ceilings. Downstairs, Bam Bou is one of Lucerne's hippest restaurants and the simple summer terrace across the street is a cool place to idle. Parking costs Sfr35 per day.

HOTEL WALDSTÄTTERHOF Hotel $$
(☎ 041 227 12 71; www.hotel-waldstaetterhof.ch; Zentralstrasse 4; s Sfr170, d Sfr270-315; P ⓦ) Behind its faux-Gothic, red-brick exterior, this hotel has smart, modern rooms with hardwood-style floors and high ceilings, plus excellent service. Each year an entire floor is renovated. Light sleepers might want to book a room in the newer, better-soundproofed annex. Wi-fi costs Sfr10 for 12 hours (total); parking is Sfr17 a day.

HOTEL ALPHA Hotel $
(☎ 041 240 42 80; www.hotelalpha.ch; Zähringerstrasse 24; s/d/tr Sfr75/150/185; P ⓦ) Easy on the eyes and wallet, this hotel is in a quiet residential area 10 minutes' walk from the Old Town. Rooms are simple, light and spotlessly clean, and there are cheaper rooms with shared bathroom. Wi-fi is free for the first hour, then Sfr1 per hour. Parking is Sfr10 per day.

Outdoor dining in Lucerne

ADINA TOVY / GETTY IMAGES ©

Around Central Lucerne

BACKPACKERS LUCERNE · Hostel $
(☎041 360 04 20; www.backpackerslucerne.ch; Alpenquai 42; dm/d Sfr32/72; @ 🛜) Could this be backpacker heaven? Right on the lake, this is a soulful place to crash with art-slung walls, bubbly staff, a well-equipped kitchen and immaculate dorms with balconies. It's a 15-minute walk southeast of the station.

PALACE LUZERN · Luxury Hotel $$$
(☎041 416 16 16; www.palace-luzern.ch; Haldenstrasse 10; r from Sfr400, ste from Sfr550; P @ 🛜) This luxury belle époque hotel on the lakefront is sure of its place in many a heart. Inside it's all gleaming marble, chandeliers, airy rooms and turn-of-the-20th-century grandeur. Parking is Sfr35 per day; wi-fi an extortionate Sfr45 for 30 hours.

 Eating

WIRTSHAUS GALLIKER · Swiss $$
(☎041 240 10 02; Schützenstrasse 1; mains Sfr24-48; ⏱lunch & dinner Tue-Sat, closed Jul–mid-Aug) Don't eat for a day before visiting this old-style tavern, passionately run by the Galliker family over four generations since 1856. It attracts a lively bunch of regulars. Motherly waitresses dish up Lucerne soul food (rösti, *chögalipaschtetli* and the like) that is batten-the-hatches filling. Book ahead for dinner.

BODU · French $$
(☎041 410 01 77; Kornmarkt 5; mains Sfr18-58; ⏱lunch & dinner) Banquettes, wood panelling and elbow-to-elbow tables create a warm ambience at this classic French-style bistro. Here locals huddle around bottles of Bordeaux and bowls of *bouillabaisse* (fish stew) or succulent sirloin steaks. Reservations strongly advised.

RESTAURANT DREI KÖNIGE · Modern European $$
(Klosterstrasse 10; mains Sfr22.80-44.50; ⏱lunch & dinner Mon-Sat) A high-ceilinged, retro-fitted bar-restaurant, this place has whopper-sized traditional and fusion meals and cheery service, attracting young hipster types and stalwart locals alike.

JAZZKANTINE · Cafe $
(www.jsl.ch, in German; Grabenstrasse 8; pasta Sfr16, sandwiches Sfr7-14.50; ⏱7am-12.30am Mon-Sat, from 4pm Sun) With its long bar, sturdy wooden tables and chalkboard menus, this is an arty haunt. Go for tasty Italian dishes and very good coffee. Check the schedule for jazz workshops and gigs, which take place downstairs.

RESTAURANT SCHIFF · Swiss $$
(Unter der Egg 8; mains Sfr26.50-44; lunch & dinner) Under the waterfront arcades and lit by tea lights at night, this restaurant has bags of charm and is a great spot to catch some sun. Try fish from Lake Lucerne and *chögalipaschtetli* (vol-au-vents stuffed with meat and mushrooms).

CONFISERIE BACHMANN · Sweets $
(Schwanenplatz 7; ⏱7am-7pm Mon-Wed & Fri, to 9pm Thu, to 5.30pm Sat, 9.30am-7pm Sun) Swiss milk chocolate flows from a fountain at this sugar-coated temple. You'll find pastries, gelati, salads and sandwiches, plus Switzerland's longest praline counter. There are other branches at the train station and throughout town.

Drinking & Entertainment

RATHAUS BRÄUEREI · Brewery
(Unter der Egg 2; ⏱8am-midnight Mon-Sat, to 11pm Sun) Sip home-brewed beer under the vaulted arches of this buzzy tavern that brews its own, or nab a pavement table and watch the river flow.

SCHÜÜR · Live Music
(www.schuur.ch, in German; Tribschenstrasse 1) Live gigs are the name of the game here: think everything from metal, garage, pop, Cuban and world, plus theme nights with DJ-spun Britpop and '80s classics. All this plus a fantastically beachy outdoors area, complete with bar.

STADTKELLER Traditional Music
(www.stadtkeller.ch; Sternenplatz 3) Alpenhorns, cowbells, flag throwing, yodelling – name the Swiss cliché and you'll find it at this folksy haunt.

🔒 Shopping

Mosey down Haldenstrasse for art and antiques or Löwenstrasse for vintage threads and souvenirs.

CASAGRANDE Souvenirs
(Grendelstrasse 6; ⊕8am-10pm Mon-Sat, 10am-7.30pm Sun) Our favourite temple of kitsch might tempt you to spend on Heidi dolls, cuckoo clocks, yodelling marmots and – heaven forbid – his 'n' hers cow mugs.

ℹ Information

Discount Cards

Lucerne Card (24/48/72hr Sfr19/27/33) Sold at the tourist office and train station, this offers unlimited travel on public transport (excluding SGV boats), 50% discount on museum entry, plus reductions on activities, city tours and car hire.

Tourist Information

Luzern Tourism (📞041 227 17 17; www.luzern.com; Zentralstrasse 5; ⊕8.30am-7.30pm Mon-Fri, 9am-7.30pm Sat & Sun) Reached from Zentralstrasse or platform 3 of the Hauptbahnhof. Offers city walking tours. Call for hotel reservations.

ℹ Getting There & Away

Frequent trains connect Lucerne to Interlaken West (Sfr56, two hours), Bern (Sfr36, one hour), Lugano (Sfr56, 2½ hours), Geneva (Sfr74, three hours) and Zürich (Sfr23, one hour).

For information on boat transport, see below. The departure points are the quays around Bahnhofplatz and Europaplatz.

ℹ Getting Around

Should you be going further than the largely pedestrianised Old Town, city buses leave from outside the Hauptbahnhof at Bahnhofplatz. Tickets cost Sfr2.20 for a short journey, Sfr3 for one zone and Sfr4.20 for two. Ticket dispensers indicate the correct fare for each destination. A

The Rigi Kaltbad–Weggis cable car on Mt Rigi (p163)

zone 101 day ticket (Sfr6) covers the city centre and beyond; Swiss Pass holders travel free. There's an underground car park at the train station.

LAKE LUCERNE

Majestic peaks hunch conspiratorially around Vierwaldstättersee – which twists and turns as much as the tongue does when pronouncing it. Little wonder English speakers use the shorthand Lake Lucerne!

To appreciate the views, ride up to Mt Pilatus, Mt Rigi or Stanserhorn. When the clouds peel away or you break through them, precipitous lookout points reveal a crumpled tapestry of green hillsides and shimmering cobalt waters below, with glaciated peaks beyond. It's especially atmospheric in autumn, when fog rises like dry ice from the lake, and in winter, when the craggy heights are dusted with snow.

ℹ Getting Around

The **Lake Lucerne Navigation Company SGV** (☏ 041 367 67 67; www.lakelucerne.ch) operates boats (sometimes paddle-steamers) daily.

From Lucerne, destinations include Alpnachstad (one-way/return Sfr25/42, 1¾ hours). Longer trips are relatively cheaper than short ones, and you can alight as often as you want. An SGV day ticket costs Sfr66 for adults and Sfr33 for children. Swiss and Eurail passes (on days selected for travel only) are valid on scheduled boat trips, while InterRail entitles you to half-price tickets.

Mt Pilatus

Rearing above Lucerne from the southwest, **Mt Pilatus** (www.pilatus.com) rose to fame in the 19th-century when Wagner waxed lyrical about its Alpine vistas and Queen Victoria trotted up here on horseback. Legend has it that this 2132m peak was named after Pontius Pilate, whose corpse was thrown into a lake on its summit and whose restless ghost has haunted its heights ever since. Poltergeists aside, it's more likely that the moniker derives from the Latin word

Detour:
Brunnen

Tucked into the folds of mountains, where Lake Lucerne and Lake Uri meet at right angles, Brunnen enjoys mesmerising views south and west. A regular guest, English artist Joseph Turner was so impressed by the vista that he whipped out his watercolours to paint *The Bay of Uri from Brunnen* (1841). As the local *föhn* wind rushes down from the mountains, it creates perfect conditions for sailing and paragliding.

By far the most pleasant way to reach Brunnen is to take a boat from Lucerne (Sfr37, 1¾ hours).

pileatus, meaning cloud covered – as the mountain frequently is.

From May to October, you can reach Mt Pilatus on a classic 'golden round-trip'. Board the lake steamer from Lucerne to Alpnachstad, then rise with the world's steepest cog railway to Mt Pilatus. From the summit, cable cars bring you down to Kriens via Fräkmüntegg and Krienseregg, where bus 1 takes you back to Lucerne. The reverse route (Kriens–Pilatus–Alpnachstad–Lucerne) is also possible. The return trip costs Sfr91 (less with valid Swiss, Eurail or InterRail passes).

Mt Pilatus is fantastic for **walking**. Hikes include a steep, partially roped 2.8km scramble (June to September) from Fräkmüntegg to the summit.

In winter, try **sledging** 6km through snowy woodlands from Fräkmüntegg to Kriens. A return ticket between Kriens and Fräkmüntegg by cable car costs Sfr38 for adults and Sfr19 for children. Free sledge hire is available at Fräkmüntegg station.

FOTOSEARCH VALUE / GETTY IMAGES ©

Don't Miss **Mt Titlis**

With a name that makes English speakers titter, Titlis is Central Switzerland's tallest mountain, has its only glacier and is reached by the world's first revolving cable car, completed in 1992. However, that's the last leg of a breathtaking four-stage journey. First, you glide up to Gerschnialp (1300m), then Trübsee (1800m). Transferring to a large gondola, you head for Stand (2450m) to board the Rotair for the head-spinning journey over the dazzling **Titlis Glacier**. As you twirl above the deeply crevassed ice, peaks rise like shark fins ahead, while tarn-speckled pastures, cliffs and waterfalls lie behind.

A glacial blast of air hits you at Titlis station (3020m) but the genuine oohs and aahs come when you step out onto the **terrace**, where the panorama of glacier-capped peaks stretches to Eiger, Mönch and Jungfrau in the Bernese Oberland. It's a 45-minute hike to the 3239m summit (wear sturdy shoes). Otherwise, enjoy the snowboarding and skiing.

The return trip to Titlis (45 minutes each way) costs Sfr86 from Engelberg. However, in fine weather, you can walk some sections. Between Stand and Trübsee, the Geologischer Wanderweg is open from July to September; it takes about two hours up and 1½ hours down. From Trübsee up to Jochpass (2207m) takes about 1½ hours, and down to Engelberg takes around the same time.

Reductions on all fares are 50% for Swiss, Eurail and InterRail pass holders.

Engelberg is at the end of a train line, about an hour from Lucerne (Sfr16.40). If on a day trip, check with the Lucerne tourist office about Mt Titlis excursion tickets.

THINGS YOU NEED TO KNOW

www.titlis.ch; ⊙8.30am-5pm daily (last ascent 3.40pm, last descent 4.50pm), but closed for maintenance for 2 weeks early Nov

Mt Rigi

Blue, no red, no dark... Turner couldn't quite make up his mind about how he preferred 1797m **Rigi** (www.rigi.ch), so in 1842 the genius painted the mountain in three different lights to reflect its changing moods. On a clear day, there are impressive views to a jagged spine of peaks including Mt Titlis and the Jungfrau giants. To the north and west, you overlook Arth-Goldau and Zugersee, which curves around until it almost joins Küssnacht and an arm of Lake Lucerne. The sunrises and sunsets viewed from the summit are the stuff of bucket lists.

At **Mineralbad & Spa Rigi Kaltbad**, the trend for major spachitecture was taking shape during our visit. Expect the Mario Botta–designed temple to relaxation to be opened during 2012.

The 33-room **Rigi Kulm Hotel** (✆ 041 880 18 88; www.rigikulm.ch; s Sfr148-203, d Sfr228-318; 🛜) is the only major establishment at the summit and commands stirring views. The natty streamlined rooms mix old and new furnishings and boast immaculate bathrooms, plus there's a good restaurant and stylishly decorated self-service cafeteria for those not staying the night.

Rigi is a magnet to hikers; for recommended routes, check www.rigi. ch. There are several easy walks (one to two hours) down from Rigi Kulm to Rigi Kaltbad, with wonderful views.

Two rival railways carry passengers to the top. One runs from Arth-Goldau (one-way/return Sfr40/64), the other from Vitznau (one-way/return Sfr45/72). The Vitznau track gives the option of diverting at Rigi Kaltbad and taking the cable car to or from Weggis instead. Holders of Swiss, Eurail and InterRail passes receive a 50% discount on fares, and children under 16 travel free when accompanied by a parent.

Valais & Zermatt

Valais landscapes leave you dumbstruck: from the unfathomable Matterhorn (4478m) to the Rhône valley's tapestry of vineyards and shimmering 23km Aletsch Glacier. With such backdrops, how can any hike, bike or ski tour be anything but great?

The Valais tale is of rags to riches, of changing seasons and celebrities, of an outdoors so wonderful it never goes out of fashion. Wedged in a remote corner of southern Switzerland, this is where farmers were so poor they didn't have two francs to rub together a century ago, where today luminaries sip Sfr10,000 champagne cocktails in the posh winter playground of Verbier.

As earthy as a vintner's boots in September and as clean as the aesthetic in Zermatt's lounge bars, this canton can be fickle. The west speaks French, the east German, united in matters of cantonal pride by fine wine and glorious cheese.

The Matterhorn, near Zermatt (p183)
GARETH MCCORMACK / GETTY IMAGES ©

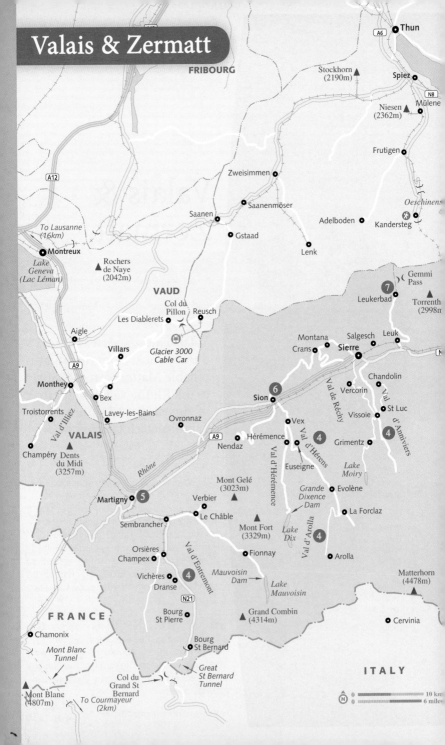

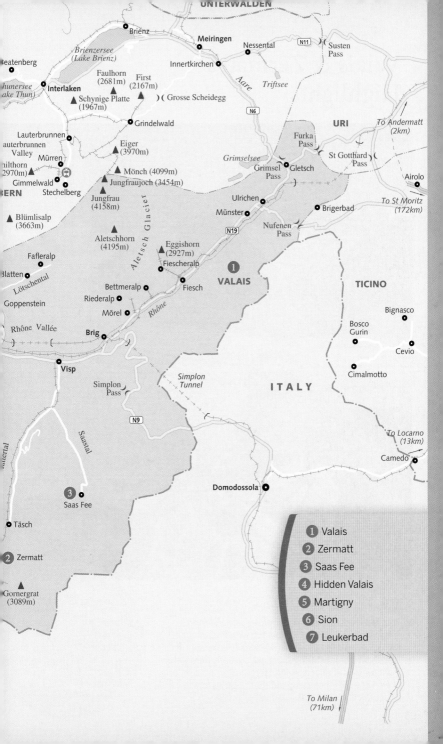

Valais & Zermatt's Highlights

① Valais Outdoors

This French-speaking corner of Switzerland (p178) is one big beautiful landscape rich with the potential for excitement at resorts like Verbier. Glacier sounds French so it's only fitting there are so many here – the most famous easily being Aletsch Glacier, a 23km-long ribbon of ice that stretches to the Jungfrau region. Above: Eggishorn (p190); Top right: Mittelallalin revolving restaurant

Valais Outdoors Don't Miss List

URS ZENHÄUSERN, LIFETIME RESIDENT AND SKI INSTRUCTOR

1 ALETSCH GLACIER

As a landscape of extraordinary beauty, the Jungfrau-Aletsch Region in the Swiss Alps is included in the list of Unesco World Natural Heritage Sites. Vacations in the **Aletsch Glacier area** (p190) are vacations in untouched nature and in an attractive hiking area. In the midst of this mountain landscape is Villa Cassel, an Information Centre for the **Pro Natura** nature conservation organisation (www. pronatura-aletsch.ch). From the summit of the **Eggishorn** (p190), at 2927m, you can enjoy beautiful views over the whole length of the Aletsch Glacier and the mighty peaks of the Eiger, Mönch and Jungfrau and as far as the Matterhorn.

2 HIGHEST REVOLVING RESTAURANT

Don't miss discovering the highest revolving restaurant in the world on the **Mittelallalin** (3500m), which offers a spectacular 360° panorama and the highest and largest Ice Pavilion in the world, containing ice sculptures and an exhibition about glacier information. It's all above the car-free resort of **Saas Fee** (p187), one of the most attractive in Valais.

3 VERBIER

As soon as the first snow falls, **Verbier** (p179) becomes a winter-sports paradise. 'Les 4 Vallées' (Four Valleys) is the name of this immense ski resort with 412 km of piste and more than 90 lifts and railways linking the train stations of Verbier, Nendaz, Veysonnaz, Thyon and La Tzoumaz. It's a fine winter playground, yet in summer it's also a place for hiking and enjoying the Alpine meadows and views.

4 PORTES DU SOLEIL

Between Switzerland and France discover the **Portes du Soleil** (www.portesdusoleil.com), the largest linked international ski area containing the mountain resorts of Champéry, Val-d'Illiez-Les Crosets-Champoussin, Morgins and Torgon. You could spend years exploring the myriad runs here.

169

Zermatt

'Wow' or some such exclamation is uttered by half the people aboard the train to car-free Zermatt (p183) the first time the Matterhorn pops into view. For such a familiar image, there's no arguing with the power the actual mountain has to amaze with its soaring clash of angles. Top right: Matterhorn Museum (p185); Bottom right: Gornergratbahn (p184)

Need to Know

BEST TIME TO VISIT
December to April for skiing and June to September for summer pleasures. **TOP TIP** Escape the crowds in Hinterdorf. **For further coverage, see p183.**

2

Zermatt Don't Miss List

JANINE IMESCH, LONGTIME
ZERMATT RESIDENT

1 MATTERHORN MUSEUM

Learn all about what Zermatt was like in 1860 at the **Matterhorn Museum** (p185). Among the many things you can see here is the broken rope from the first ascent by Edward Whymper. In 2015 the 150th anniversary of the first ascent of the Matterhorn will be celebrated all over the village.

2 IN EDWARD WHYMPER'S FOOTSTEPS

Want to learn even more history of mountaineering? Then visit the historic **Hotel Monte Rosa** (www. monterosazermatt.ch) for its guided tours, which take place every Thursday. Step into the era of Belle Époque in Zermatt and experience Whymper's time in town and hear many fascinating tales.

3 MATTERHORN GLACIER PARADISE

There's no need to wait until winter to touch snow. Head up to this very popular attraction, **Matterhorn Glacier Paradise** (p186), which at a soaring 3883m is a must. There is also a glacier palace where you can see ice sculptures. Don't miss the platform where you can admire almost 40 peaks that are higher than 4000m. You can even see all the way south to Italy. And on the way up there's an audio guide that explains about the Alpine world around you. It's a pain-free way to learn.

4 GORNERGRATBAHN

You can climb up to the **Gornergrat** on the highest open-air cogwheel railway in Europe (p184). Up top the view on the glaciers is breathtaking. Don't forget to take a picture with the St Bernard dogs in front of the Matterhorn.

5 GORNERSCHLUCHT

To explore the force of nature, a visit to the **Gorner Gorge** is a must. The rock here, with its amazing serpentine shapes, is around 220 million years old. It's a natural spectacle and it's only 15 minutes from Zermatt.

Saas Fee

Without the glitz of resorts like Verbier, Saas Fee (p187) makes do with its location amid 13 peaks over 4000m. Cleaving between the summits and carving their way down the granite valleys are nine glaciers. It's an ideal location for every kind of sporty mischief you can conceive. The ski runs attract more acolytes every year and the hiking is simply endless.

Hidden Valais

There's a hidden Valais too, where roads corkscrew up the side of mountains and plunge into dark crevices before emerging into the daylight and a new view of some slice of heaven. Valais is lined with tiny routes that only open in summer, but can carry you to little Swiss corners where you discover the most extraordinary hidden places (p182) tucked into tiny valleys like Val d'Entremont, Val d'Arolla and Val d'Anniviers.

GÜNTER GRAFENHAIN / 4CORNERS ©

Martigny

Woof! Although the clichéd image of the St Bernard dog appearing to rescue the upended winter adventurer while wearing a tiny keg of brandy around the neck is barely even mythical, there's no denying the appeal of these big, lovable droolers. Martigny (p178) honours the big pooch with museums and attractions while also offering exceptional art and tangible links to the era when Romans stomped about.

OLIVIER MAIRE / CORBIS ©

AGE FOTOSTOCK / ROBERT HARDING ©

Sion

Thanks to the glittery Rhône River weaving its way through the centre of town, Sion (p181) can readily quench the thirst of its surrounding vineyards. A quick ramble and you can taste some of Switzerland's finest whites. Or march on either of two castles that surmount meandering little lanes lined with outdoor cafes where, yes, you can enjoy more of the local vintages.

Soaking in Leukerbad

In a country renowned for its spas, Leukerbad (p191) stands out. Water heated at untold depths of the earth bubbles forth at a temp of 36°C into a series of soaking and therapy pools. Stripping off your clothes is just a prelude to stripping away your aches, pains and cares. Saunas, whirlpools and cold baths add to the pleasures that often come with a minute dash of soul-cleansing pain.

Valais & Zermatt's Best...

Skiing

○ **Verbier** (p180) A winter wonderland of fab powder and more than 400km of runs served by almost 100 lifts.

○ **Zermatt** (p185) The Matterhorn is a backdrop for 350km of ski runs for every taste and skill level.

○ **Saas Fee** (p188) Excellent snow on the slopes around a lovely old traditional town.

○ **Bettmeralp** (p190) Family-friendly skiing on the dramatic edge of the Aletsch Glacier.

Scenery

○ **Zermatt** (p183) The Matterhorn in all its imposing majesty looms large over town, beckoning you closer.

○ **Aletsch Glacier** (p190) One of the world's largest, a sweeping superhighway of ice.

○ **Pyramides d'Euseigne** (p182) Bizarre glacier-carved rock formations defy logic.

○ **Leukerbad** (p191) The remarkable spa is set amidst even more remarkable mountain beauty.

Hiking

○ **Zermatt** (p185) One of Switzerland's best places to hike with oodles of well-marked trails.

○ **Salgesch** (p183) A bevy of wineries linked by a beautiful 6km walk. Stroll and taste.

○ **Fiesch** (p190) Begin hikes here that take in the spectacle of the Aletsch Glacier.

○ **Bettmeralp** (p190) Catch a cable car up to beautiful walks with glacier views.

Need to Know

Food & Wine

⊙ **Verbier** (p180) This playground for the stars has plenty of stellar places to dine and carouse.

⊙ **Salgesch** (p183) The many wineries offer tastings; try the Pinots or the Fendants.

⊙ **Zermatt** (p182) Views of the Matterhorn only enliven the many choices in this lugubrious mountain town.

⊙ **Sion** (p182) In summer, restaurants use bounty grown in Valais and serve local wines.

ADVANCE PLANNING

⊙ **Five months before** If travelling to any of the top ski resorts like Zermatt or Verbier during peak season (Christmas to March), nail down your accommodation.

⊙ **Three months before** For summertime Matterhorn excursions, beat the crowds by lining up your ideal Zermatt room early.

RESOURCES

⊙ **Valais Tourism** (www.valais.ch) The region's tourism authority.

⊙ **Verbier Booking** (www.verbierbooking.com) Book early during peak winter skiing season.

⊙ **Ski Zermatt** (www.ski-zermatt.com) Skiing info plus live cams of the Matterhorn.

GETTING AROUND

⊙ **Train** The major towns are all connected by efficient train service (for Zermatt you have no choice!). Zermatt is also the western terminus for the popular Glacier Express train (p286), which runs east all the way to St Moritz.

⊙ **Car** Travelling around the Valais is a grandiose experience thanks to the astonishing road links – high mountain passes, snowbound in winter, and masterfully engineered tunnels – it shares with neighbouring Italy. For exploring intriguing hidden valleys, you'll want a car.

BE FOREWARNED

⊙ **Parking** Some popular areas such as Zermatt, gateway to the Matterhorn, are car-free and you have to leave your car in remote parking areas and catch a train in.

⊙ **Peak Seasons** Christmas to March and July and August are busy, busy, busy any place that's beloved for winter skiing or hiking under azure blue summer skies. Plan accordingly. (Locals in the know suggest the golden, uncrowded days of September and October for enjoying the outdoors.)

Left: Vines around Salgesch (p183);
Above: Skiing in the Swiss Alps

Valais & Zermatt Itineraries

The Matterhorn serves as a sentinel to start the first tour and finish the second. The first tour includes a spectacular glacier that leads back to the Jungfrau region while the second tour has all that's best about Valais.

ZERMATT TO EGGISHORN
Matterhorn

3 DAYS

It's the **Matterhorn** baby! And the lure of this international symbol of Switzerland rightfully draws people to **(1) Zermatt** literally by the trainload. From this car-free village on the side of the slopes, you can wander myriad **trails** in summer and **ski** myriad runs in winter. It's a beautiful playground year-round. Too many people zoom in, grab an eyeful of the mountain through their viewfinder and zoom out again. Instead, spend a couple of nights here so you can explore this beautiful patch of Valais at your leisure and take yourself far from the maddening crowds. But be sure to join the mobs riding the cable car to **Matterhorn**

Glacier Paradise, an icy landscape with spectacular views 4000m up.

Ride the train back down from Zermatt and start connecting the dots of Swiss Alpine treasures at **Aletsch Glacier**. Drive or catch a train to the cute little valley village of **(2) Fiesch**. From here catch a cable car and gondola up to **(3) Eggishorn** and clamp your hand over your mouth so nothing will fly in when your jaw drops – the views of the 23km glacier, which curves in a huge ribbon of ice back towards **Jungfrau**, are simply magnificent.

5 DAYS

MARTIGNY TO ZERMATT

Valleys & Peaks

Woof! Start your Valais adventure in the home of St Bernard dogs, **(1) Martigny**. The **Musée et Chiens du Saint-Bernard** honours the brandy-proffering, drooling pooch of lore. It's a short ride by train and bus or car to one of those places that never seems far from the gossip mags: **(2) Verbier**. By equal measure posh and plebeian, this ski resort justifies the hype with spectacular powder in winter.

Back in the valley, pause for a vineyard ramble from spring to autumn at the wineries in the hills surrounding **(3) Sion**. The **Bisse de Clavau** is a centuries-old canal that today waters the grapes and leads to

restaurants amid the vines. **(4) Salgesch** is another fine place to enjoy the local wines, particularly along the 6km-long **Sentier Viticole**, a trail through the vineyards.

If you're ready for a restorative break, take it at **(5) Leukerbad**, a lovely thermal spa set in the middle of staggering Alpine beauty. Return to the valley and catch a bus to (or park on the outskirts of) car-free **(6) Saas Fee**. Thirteen peaks and nine glaciers create a festival of natural beauty. From here, it's a short jaunt over to **(7) Zermatt** and the essential prospect of the **Matterhorn**.

Gornergrat (p184)

Discover Valais & Zermatt

At a Glance

○ **Verbier** (p179) Some of Europe's best powder draws famous names and regular folk all winter.

○ **Zermatt** (p183) The village at the base of the iconic Matterhorn makes visiting a pleasure.

○ **Aletsch Glacier** (p190) A 23km Unesco-listed river of ice.

○ **Sion** (p181) Walk amidst vineyards.

Verbier, at the heart of the Quatre Vallées (Four Valleys)
GAVIN HELLIER / GETTY IMAGES ©

LOWER VALAIS

Stone-walled vineyards, tumbledown castle ruins and brooding mountains create an arresting backdrop to the meandering Rhône valley in western Valais. Running west to east, the A9 motorway links towns such as Roman-rooted Martigny and vine-strewn Sion, where the French influence shows not only in the lingo but also in the locals' passion for art, wine and pavement cafes.

Martigny

POP 15,900 / ELEV 476M

Once the stomping ground of Romans in search of wine and sunshine en route to Italy, small-town Martigny is Valais' oldest town. Look beyond its concrete high-rises to enjoy a world-class art gallery, Roman amphitheatre and a posse of droopy St Bernard dogs to romp up the surrounding mountains with.

 **Sights & Activities**

The tourist office has details of vineyard walks and cycling trails.

FONDATION PIERRE GIANADDA　　　Gallery
(www.gianadda.ch; Rue du Forum; adult/10-25yr Sfr20/12; ☺9am-7pm) Set in a spacey concrete edifice, this renowned gallery harbours a star-studded art collection. A copy of Rodin's *The Kiss* sculpture by the entrance promises great things and the gallery delivers with works by Picasso, Cézanne and van Gogh, occasionally shifted to make space for blockbuster exhibitions.

Admission also covers the permanent exhibition of Roman milestones, vessels and so on.

MUSÉE ET CHIENS DU SAINT-BERNARD
Museum

(📞027 720 49 20; www.museesaintbernard.ch; Route du Levant 34; museum adult/child Sfr12/7, dog walking & museum adult/child Sfr45/9, audioguide Sfr3; ⏰10am-6pm) A tribute to the lovably dopey St Bernard, this museum across from the Roman amphitheatre includes real-life fluff bundles in the kennels. If you're lucky, you might be able to stroke them.

 **Sleeping**

L'ÉRABLE ROUGE
B&B $

(📞027 746 16 08; erablerouge@mycable.ch; Rue St-Ours 49, Fully; dm/s/d Sfr40/50/100) Dreamily set amid terraced vines, this old winemaker's house with all the right rustic fixtures and fittings is an oasis of peace and tranquillity. Find it 9.5km north of Martigny, in the viticultural hamlet of Branson, near Fully.

LA RÉSIDENCE
Guesthouse $

(📞027 723 16 00; www.residence-martigny. ch; Les Creusats, Martigny-Croix; s/d Sfr70/140; 🅿🛜) Sitting pretty in its vineyard setting, this rosy guesthouse has big sunny rooms with garden-facing terraces. The rooms are all named after local Valais vines and wines, and breakfasts of homemade jam, local cheese and ham are a delight.

Eating & Drinking

Everything happens on plane-tree-flanked Place Centrale, framed with pavement cafes, bistros and bars.

CAFÉ DU MIDI
Cafe $

(📞027 722 00 03; www.cafedumidi.ch; Rue des Marronniers 4; fondue Sfr21-29; ⏰noon-11pm Wed-Mon) This shabby-chic cafe run by Brigida and Steve across from the church is a great address. Guzzle Trappist brews and gorge on as much raclette as you can handle or dip into one of 10 different fondues.

LA VACHE QUI VOLE
Gallery, Bistro $$

(📞027 722 38 33; Place Centrale 2b; mains Sfr25-45; ⏰10.30am-1am Mon-Sat) Martigny's 'Flying Cow' is a theatrical gallery-style bistro and bar with Boho ambience and cult cow kitsch: from the angelic bovine beauty suspended from the ceiling to snazzy cowbell lights.

ⓘ Information

Tourist office (📞027 720 49 49; www.martigny tourism.ch; Ave de la Gare; ⏰9am-6pm Mon-Fri, to 7pm Sat, 10am-12.30pm & 3-5pm Sun)

ⓘ Getting There & Away

Martigny is on the main train line running from Lausanne (Sfr23, 50 minutes) to Brig (Sfr25, 55 minutes).

From Martigny the panoramic Mont Blanc Express (📞027 783 11 43; www.tmrsa.ch) goes to Chamonix (1½ hours) in France.

Verbier
POP 3000 / ELEV 1500M

Ritzy Verbier is the diamond of the Valaisian Alps: small, stratospherically expensive and cut at all the right angles to make it sparkle in the eyes of accomplished skiers and piste-bashing stars. Yet despite its ritzy packaging, Verbier is that rare beast of a resort – all things to all people. It swings from schnapps-fuelled debauchery to VIP lounges, bunker hostels to design-oriented hotels, burgers to Michelin stars. Here ski bums and celebs slalom in harmony on powder that is legendary.

Unlike smaller resorts, Verbier shuts down between seasons.

 **Activities**

Something of a recreation mecca, there is an activity to suit every outdoor urge. For an overview and on-the-ground guidance hook up with a local mountain guide at **Les Guides de Verbier** (📞027 775 33 70; www.guideverbier.com; Place de Médran).

Savvy Skiing: Best Queue-Free Resorts

Valais enjoys the luxury of having it all when it comes to ski resorts: from star-studded high-flyers firmly on the paparazzi map, such as Zermatt (p183) and Verbier (p179), to tiny villages down lost valleys where you can dress as you want and don't have to queue. Oh, and ski passes don't cost the earth.

The perfect mix of big skiing and storybook charm, Bettmeralp (p190) is a pearl of Swiss mountain charm where cars are banned, kids are towed about on wooden Davos sledges and high-altitude slopes cruise breathlessly above the Aletsch Glacier. Car-free Saas Fee (p187) is posher, pricier, bigger and better known but has that same 'go slow, real village' vibe.

Skiing

Verbier's skiing is justifiably billed as some of Europe's finest. The resort sits at the heart of the Quatre Vallées (Four Valleys), comprising a cool 412km of runs and 94 ski lifts. A regional ski pass costs Sfr65 per day. Cheaper passes excluding Mont Fort are also available. The terrain is exciting and varied, with beginners on gentle slopes at **Le Rouge** and intermediates carving long slopes at **La Chaux**. Boarders make for the latter to catch big air on kickers and rails.

Hiking

The walking here is naturally superb. From Les Ruinettes, it takes 1½ hours to ascend to the ridge at Creblet, and down into the crater to Lac des Vaux.

 **Sleeping**

Verbier is doable for ski bums on a budget with pre-planning. If money isn't an issue, there are posh-digs galore. Rates nose-dive by 30% to 50% in July and August.

LE STOP Hostel $
(☎ 079 549 72 23; www.le-stop.ch; Le Châble; dm Sfr34, breakfast/dinner Sfr11/15) This former bunker has a new raison d'être with no-frills dorms. What you'll get is four walls, a queue for the loo and a rickety bunk, but with Verbier just a cable-car ride away,

frankly it's a gift. Important: bring your own sleeping bag.

LES TOURISTES Hotel $
(☎ 027 771 21 47; www.hoteltouristes-verbier.ch; s/d Sfr75/150, d with shower Sfr180; **P**) If you think *le chic c'est freak,* try this rustic chalet next to a *fromagerie* (cheese dairy) – the *only* Verbier hotel with less than three stars and to be open year-round. Rooms are modest but comfy with pine trappings, floral bedding and washbasins. Find it a 15-minute walk downhill from Verbier Station.

Eating & Drinking

The best addresses to dine (bar one) are piste-side, while Verbier's full-throttle après-ski scene kicks off on the slopes before sliding down to Place Centrale. Out of season (mid-December to April, July and August), pretty much everything is shut.

LE NAMASTÉ Swiss $$
(☎ 027 771 57 73; www.namaste-verbier.ch; Les Planards; mains Sfr20-35; ⊙ daily in season, Thu-Sun mid-May–Jun, Sep & Oct) With a name that means 'Welcome' in Tibetan it is no wonder that this cosy mountain cabin is always packed. Jean-Louis and his wife Annick are the creative energy behind the place and cuisine is 100% traditional – think fondue, raclette and a wonderful *croûte Namasté.*

LE FER À CHEVAL
Pizzeria $

(☎ 027 771 26 69; Rue de Médran; mains Sfr20-30; ⏰ 11.30am-11.30pm) Thank goodness for the Horseshoe, a wholly affordable, down-to-earth and tasty pizzeria with buzzing sunny terrace, electric atmosphere and fabulous pizza any hour. Ask anyone in the know where to eat and this is where they'll send you. Find it footsteps from Place Centrale towards the Médran cable car.

PUB MONT FORT
Pub

(Chemin de la Tinte 10; ⏰ 3pm-1.30am) In winter, this après-ski heavyweight sells the most beer in Switzerland. Enough said.

ⓘ Information

Tourist office (☎ 027 775 38 88; www.verbier.ch; Place Centrale; ⏰ 8.30am-12.30pm & 1.30-6pm Mon-Sat)

ⓘ Getting There & Away

Trains from Martigny run hourly year-round to Le Châble (30 minutes) from where you can board a Verbier-bound bus (30 minutes) or, when it's running, the Le Châble-Verbier cable car.

Skiing around Verbier

Sion

POP 29,700 / ELEV 490M

French-speaking Sion is bewitching. The serpentine Rhône River bisects Sion and a twinset of 13th-century hilltop châteaux play guard atop a pair of craggy rock hills.

Sion moves to a relaxed beat, with winemaking (and tasting) playing an essential role in the town's mantra and pavement cafes lining the helter-skelter of quaint lanes that thread sharply downhill from its castles to medieval Old Town.

◎ Sights

CHÂTEAU DE TOURBILLON
Castle

(Rue des Châteaux; ⏰ 10am-6pm May-Sep, 11am-5pm mid-Mar–Apr & Oct–mid-Nov) Lording it over the fertile Rhône valley from its hilltop perch above Sion, the crumbling remains of this medieval stronghold, destroyed by fire in 1788, are well worth the stiff trudge for the postcard views alone – wear solid shoes as the rocky path is decidedly hairy in places.

GLENN VAN DER KNIJFF / GETTY IMAGES ©

If You Like...
Hidden Places

If you like the off-the-beaten path charms of Salgesch (p183), there are many more hidden joys tucked away deep in the little valleys between the jutting peaks of Valais:

1 VAL D'ENTREMONT & VAL FERRET
The St Bernard Express train from Martigny to Orsières branches south at Sembrancher, chugging along the Val d'Entremont through classic Alpine scenery to the Italian border. Orsières marks the beginning of pine-brushed Val Ferret. It's a 1¾-hour walk to Champex (1471m), a mountain village with a beautiful glassy lake.

2 VAL D'HÉRENS & VAL D'AROLLA
These thickly wooded valleys hide many peculiarities and pastures mown by silky black Hérens cattle. The road wriggles up from Sion through Vex and then Euseigne, passing the wondrous Gaudí-esque rock pinnacles Pyramides d'Euseigne.

3 VAL D'ANNIVIERS
Brushed with pine and larch, scattered with dark-timber chalets and postcard villages and set against glistening 4000m peaks, this strikingly beautiful, little-explored valley beckons skiers eager to slalom away from the crowds and hikers seeking big nature. The road south from Sierre corkscrews precipitously past postage-stamp orchards and vineyards, arriving after 13km in the medieval village of Vissoie.

CHÂTEAU DE VALÈRE Castle
(Rue des Châteaux; guided tour adult/child Sfr4/2; ⊙11am, noon, 2pm & 4pm Mon-Sat, 2pm & 4pm Sun Jun-Sep, 2pm & 4pm Sun Oct-May) Slung on a hillock across from Château de Tourbillon is this 11th- to 13th-century château that grew up around a fortified basilica. The church interior reveals beautifully carved choir stalls and a brightly frescoed apse.

Activities

What makes trails in this part of the Rhône Valley so unique are the *bisses* – miniature canals built from the 13th century to irrigate the steeply terraced vineyards and fields.

Best known is the Bisse de Clavau, a 550-year-old irrigation channel that carries water to the thirsty, sun-drenched vineyards between Sion and St Léonard. Vines, planted on narrow terraces supported by drystone retaining walls, are devoted to the production of highly quaffable Valaisian dôle (red) and Fendant (white) wines. Taste them alone or with lunch at **Le Cube** (☎079 566 95 63; www.verone.ch; mains without/with wine Sfr25/29, tasting menu incl wine Sfr69; ⊙5-9pm Fri, 11am-9pm Sat, 11am-6pm Sun May-Oct), an old winegrower's hut once used to store tools and now transformed into a fabulously stylish address in the vines to wine and dine. The Cube sits on the Bisse de Clavau footpath (7.5km, 2½ hours), part of the Chemin du Vignoble.

Sleeping & Eating

Food and wine are big reasons to linger. Rue du Grand-Pont, so-called because of the river that runs beneath its entire length, is peppered with tasty places to eat well and drink fine Valais wine.

HÔTEL ELITE Hotel $$
(☎027 322 03 27; www.hotelelite-sion.ch; Ave du Midi 6; s/d/tr/q Sfr111/150/220/240; [P]) Aptly named, this bright, modern two-star address just off the main street is the best place to stay in town. Rooms, painted soft apricot hues, are not quite as bold as the pillar-box-red reception.

AU CHEVAL BLANC Swiss $$
(☎027 322 18 67; www.au-cheval-blanc.ch; Rue du Grand-Pont 23; beef Sfr26-59, mains Sfr30-40; ⊙10am-midnight Tue-Fri, 11am-midnight Sat) An

institution among locals for its great food and convivial vibe, this old-style bistro with the biggest pavement terrace on Rue du Grand-Pont only uses the best local produce. The icing on the cake is its Val d'Hérens beef prepared just as you like it.

LA SITTERIE Swiss $$

(027 203 22 12; www.lasitterie.ch; Rue du Rawil 41; menus Sfr65 & Sfr85; lunch & dinner Tue-Sun) A 10-minute uphill walk from the Old Town is this salmon-pink townhouse with red-wine wooden shutters – Sion's most exciting gastronomic address. Young chef Jacques Bovier works with strictly seasonal and local products to create a dining experience that thrills every time. Summer dining is in a dreamy flowery garden with terraced vineyard view. Advance reservations essential.

Information

Tourist office (027 327 77 27; www.sion tourism.ch; Place de la Planta; 9am-12.30pm & 1.30-6pm Mon-Fri, 9am-12.30pm Sat)

Getting There & Around

Train

All trains on the express route between Lausanne (Sfr29, 50 to 80 minutes) and Brig (Sfr18.60, 25 to 35 minutes) stop in Sion.

UPPER VALAIS

In a xylophone-to-gong transition, the soothing loveliness of vineyards in the west gives way to austere beauty in the east of Valais. Bijou villages of woodsy chalets stand in collective awe of the drum-roll setting of vertiginous ravines, spiky 4000m pinnacles and monstrous glaciers. The effervescent thermal waters of Leukerbad, the dazzling 23km Aletsch Glacier and the soaring pyramid of the Matterhorn are natural icons that invite spontaneous applause.

Zermatt

POP 5830 / ELEV 1605M

You can almost sense the anticipation on the train from Täsch: couples gaze

Detour:
Salgesch

As dreamy as a Turner watercolour in the golden autumn light, the winegrowing hamlet of Salgesch produced the first-ever Swiss grand cru in 1988. Blessed with chalky soil and sunshine, Salgesch yields spicy Pinot noirs, fruity dôles and mineral Fendants. Many cellars open their doors for tastings.

A real must for wine buffs is the scenic **Sentier Viticole** (wine trail; 6km) that leads through vineyards from the wine museum inside Sierre's Château de Villa to the gabled **Weinmuseum** (Wine Museum; adult/child Sfr6/free, free with Sierre wine museum ticket; 2-5pm Tue-Sun Apr-Nov) in Salgesch – allow 2½ hours for the walk, which takes in 80 explanatory panels about the vines, local winegrowing techniques, the harvest and so on.

Hourly trains link Salgesch and Sierre (Sfr3, three minutes), which are in the geographic centre of Valais.

wistfully out of the window, kids fidget and stuff in Toblerone, folk rummage for their cameras. And then, as they arrive in Zermatt, all give little whoops of joy at the pop-up book effect of the one-of-a-kind **Matterhorn** (4478m). Trigonometry at its finest, topographic perfection, a bloody beautiful mountain – call it what you will, the Matterhorn is hypnotic.

Since the mid-19th century, Zermatt has starred among Switzerland's glitziest resorts. Today it attracts intrepid mountaineers and hikers, skiers who cruise at snail's pace spellbound by the scenery, and style-conscious darlings flashing designer togs in the lounge bars.

Zermatt

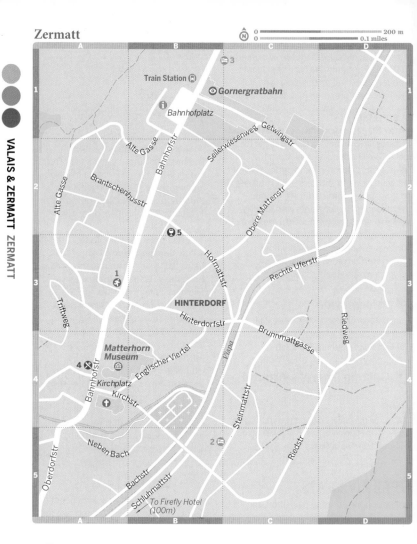

Sights

It pays to meander away from main strip **Bahnhofstrasse** with its flashy boutiques and stream of horse-drawn sleds or carriages and electric taxis. Head towards the river along side streets in **Hinterdorf**, crammed with archetypal Valaisian timber storage barns propped up on stone discs and stilts to keep out the rats.

GORNERGRATBAHN   Railway

(www.gornergrat.ch; Bahnhofplatz 7; adult/child one way Sfr39/19.50; journey time 35 to 45 min; ⏰2 or 3 departures hourly 7am-6pm May & mid-Oct–Nov, 7am-10pm Jun-Sep, every 20 min 7am-5.15pm Dec-Apr) This splendid cogwheel railway – Europe's highest – climbs through picture-postcard scenery to **Gornergrat** (3089m). Tickets allow you to get on and off en route.

Zermatt

MATTERHORN MUSEUM Museum
(www.matterhornmuseum.ch; Kirchplatz; adult/
child Sfr10/5, audioguide Sfr5; ⏰11am-6pm,
closed Nov) This crystalline, state-of-the-art
museum provides a fascinating insight
into Valaisian village life, mountaineering,
the dawn of tourism in Zermatt and the
lives the Matterhorn has claimed.

 **Activities**

An essential stop in activity planning is
Zermatt Alpin Center (📞027 966 24 60;
www.alpincenter-zermatt.ch; Bahnhofstrasse
58; ⏰9am-noon & 3-7pm mid-Nov–Apr & Jul-
Sep), home to Zermatt's ski school and
mountain guides. In winter you can buy
lift passes here (Sfr75/371 for a one-/six-
day pass excluding Cervinia, Sfr86/423
including Cervinia).

Skiing

Zermatt is cruising heaven, with mostly
long, scenic red runs, plus a smattering of
blues for ski virgins and knuckle-whitening blacks for experts. The main skiing areas in winter are **Rothorn**, **Stockhorn** and
Klein Matterhorn – 350km of ski runs in
all with a link from Klein Matterhorn to the
Italian resort of **Cervinia** and a freestyle
park with half-pipe for snowboarders.

Summer skiing (20km of runs) and
boarding (gravity park at Plateau Rosa

on the Theodul glacier) is Europe's most
extensive.

Hiking

Zermatt is a hiker's paradise in summer
with 400km of trails through some of the
most incredible scenery in the Alps – the
tourist office has trail maps. For Matterhorn close-ups, the ultimate day trek is
Höhenweg Höhbalmen.

 **Sleeping**

Book well ahead in winter, and bear in
mind that nearly everywhere closes from
May to mid- or late June and October to
November or early December.

HOTEL BAHNHOF Hotel $
(📞027 967 24 06; www.hotelbahnhof.com; Bahnhofstrasse; dm Sfr40-55, s/d/q Sfr80/110/210;
📶) Opposite the train station, these five-
star budget digs have proper beds and
spotless bathrooms that are a godsend
after scaling or schussing down mountains all day. Rooms for four are fabulous
for families.

FIREFLY HOTEL Boutique Hotel $$$
(📞027 967 76 76; www.firefly-zermatt.com;
Schluhmattstrasse 55; d/q from Sfr770/1250)
Oh to have oodles of cash to while away a
few dreamy weeks in this glorious hotel,
named after a bar on a paradise island
where the owners spent many a happy
moment one holiday! Rooms, all with
kitchenette, sleep two to eight.

CHESA VALESE Chalet $$
(📞027 966 80 80; www.chesa-valese.ch;
Steinmattstrasse 2; s/d Sfr165/260) A dreamy
address the other side of the river, this
traditional burnt-red wood chalet with
traditional slate-roof conservatory and
flowery garden is romantic, charming
and ablaze with red geraniums in
summer. Rooms are cosy country style
and the very best stare brazenly at the
Matterhorn.

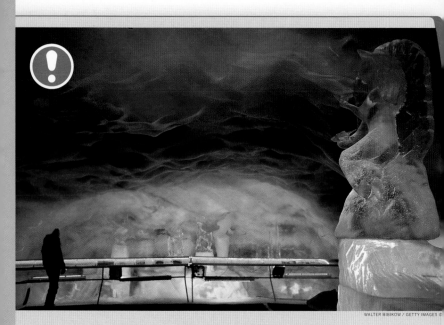

WALTER BIBIKOW / GETTY IMAGES ©

Don't Miss **Matterhorn Glacier Paradise**

Views from Zermatt's cable cars and gondolas are all pretty remarkable, but the Matterhorn Glacier Paradise is the icing on the cake. Ride Europe's highest-altitude cable car up to 3883m and gawp at a top-of-the-beanstalk panorama of 14 glaciers and 38 mountain peaks over 4000m from the Panoramic Platform. Don't miss the Glacier Palace, an ice palace complete with glittering ice sculptures, a glacier crevasse to walk through and – one for the kids – an ice slide to swoosh down bum first.

THINGS YOU NEED TO KNOW

www.matterhornparadise.ch; adult/child one way Sfr63/31.50, afternoon-return available from 1.30pm Sfr78.50/39; ⏰7am-4.20pm Jul & Aug, 8.30am-3.35pm mid-Oct–Dec, 8.30am-4.20pm rest of year

 Eating

CHEZ VRONY — Swiss $$

(☎027 967 25 52; www.chezvrony.ch; mains Sfr25-60) Ride the Sunnegga Express to 2288m then ski halfway down blue piste 6 to what must be Zermatt's cosiest, toastiest, tastiest address on the slopes (Robbie Williams loves the place). Its dried meat, homemade cheese and sausage – all organic – come from their own cows that graze away the summer on the high alpine pastures (2100m) surrounding it. Advance reservations essential in winter.

WHYMPER STUBE — Valaisian $$

(☎027 967 22 96; www.whymper-stube.ch; Bahnhofstrasse 80; fondue Sfr25-27, mains Sfr22-43) An advance reservation is essential at this legendary address, known for its excellent raclette and fondues, both cheese and meat. Service is relaxed and friendly, tables are packed tightly together, and the place has a real buzz.

 **Drinking**

Still fizzing with energy after schussing down the slopes? Zermatt pulses in

party-mad après-ski huts, suave lounge bars and Brit-style pubs. Most close (and some melt) in low season.

VERNISSAGE BAR   Lounge Bar
(www.vernissage-zermatt.ch; Hofmattstrasse 4; ⏱5pm-2am) The ultimate après-ski antithesis, Vernissage exudes grown-up sophistication. Local artist Heinz Julen has created a theatrical space with flowing velvet drapes, film-reel chandeliers and candlelit booths. Catch an exhibition, watch a Bond movie in the decadent cinema, then practise your 007 martini pose in the lounge bar.

ℹ Information

Tourist office (☏027 966 81 00; www.zermatt.ch; Bahnhofplatz 5; ⏱8.30am-6pm mid-Jun–Sep, 8.30am-noon & 1-6pm Mon-Fri, 8.30am-6pm Sat, 9.30am-noon & 4-6pm Sun rest of year)

ℹ Getting There & Away

Car

Zermatt is car-free. Motorists have to park in Täsch (www.matterhornterminal.ch; Sfr14.50/day), load luggage onto a trolley (Sfr5) and ride the Zermatt Shuttle train (adult/child Sfr7.80/3.90, 12 minutes, every 20 minutes from 6am to 9.40pm) the last 5km to Zermatt.

Train

Trains to Täsch depart roughly every 20 minutes from Brig (Sfr31, 1½ hours), stopping at Visp en route. Zermatt is also the starting point of the Glacier Express to Graubünden, one of the most spectacular train rides in the world.

Saas Fee

POP 1700 / ELEV 1800M
Hemmed in by a magnificent amphitheatre of 13 implacable peaks over 4000m and backed by the threatening tongues of nine

glaciers, this village looks positively feeble in the revealing light of summer.

Today Saas Fee is a chic, car-free resort where every well-to-do skier and hiker wants to be. Modern chalets surround the village but its commercial heart, well-endowed with old timber chalets and barns on stilts (once used to store hams and grain), retains a definite old-world, Heidi-style charm.

◉ Sights

ALLALIN   Glacier
Year-round, an underground funicular steadily climbs up to an icy 3500m, where the world's highest revolving restaurant on the Allalin glacier basks in glorious 360-degree views of Saas Fee's 4000m glacial giants. Whatever the season, wrap up warm to visit the subzero **Eispavillion** (Ice cave; adult/child Sfr5/3 or free for non-skiers with return cable-car ticket), hollowed out 10m below the ice surface. To reach the glacier, take the cable car up

VALAIS & ZERMATT SAAS FEE

Hiking (p185) with Matterhorn views
BUENA VISTA IMAGES / GETTY IMAGES ©

to Felskinn (3000m) then the Mittelallin funicular to the top; a Saas Fee-Allalin return costs Sfr106.

 **Activities**

Saas Fee's slopes are snow-sure, with most skiing taking place above 2500m and the glacier acting like a deep freeze. The 145km of groomed, scenic pistes are more suited to beginners and intermediates. The resort is a snowboarding mecca and regularly hosts world championships. Boarders gravitate towards the kickers, half-pipe and chill-out zone at the glacial **freestyle park** on Allalin in summer and lower down the slopes at Morenia (2550m) in winter. A one-day ski-lift pass costs Sfr68 and a six-day ski-lift pass costs Sfr346; kids aged under nine ride for free.

 Sleeping

In season (December to April, July and August) hotels only offer half-board. Most close completely in May and November. Hotel guests get a free Visitor's Card which yields a bonanza of savings, including on car parking fees, cable cars and so on.

**VERNISSAGE BERGHAUS
PLATTJEN**   Mountain Hotel $$
(☎ 027 957 12 05; www.vernissage-berghaus. ch; Plattjen; dm/tr incl half-board Sfr100/360) 'Where dreams have no end' is the apt strapline of this stylish, design-driven address half-way up the mountain at 2418m, near the Plattjen cable-car station (2567m). Sheepskins dress lounge chairs on the terrace and rooms fuse cosy alpine with clean-cut contemporary. Its terrace restaurant is one of the top addresses to lunch on the slopes.

HOTEL
WALDESRUH   Chalet $$

(☎027 958 64 64; www.hotelwaldesruh.
ch; Gletscherstrasse 14; s/d incl half-board
Sfr169/338) This three-star chalet is an
ecstatic I'll-be-first-in-the-queue hop
from the ski lifts. The family that runs it
is affable and old-style hotel rooms are
comfy with balconies overlooking the
glacial slopes.

 **Eating**

ZUR MÜHLE   Swiss $$
(☎027 957 26 76; Dorfstrasse 61; mains
Sfr15-30) From the village church follow
Dorfstrasse downhill to this snug riverside
address bedecked with sheepskins,
cow-print curtains and copper pans. Rösti
is the mainstay and comes in various
creative guises.

LA FERME   Valaisian $$
(☎027 958 15 69; Obere Dorfstrasse 32; mains
Sfr20-59) Dirndl-clad maidens bring tra-

ditional Valaisian specialities to the table
at this barn-style restaurant, decked out
with hops, cowbells and farming imple-
ments. Try tender lamb loin cooked in
Alpine hay or fresh river trout.

 Information

Tourist office (☎027 958 18 58; www.saas-fee.
ch; Obere Dorfstrasse 2; ☺8.30am-noon & 2-6pm
Mon-Fri, 8am-6pm Sat, 9am-noon & 3-6pm Sun,
shorter hours low & mid-season) Opposite the
post office and bus station.

Getting There & Away

Buses depart half-hourly from Brig (Sfr18.60, 1¼
hours) and Visp (Sfr16.20, 45 minutes). You can
transfer to/from Zermatt at Stalden Saas.

Saas Fee is car-free; park at the village
entrance (Sfr17/12.50 per day winter/summer)
and walk or pay around Sfr23 for an electric taxi
(☎079 220 21 37) to take you to your hotel.

Aletsch Glacier

As you approach the source of the mighty Rhône and gain altitude, the deep valley narrows and the verdure of pine-clad mountainsides and south-facing vineyards that defines the west of the canton switches to rugged wilderness. Along the way is a string of bucolic villages of geranium-bedecked timber chalets and onion-domed churches.

Out of view from the valley floor lies the longest and most voluminous glacier in the European Alps. The Aletsch Glacier (Aletschgletscher) is a seemingly never-ending, 23km-long swirl of deeply crevassed ice that slices past thundering falls, jagged spires of rock and pine forest. It stretches from Jungfrau in the Bernese Oberland to a plateau above the Rhône and is, justly so, a Unesco World Heritage Site.

Fiesch & Eggishorn

Most people get their first tantalising glimpse of Aletsch Glacier from Jungfraujoch, but picture-postcard riverside Fiesch on the valley floor is the best place to access it. From the village, ride the **cable car** (www.eggishorn.ch; adult/child return Sfr42.80/21.40) up to **Fiescheralp** – a hot spot for paragliding – and continue up to **Eggishorn** (2927m). Nothing can prepare you for what awaits on exiting the gondola.

Streaming down in a broad curve around the Aletschhorn (4195m), the glacier is just like a frozen five-lane superhighway. In the distance, to the north, rise the glistening summits of Jungfrau (4158m), Mönch (4107m), the Eiger (3970m) and Finsteraarhorn (4274m). To the west of the cable-car exit, spy Mont Blanc and the Matterhorn.

Bettmeralp & Riederalp

This twinset of family-friendly car-free hamlets, accessible only by cable car, is the stuff of Swiss Alpine dreams. Paved with snow December to March, kids are pulled around on traditional wooden Davos sledges and skis are the best way to get to the local supermarket. With the run at the top of the Bettmerhorn cable car (2647m) skirting the edge of the Aletsch Glacier, skiing here is a sensationally picturesque and dramatic affair – 104km of intermediate or easy ski runs in all the

Bettmeralp

Detour:
Leukerbad

The road that zigzags 14km up from Leuk past breathtakingly sheer chasms and wooded crags is a spectacular build-up to Leukerbad. Gazing up to an amphitheatre of towering rock turrets and canyon-like spires, Europe's largest thermal spa resort is pure drama.

Lindner Alpentherme (☎027 472 10 10; www.alpentherme.ch; Dorfplatz; thermal baths 3hr/day Sfr23/28, with sauna village Sfr39/53, Roman-Irish bath with/without soap-brush massage Sfr74/54; ☺pools 8am-8pm, sauna village & Roman-Irish baths 10am-8pm) offers a twinset of pools – one in, one out, both 36°C – with whirlpools, jets, Jacuzzi and mountain views you just can't get enough of. To lounge in the traditional Valais Sauna Village – all wood and rustic cartwheels, with several saunas, mill, ice-cold stream and herbal steam rooms – you must be naked. Equally invigorating is the Roman-Irish bath, a two-hour nude bathing ritual.

Hourly postal buses link Leukerbad with Leuk (Sfr11.20, 30 to 35 minutes). These are near Salgesch and the Rhône Valley.

so-called **Aletsch Arena** (www.aletscharena. ch) ski area, with a one-day ski pass costing Sfr53 (Sfr58 including cable car up from the valley).

Hiking in the summer is equally mind-blowing. From **Bettmeralp** (1950m) take the cable car to **Bettmerhorn** (adult/child return Sfr20/15) for a dramatic bird's-eye glacier view. Exit the station and follow the wooden walkway through cinematically oversized boulders to the so-called *Eis Terrasse* (Ice Terrace) where information panels tell you about the glacier and several marked footpaths start.

Sleeping & Eating

VILLA CASSEL   Historic Hotel $$
(☎027 928 62 20; d with breakfast/half-board Sfr160/210, dm with breakfast/half-board Sfr50/70; ☺mid-Jun–mid-Oct) Short but sweet is the season at this fabulous mountainside villa, the stunning summer pad of wealthy Englishman Ernest Cassel who – so the story goes – had to pay local farmers to stuff the bells of their cows with hay after their incessant ringing upset one of his house guests – a young Winston Churchill no less. Rooms today are simple pine with shared bathrooms.

**MOUNTAIN RESORT
RIEDERFURKA**   Mountain Hotel $
(☎027 929 21 31; www.artfurrer.ch; Riederfurka; dm incl breakfast Sfr60, d Sfr80) Planted firmly on the *alpages* (pasture) up high in Riederfurka, this oasis of peace, tranquillity and Alpine tradition has been around with the cows since the mid-19th century. Rooms are cosy, with lots of wood, and the restaurant – hearty mountain fare – is one of the best on the slopes.

ⓘ Getting There & Away

The base stations for these resorts – Mörel (for Riederalp), Betten (Bettmeralp) and Fiesch – are on the train route between Brig and Andermatt. Cable-car departures (Sfr9.20) are linked to train arrivals.

Zürich, Lake Constance & the Northeast

Switzerland's biggest city, Zürich, is not only efficient, it's also hip. The locals are hard-working early risers but, come clock-off time, they throw themselves wholeheartedly into a festive vortex.

Much of the ancient centre, with its tall church steeples and winding lanes, remains intact. Winterthur, to the northeast, is a cultural powerhouse, with major museums.

Northeastern Switzerland is the place to tiptoe off the map and back to nature for a few days. Here country lanes unravel like spools of thread, weaving through Appenzell's patchwork meadows and past the fjord-like waters of Walensee.

From the thunderous Rheinfall to the still waters of Lake Constance, nature is on a grand scale here. Completing the storybook tableau are castle-topped towns like Stein am Rhein and Schaffhausen, their facades festooned with frescos; while in St Gallen, the abbey library literally catches your breath with its rococo splendour.

Fraumünster cathedral (p204), Zürich

193

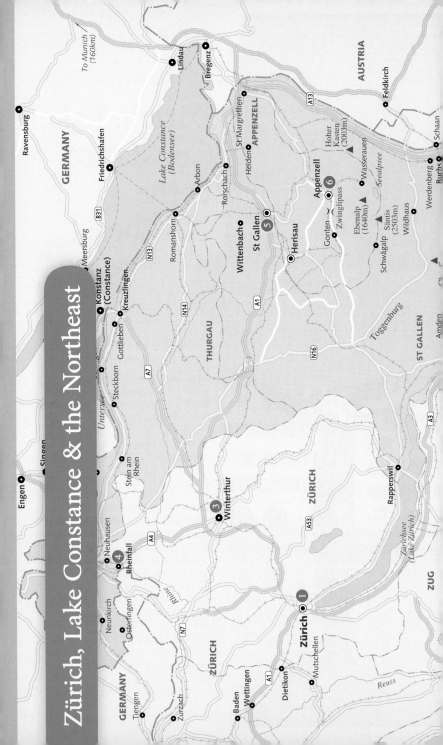

Zürich, Lake Constance & the Northeast

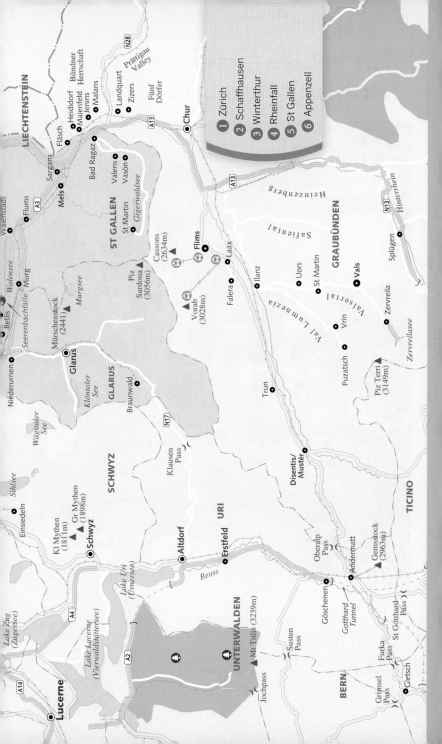

Zürich, Lake Constance & the Northeast's Highlights

1 Zürich

Switzerland's number-one city, Zürich (p204) has an image of suited bankers so conservative that they could be from another era. And while partly true, those suits do come off and the locals certainly know how to enjoy themselves. Cutting-edge bars, restaurants and boutiques can be found across town. Above: Rote Fabrik (p212), Zürich

Need to Know

BEST TIME TO VISIT Zürich is a year-round city; in colder months it throbs with life indoors. **TOP TIP** Go carless in Zürich. **For further coverage, see p204.**

Zürich Don't Miss List

JANINA BARUTH, ZÜRICH RESIDENT
AND MEDIA EXECUTIVE

1 LAKE ZÜRICH SWIMMING

One of the most beautiful spots during summertime is **Seebad Enge**. By day you can swim in Lake Zürich while watching the Alps with their snowy tops in the background. There are trendy people and almost no kids. It gets packed during the weekend when it's sunny. In the afternoon the bar is open, plus there are many events such as readings and little concerts. It's a 10-minute walk from the tram station Bürkliplatz.

2 UETLIBERG: ZÜRICH'S MOUNTAIN

Only a few minutes away by train from the main station by S-Bahn (No 10, station: Uetliberg) you get a break from the urban stress and still have the feeling of being in the city. From the **Uetliberg** hill you have a beautiful view all over the city and lake. There's a great restaurant too.

3 LANGSTRASSE IN KREIS 4 AND 5

In Zürich's most colourful and lively area you'll find bars, restaurants and clubs. Arthouse movies are big here, including the summertime **Kino Röntgenplatz** (www.sommerkinoröntgenplatz.ch), which is an open-air cinema showing classics. It's been going for almost 30 years and the tradition is that it rains, so bring a jacket. It's free but a hat is passed around.

4 LAKESIDE ZÜRICH

A walk along the lake from **Bellevue** to **Zürichhorn** is one of the most impressive things to do in Zürich. It takes maybe 45 minutes and you'll pass by musicians, BBQ places, people having a picnic, ice-cream vendors and guys selling Zürich's classic Cervelat sausage. Take a tram to Bellevue.

5 SHOPPING IN NIEDERDORF

For shopping that's not like everywhere else, go to the **Niederdorf area** (p213). Here you find little shops, wine and chocolate shops, clothes and shoe shops, art ateliers, jewellery stores and great bars, hotels and restaurants, theatres, arthouse cinemas...

Schaffhausen's Swiss Food

Who doesn't like cheese? A pot of lightly simmering fondue is one of the core pleasures of Switzerland. Raclette – the heated (often by flame) cheese you enjoy with fresh potatoes – another local favourite that can warm the chilliest bones on a frosty night. Schaffhausen ar the surrounding region are dotted with ageless traditional havens for Swiss food (p216).

2

Artful Winterthur

Zürich has its stolid, suitably grand museums but a mere 30 minutes away by train, Winterthur (p214) has a dynami collection of galleries and museums that together offer the country's mos provocative exhibits. The Sammlung Oskar Reinhart am Römerholz mixes and new masterpieces – think Ruben meets Renoir – while the Fotomuseur shows images that will stay with you lc after your visit. Renoir Sculpture, Sammlung O Reinhart am Römerholz (p215), Winterthur

3

REINHARD SCHMID / 4CORNERS ©

Thundering Rheinfall

Watched over by castles, Rheinfall (p220) always surprises: northeastern Switzerland is not that hilly yet here is a long pounding waterfall that throws up enough spray to grow a rainforest. Walk out on platforms that put you in the midst of the gravity-fed fury and *feel* the thundering power. Summertime ferries get you close to the pounding action.

St Gallen's Stiftsbibliothek

In *A World Lit Only by Fire*, the historian William Manchester writes about how the facts of the ancient world survived to the modern age. One of the places where monks tirelessly wrote out mankind's knowledge to pass on to future generations was right here in St Gallen's extraordinary Stiftsbibliothek (p223). Amid Unesco-recognised rococo splendour you can see some of the 150,000 surviving books on display.

Appenzell

Even the name is melodic: Appenzell (p225). This lovely little town, surrounded by Alpine beauty, harmoniously blends a rainbow of pastel-coloured vintage buildings in its Old Town. At the centre of town is the Landsgemeindeplatz, an all-star of a main square, where one of the nation's purest forms of democracy is practised. Pick any trail leading out of town and soon you'll be in glorious mountains.

Zürich, Lake Constance & the Northeast's Best...

Museums

○ **Stiftsbibliothek** (p223) St Gallen's star attraction was a repository for knowledge in medieval times.

○ **Schloss Kyburg** (p215) Try on a suit of armour at this castle overlooking Winterthur.

○ **Kunsthaus** (p207) A huge and deep collection that reflects Zürich's wealth.

○ **Schweizerisches Landesmuseum** (p204) A wonderful romp through Swiss history.

Old Towns

○ **Appenzell** (p225) Beautiful Old Town with colourful buildings around a square lined with cafes.

○ **Stein am Rhein** (p219) Cobblestone streets and gingerbread houses are among the details that yell 'cute' and 'quaint'!

○ **Werdenberg** (p226) A 13th-century town with the oldest Swiss collection of timber houses.

○ **Schaffhausen** (p216) Tidy streets dating from the 16th to 18th centuries make this a stroller's dream.

Outdoor Fun

○ **Lake Constance Ferries** (p221) Hop around the lake aboard boats that offer beautiful views.

○ **Bodensee-Radweg** (p222) A 273km easy-peasy bike and walking path around Lake Constance.

○ **Rhine Cycling** (p218) Several routes take you past ancient treasures and natural wonders.

○ **Lake Zürich** (p207) Join bankers removing their pinstripes for a dip in the crystal-clear waters right in the centre.

Need to Know

Natural Wonders

○ **Rheinfall** (p220) Huge falls never fail to stun first-time visitors.

○ **Lake Constance** (p221) A vast lake bordering Switzerland, Germany and Austria mirrors the Alps and is lined with sights.

○ **Seerenbachfälle** (p227) A series of three massive waterfalls tumble down in a beautful remote setting near Walensee.

○ **Braunwald** (p225) A car-free town with mountain and meadow views.

ADVANCE PLANNING

○ **Two months before** Check for any blockbuster exhibitions in Zürich and buy tickets.

RESOURCES

○ **Zürich** (www.zuerich.com) Full details on the big city.

○ **Züritipp** (www.zueritipp.ch) Jammed with info on what's on in Zürich.

○ **Art in Zürich** (www.artinzurich.ch) What's up and on in the city's museums.

○ **Ostschweiz Tourismus** (Eastern Switzerland Tourism; www.ostschweiz.ch) From St Gallen to Appenzell and beyond.

○ **Lonely Planet** (www.lonelyplanet.com/switzerland/zurich) Reader tips and more.

GETTING AROUND

○ **Train** All the main towns are well-linked to each other and Zürich.

○ **Ferry** Lake Constance is criss-crossed by a web of ferries, many of which hop along the shore from one stop to the next, so you can sit back on deck and enjoy a cruise. On foggy days there's a touch of mystery and drama as a cute little village materialises in the mist.

○ **Cable Cars** The Galurs Alps, an hour east of Zürich, are threaded by all manner of peak-seeking cable cars.

BE FOREWARNED

○ **Christmas** The region draws fully on its Germanic heritage as every town has a delightful Christmas market on its main square. Zürich has several, including a great one in the main station you can pop through between trains.

○ **Summer** People pour outside and central squares are filled with cafes, while special events – like fireworks – happen in the countryside and along the lakeshore.

Left: Schweizerisches Landesmuseum (Swiss tional Museum; p204), Zürich; **Above:** Views across the city and lake from Uetliberg (p197)

Zürich, Lake Constance & the Northeast Itineraries

Whether you're fresh off a plane or train, Zürich is an excellent starting point for tours around the region. The first tour takes it easy, while the second packs in plenty of pleasures.

ZÜRICH TO ST GALLEN
Old Switzerland

3 DAYS

Start your **(1) Zürich** day with a stroll around the namesake lake. Watch bankers officiously heading to work and revel in the knowledge that you're on holiday. Wander the Old Town, popping into the **Fraumünster**, the 13th-century cathedral. Soak up some of the city's rich culture at museums such as **Schweizerisches Landesmuseum**, **Museum für Gestaltung** and **Museum Rietberg**. Laze away in a tidy cafe before having a hearty Swiss meal in one of Zürich's traditional restaurants. In summer, head out to a lakeside place for a drink under the stars.

Catch a quick and early train to nearby **(2) Winterthur** and make the walk up to **Schloss Kyburg**, a classic old castle with good views. Consider visits to some of the fine local museums or head right on to pretty **(3) Schaffhausen**, where you can make an easy transfer to see the thundering wonder that is **(4) Rheinfall**, a 150m-wide waterfall on the **Rhine River**. Continue on to **(5) St Gallen**, one of Switzerland's finest Old Towns, where you can enjoy a delicious dinner. In the morning be ready for the rococo confection that is the Unesco-listed **Stiftsbibliothek**, a medieval treasure worthy of all the accolades.

ZÜRICH TO WALENSEE

Northeast Ramble

5 DAYS

Whirl through **(1) Zürich's** Old Town, buy something shamelessly expensive in the luxe shops and head for **(2) Schaffhausen**. Soak up the ancient charms of the walkable centre, then get spray in your face at the waterfall spectacular at **(3) Rheinfall**. Now for the silvery blue beauty of **Lake Constance**. Cross over from **(4) Kreuzlingen** to the beautiful medieval German town of **(5) Konstanz**. Catch a lake boat and explore. Various German towns might tempt you to get off for a look around (there's always another boat coming behind you), or just sit back and enjoy the Alpine views across the lake.

Spend a restful night in **(6) St Gallen** and ponder the magnificence of the **Stiftsbibliothek**, which was the western world's equivalent of a mainframe back in the day. **(7) Appenzell** is a good place for a long lunch; in fact, you might just slow down, stay the night and enjoy an invigorating morning hike into the surrounding Alps.

Timeless 13th-century houses line the little lanes of **(8) Werdenberg**. Get a gander over it all from the peak at **(9) Säntis** and then settle back along beautiful **(10) Walensee**.

Relaxing on the shores of Lake Zürich

Discover Zürich,
Lake Constance & the Northeast

View from the edge of Lake Zürich to Fraumünster and St Peterskirche (p207)

ZÜRICH

Zürich is an enigma. A savvy financial centre with possibly the densest public transport system in the world, it also has a gritty, post-industrial edge that always surprises. The nation's largest city has an evocative Old Town and lovely lakeside location. Its museums, shops and myriad restaurants can easily keep you busy for a few days.

 Sights

The city spreads around the northwest end of Zürichsee (Lake Zürich), from where the Limmat river runs further north still, splitting the medieval city centre in two. The narrow streets of the Niederdorf quarter on the river's east bank are crammed with restaurants, bars and shops. The central areas around the lake, especially Niederdorf, are best explored on foot.

FRAUMÜNSTER   Cathedral

(www.fraumuenster.ch, in German; Münsterhof; ◷10am-6pm Apr-Oct, to 4pm Nov-Mar) The 13th-century cathedral is renowned for its distinctive stained-glass windows, designed by the Russian-Jewish master Marc Chagall (1887–1985). He did a series of five windows in the choir stalls in 1971 and the rose window in the southern transept in 1978. The rose window in the northern transept was created by Augusto Giacometti in 1945.

SCHWEIZERISCHES LANDESMUSEUM   History Museum

(Swiss National Museum; ☎044 218 65 11; www.musee-suisse.ch; Museumstrasse 2; adult/child Sfr10/free; ◷10am-5pm Tue-Sun) Inside a

Zürich

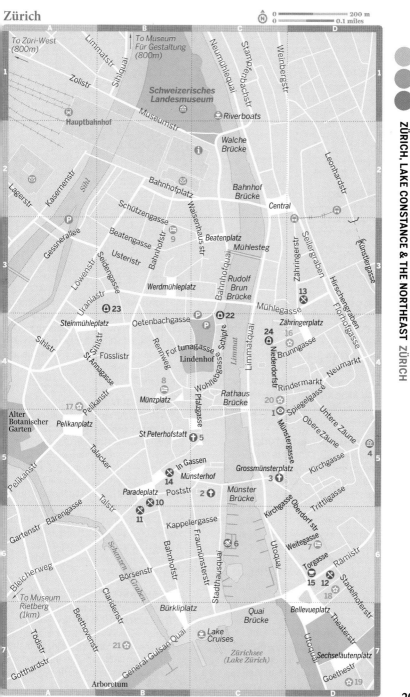

0   200 m
0   0.1 miles

To Züri-West
(800m)

To Museum
Für Gestaltung
(800m)

Limmatstr

Zolistr

Sihlquai

Limmatquai

Neumühlequai

Stampfenbachstr

Weinbergstr

**Schweizerisches
Landesmuseum**

Hauptbahnhof

Museumstr

Riverboats

Walche
Brücke

Leonhardstr

Lagerstr

Kasernenstr

Sihl

Bahnhofplatz

Bahnhof
Brücke

Central

Künstlergasse

Gessnerallee

Schützengasse

Wasenhaus str

Beatenplatz

Zähringerstr

Seilergraben

Hirschengraben

Florhofgasse

Beatengasse

Bahnhofstr

9

Mühlesteg

Beatenplatz

Löwenstr

Seidengasse

Usteristr

Werdmühleplatz

Bahnhofquai

Rudolf
Brun
Brücke

13

Mühlegasse

Zähringerplatz

16

Uraniastr

23

Oetenbachgasse

22

24

Niederdorfstr

Brunngasse

Steinmühleplatz

Renweg

Schipfe

Limmatquai

Neumarkt

Sihlstr

St Annagasse

Füsslistr

Sihlstr

Pelikanstr

17

8

Fortunagasse
Lindenhof

Wohllebgasse

Limmat

Rindermarkt

Spiegelgasse

Untere Zäune

Alter
Botanischer
Garten

Pelikanplatz

Münzplatz

Pfalzgasse

Rathaus
Brücke

20

1

Münstergasse

Obere Zäune

4

St Peterhofstatt

5

Grossmünsterplatz

Kirchgasse

Talacker

In Gassen

14

Münsterhof

3

Trittligasse

Pelikanstr

Paradeplatz

Poststr

2

Münster
Brücke

Kirchgasse

Oberdorf str

Gartenstr

Bärengasse

Talstr

10

11

Kappelergasse

Bahnhofstr

Fraumünsterstr

Utoquai

Weitegasse

7

Torgasse

Rämistr

Bleicherweg

Börsenstr

Schanzengraben

6

15

12

Stadelhoferstr

18

To Museum
Rietberg
(1km)

Beethovenstr

Claridenstr

21

Bürkliplatz

Quai
Brücke

Stadthausquai

Bellevueplatz

Theaterstr

Tödistr

Gotthardstr

General Gulsan Quai

Lake
Cruises

Zürichsee
(Lake Zürich)

Utoquai

Sechseläutenplatz

Goethestr

19

Arboretum

Zürich

purpose-built cross between a mansion and a castle sprawls an eclectic and imaginatively presented permanent collection that includes an extensive tour through Swiss history. Collections range from ancient arms to coins, and traditional crafts to a series of rooms recreating the interiors of everything from a 15th-century convent to contemporary pads crammed with designer furniture.

MUSEUM FÜR GESTALTUNG   Museum
(Design Museum; ☎043 446 67 67; www.museum-gestaltung.ch; Ausstellungstrasse 60; adult/concession Sfr9/6; ☺10am-8pm Wed, 10am-5pm Tue & Thu-Sun) Consistently impressive and wide-ranging, the exhibitions at this design museum include anything from works by classic photographers like Henri Cartier-Bresson to advertising for design furniture of yesteryear. Graphic and applied arts dominate the permanent collections, with anything from canned fruit tins to typewriters on display. Take trams 4 or 13.

MUSEUM RIETBERG   Art Museum
(☎044 206 31 31; Gablerstrasse 15; adult/concession permanent collection Sfr12/10, special exhibitions Sfr16/12; ☺10am-5pm Tue & Fri-Sun, to 8pm Wed & Thu) Set in three villas

in a leafy park and fronted by a striking emerald glass entrance, the museum houses the country's only assembly of African, Oriental and ancient-American art. This wide-ranging collection is frequently complemented by temporary exhibitions. Take tram 7.

CABARET VOLTAIRE   Gallery
(☎043 268 57 20; www.cabaret voltaire.ch; Spiegelgasse 1; admission varies; ☺12.30-6.30pm Tue-Sun) Birthplace of the zany Dada art movement, this bar-cum-art-space came back to life in 2004 as a hotbed of contentious art exhibitions and socially critical artistic ferment. In a sense, it sums up the city's contemporary trick of combining its obvious wealth with a sense of devilish social-artistic trouble-making. Entry to the bar is free and it's open until midnight Tuesday through Saturday.

GROSSMÜNSTER   Cathedral
(www.grossmuenster.ch; Grossmünsterplatz; ☺10am-6pm Mar-Oct, to 5pm Nov-Feb) More of Augusto Giacometti's work is on show across the river from Fraumünster in the twin-towered landmark cathedral founded by Charlemagne in the 9th century.

ANDREA PISTOLESI / PHOTOSHOT ©

Don't Miss **Kunsthaus**

Zürich's impressive fine-arts gallery boasts a rich collection of largely European art that stretches from the Middle Ages through a mix of Old Masters to Alberto Giacometti stick-figure sculptures, Monet and Van Gogh masterpieces, Rodin sculptures and other 19th- and 20th-century art. The museum is free on Wednesdays.

THINGS YOU NEED TO KNOW

Museum of Fine Arts; ☑ 044 253 84 84; www.kunsthaus.ch; Heimplatz 1; adult/child Sfr16/free; ☺10am-8pm Wed-Fri, to 6pm Tue, Sat & Sun

The firebrand preacher from the boondocks, Huldrych Zwingli (1484–1531), began speaking out against the Catholic Church here in the 16th century, and thus brought the Reformation to Zürich. You can also climb the southern tower, the **Karlsturm**. **Zwingli's house**, where he lived and worked, is nearby at Kirchgasse 3.

ST PETERSKIRCHE   Church

(St Peter's Church; St Peterhofstatt; ☺8am-6pm Mon-Fri, to 4pm Sat, 11am-5pm Sun) From any position in the city, it's hard to overlook the 13th-century tower of this church. Its prominent clock face, 8.7m in diameter, is the largest in Europe. Inside, the choir

stalls date from the 13th century but the rest of the church is largely an 18th-century remake.

Activities

Zürich comes into its own in summer, when the parks lining the lake are overrun with bathers, sun seekers, in-line skaters, footballers, lovers, picnickers, party animals and preeners. Police even patrol on rollerblades!

From May to mid-September, official swimming areas known locally as *Badis* open around the lake and up the Limmat river. There are also plenty of free,

207

Zürich with Children

In summer, spending time having a dip in the **Limmat river** or lake is a pleasant investment for the whole family. A walk along the Planetenweg in **Uetliberg** combines views with exercise and education on the planets. Uetliberg is on a 870m mountain top at the namesake stop on the S10 line.

Parents wanting a one-stop lesson in Swiss history should take their children to the **Schweizerisches Landesmuseum** (p204), a clever and attractively laid out museum with interactive screens, book corners and even a short slide from the highest part of the history section down to the beginning. With its garden setting, the **Museum Rietberg** (p206) can also be a clever compromise between art and the outdoors.

unofficial places to take a dip. Official swimming areas are usually wooden piers with a pavilion and most offer massages, yoga, saunas and snacks. Admission is Sfr6, and swimming areas are generally open from 9am to 7pm in May and September and 9am to 8pm from June to August.

🛏 Sleeping

Prices sometimes head north for various major trade fairs (including those in Basel).

TOWNHOUSE　　Boutique Hotel $$$
(✆044 200 95 95; www.townhouse.ch; Schützengasse 7; r Sfr195-425; 🛜) With luxurious wallpapers, wallhangings, parquet floors and retro furniture, the 21 rooms in these stylish digs come in an assortment of sizes from 15 sq m to 35 sq m. Located close to the main train station, it offers such touches as a DVD selection and iPod docking stations.

HOTEL OTTER　　Hotel $$
(✆044 251 22 07; www.hotelotter.ch; Oberdorfstrasse 7; s Sfr125, d Sfr155-175) The Otter has 17 rooms with a variety of colour schemes ranging from white and blue stripes to olive green. You might get pink satin duvet covers. Studio apartment–style rooms with kitchens are another option.

LADY'S FIRST　　Hotel $$
(✆044 380 80 10; www.ladysfirst.ch; Mainaustrasse 24; s Sfr230-270, d Sfr290-395; 🛜) Immaculate and generally spacious rooms provide a pleasant mixture of traditional parquet flooring and designer furnishings. The hotel spa and its accompanying rooftop terrace are for female guests only.

HOTEL WIDDER　　Hotel $$$
(✆044 224 25 26; www.widderhotel.ch; Rennweg 7; s/d from Sfr560/755; P ✳ @ 🛜) A stylish hotel in the equally grand district of Augustiner, the Widder is a pleasing fusion of modernity and traditional charm. Rooms and public areas across the eight town houses that make up this place are stuffed with art and designer furniture.

KAFI SCHNAPS　　Hotel $
(www.kafischnaps.ch; Kornhausstrasse 57; r per person Sfr44-59) Set in a onetime butcher's shop, this is a bustling little spot that happens to have a collection of five cheerful little rooms, each named and decorated after a fruit-based liquor.

HOTEL SEEGARTEN　　Hotel $$
(✆044 388 37 37; www.hotel-seegarten.ch; Seegartenstrasse 14; s Sfr195-295, d Sfr295-405; 🛜) Rattan furniture and vintage tourist posters give this place an airy Mediterranean atmosphere, which is reinforced by its proximity to the lake and the on-site Restaurant Latino.

ROMANTIK HOTEL FLORHOF Hotel $$$
(☏044 250 26 26; www.florhof.ch; Florhofgasse 4; s Sfr245-330, d Sfr395-570; 🛜) Set in a lovely garden, this one-time noble family's mansion contains 35 tastefully appointed rooms and is a stone's throw from the Kunsthaus.

Eating

Denizens of Zürich have the choice of an astounding 2000-plus places to eat and drink. Traditional local cuisine is very rich, as epitomised by the city's signature dish, *Zürcher Geschnetzeltes* (sliced veal in a creamy mushroom sauce).

ALPENROSE Swiss $$
(☏044 271 39 19; Fabrikstrasse 12; mains Sfr25-45; 🕑lunch & dinner Wed-Sun) With its timber-clad walls, 'No Polka Dancing' warning and fine cuisine from regions all over the country, the Alpenrose makes for an inspired meal out. You could try risotto from Ticino, *Pizokel* (aka *Bizochel,* a kind of long and especially savoury *Spätzli*) from Graubünden, or fresh perch filets.

COCO European $$
(☏044 211 98 98; www.coco-grill.ch; Bleicherweg 1a am Paradeplatz; mains Sfr25-45; 🕑lunch & dinner Mon-Fri, dinner Sat) For straightforward, juicy grilled meats and fish, this is the place to be. Secreted down a short alley just off Paradeplatz, you first encounter a teeny front bar, good for a pre-dinner wine. The almost conspiratorial dining area is out the back.

KRONENHALLE Swiss $$$
(☏044 251 66 69; Rämistrasse 4; mains Sfr28-65; 🕑noon-midnight) A haunt of city movers and shakers in suits, the Crown Hall is a brasserie-style establishment with an old-world feel, white tablecloths and lots of dark wood. Impeccably mannered waiters move discreetly below Chagall, Miró, Matisse and Picasso originals. Push the boat out for a Chateaubriand in Béarnaise sauce (Sfr152).

CAFÉ SPRÜNGLI Cafe $$
(☏044 224 47 46; www.spruengli.ch; Bahnhofstrasse 21; 🕑7.30am-5.30pm Mon-Fri, 8am-3pm Sat) Sit down for cakes, chocolate and coffee at this epicentre of sweet Switzerland, in business since 1836. You can have a light lunch too, but whatever you

Alpenrose restaurant, Zürich

do, don't fail to check out the heavenly chocolate shop around the corner on Paradeplatz.

RACLETTE STUBE Swiss $$
(☎ 044 251 41 30; www.raclette-stube.ch; Zähringerstrasse 16; mains Sfr28-40; ⏱ dinner) For the quintessential Swiss cheese experience, raclette, pop by this welcoming *Stube*, which feels like a warm country restaurant. They do fondue too.

ZEUGHAUSKELLER Swiss $$
(www.zeughauskeller.ch; Bahnhofstrasse 28a; mains Sfr18.50-34.50; ⏱ 11.30am-11pm) The menu (in eight languages) at this huge, atmospheric beer hall offers 20 different kinds of sausages, as well as numerous other Swiss specialities, including some of a vegetarian variety. There's no shortage of fine frothy beers either.

FRIBOURGER FONDUE-STÜBLI Swiss $
(☎ 044 241 90 76; www.fondue-stuben.ch; Rotwandstrasse 38; mains Sfr23-28; ⏱ closed Jun-Aug) One of three branches of this minichain located around town, this

is a cosy, warm spot for indulging in your fondue fantasy. Bright gingham adorns the timber tables and matches the steaming red pots of delicious hot melted cheese.

🍷 Drinking

Options abound across town, but the bulk of the more-animated drinking dens are in Züri-West, especially along Langstrasse in Kreis 4 and Hardstrasse in Kreis 5.

CAFÉ ODEON Cafe
(www.odeon.ch; Am Bellevueplatz; ⏱ daily) This one-time haunt of Lenin and the Dadaists is still a prime people-watching spot for gays and straights alike. Come for the art-nouveau interior, the OTT chandeliers and a whiff of another century. It serves food too.

LONGSTREET BAR Music Bar
(www.longstreetbar.ch; Langstrasse 92; ⏱ 8pm-late Tue-Sat) The Longstreet is a music bar

with a varied roll call of DJs coming in and out. Try to count the thousands of light bulbs in this purple-felt-lined, one-time cabaret. The biggest nights are Tuesday, Wednesday, Friday and Saturday.

CITY BEACH Bar
(www.city-beach.ch; Förrlibuckstrasse 151; ⊙noon-midnight mid-May–Aug) Head to the car-park roof to discover tropical Zürich – two pools, a sandy 'beach', bars and chilled music – for the perfect start to a long evening that could finish in the Q Zürich clubbing to the wee hours.

LIQUID Lounge
(www.liquid-bar.ch; Zwinglistrasse 12; ⊙5pm-late Mon-Sat) With its striped wallpaper and moulded plastic chairs in the form of boiled eggs broken in half, this is a kitsch kind of setting, with mostly lounge-oriented music nights. A groovy way to get ready for the latter half of the night.

⭐ Entertainment

Clubs

Generally dress well and expect to pay Sfr15 to Sfr30 admission.

ZÜRI-WEST

Q ZÜRICH Club
(www.qzurich.ch; Förrlibuckstrasse 151; ⊙11pm-late Fri & Sat, 5-10pm Sun) This car-park club is for those who take their dancing – to house, hip hop, mash up, electro and R&B – more seriously than seeing and being seen. The closing times are less radical than in days of yore, but the crowd remains as enthusiastic as ever. For pre-clubbing drinks and a dip, try the nearby City Beach.

CLUB KOMPLEX 457 Club
(www.komplex457.ch; Hohlstrasse 457; ⊙8pm-late Wed-Sun) The latest addition to Zürich's busy club circuit is also the scene of

211

Waterside Tippling

The **Frauenbad** (Stadthausquai) and **Männerbad** (Schanzengraben) public baths are open only to women and men respectively during the day, but they open their trendy bars to both sexes at night. At the former, up to 150 men are allowed into the **Barfussbar** (Barefoot Bar; ☎ 044 251 33 31; www.barfussbar.ch; ⏰8pm-midnight Wed-Thu & Sun mid-May-mid-Sep). You leave shoes at the entrance – drink while you dip your feet in the water! Sunday night is open-air disco night.

occasional live concerts, generally of a powerful rock variety. DJs spin all sorts, with techno taking pride of place. In summer, you can come along early (from 5pm) for a drink on the upstairs terrace (also open lunchtime when the weather is nice). Take bus 31 from Hauptbahnhof.

CENTRAL ZÜRICH

KAUFLEUTEN   Club
(www.kaufleuten.com; Pelikanstrasse 18; ⏰11pm-late Tue-Sun) An opulent art-deco theatre with a stage, mezzanine floor and bars arranged around the dance floor, Zürich's 'establishment' club plays house, hip hop and Latin rhythms to a slightly older crowd.

MASCOTTE   Club
(www.mascotte.ch; Theaterstrasse 10; ⏰9.30pm-late Mon, Wed & Fri-Sun) The old variety hall 'Corso' is now a popular club with huge windows facing Sechseläuten-platz and the lake. The Monday night session, with funk, soul and dancefloor jazz, is a mellow way to start the week.

Cultural Centres

ROTE FABRIK   Performing Arts
(www.rotefabrik.ch; Seestrasse 395) This once counter-cultural and now largely mainstream institution stages rock concerts, original-language films, theatre

and dance performances. There's also a bar and a restaurant. Take bus 161 or 165 from Bürkliplatz.

Gay & Lesbian Venues

Zürich has a lively gay scene, which includes Café Odeon.

BARFÜSSER   Bar
(http://barfuesser.ch; Spitalgasse 14; ⏰11.30am-late Mon-Fri, 2pm-2am Sat, 3.30-11.30pm Sun) One of the first gay bars in the country and still going strong, Barfüsser now incorporates a sushi bar and has mellowed over the years – gays and straights feel equally at home.

PIGALLE   Bar
(www.pigalle-bar.ch; Marktgasse 14; ⏰6pm-late) In business since the 1950s, this cupboard of a bar hosts a jukebox with boisterous hits of years gone by and a regular clientele that can get good-naturedly rowdy at times. Some punters tipple on the street but duck inside to soak in the music-hall-style decor.

DANIEL H   Bar
(☎ 044 241 41 78; www.danielh.ch; Müllerstrasse 51; ⏰5pm-late Mon-Fri, 7pm-2am Sat) An easygoing lounge-bar arrangement (with a tiny courtyard at the side), the 'Dani H' is a cruisy place to start the night. It is hetero-friendly.

Live Music

Aside from the high-brow stuff, Zürich has an effervescent live-music scene. Many of the bars and clubs mentioned earlier in this chapter offer occasional gigs.

MOODS   Jazz
(www.moods.ch; Schiffbaustrasse 6; ⏰7.30pm-late Mon-Sat, 6-10pm Sun mid-Sep–mid-Jun) One of the city's top jazz spots, although other musical genres such as Latin and world music grab the occasional spot on its busy calendar.

TONHALLE   Music
(www.tonhalle-orchester.ch; Claridenstrasse 7) An opulent venue used by Zürich's orchestra and chamber orchestra.

OPERNHAUS
Opera

(www.opernhaus.ch; Falkenstrasse 1) The city's premier opera house enjoys a worldwide reputation.

 Shopping

For high fashion, head for Bahnhofstrasse and surrounding streets. Across the river funkier boutiques are dotted about the lanes of Niederdorf. For grunge, preloved gear and some none-too-serious fun young stuff, have a stroll along Langstrasse in Kreis 4.

The leading markets include the flea market at **Bürkliplatz** (☉8am-4pm Sat May-Oct), the year-round **Flohmarkt Kanzlei** (www.flohmarktkanzlei.ch; Kanzleistrasse 56; ☉8am-4pm Sat) and **Rosenhof** (www.rosenhof.ch; Rosenhof; ☉10am-8pm Thu, to 5pm Sat Mar-Dec), but the tourist office has details of more options.

HEIMATWERK
Souvenirs

(www.heimatwerk.ch; Uraniastrasse 1) Good-quality, if touristy, souvenirs are found here, including fondue pots, forks, toys and classy handbags.

JELMOLI
Department Store

(www.jelmoli.ch; Bahnhofstrasse) The basement food hall is the highlight of this legendary department store, Zürich's first, biggest and best.

ℹ️ Information

Discount Card

ZürichCard (adult/child per 24hr Sfr20/14, per 72hr Sfr40/28) Available from the tourist office and the airport train station, this provides free public transport, free museum admission and more.

Tourist information

Zürich Tourism (☎044 215 40 00; www.zuerich.com; Hauptbahnhof; ☉8am-8.30pm Mon-Sat & 8.30am-6.30pm Sun) For hotel reservations through the tourist office, call ☎044 215 40 40.

ℹ️ Getting There & Away

Air

Zürich Airport (☎043 816 22 11; www.zurich-airport.com) is 9km north of the centre, with flights to most European capitals as well as some in Africa, Asia and North America.

Train

Direct trains run to Stuttgart (Sfr64), Munich (Sfr95), Innsbruck (Sfr48) and other international destinations. There are regular direct departures to most major Swiss towns, such as Lucerne (Sfr23, 45 to 50 minutes), Bern (Sfr47, 56 minutes) and Basel (Sfr31, 55 minutes).

Outdoor dining (p209) in Zürich
INGOLF POMPE / GETTY IMAGES ©

ⓘ Getting Around

To/From the Airport

Up to nine trains an hour go to/from the Hauptbahnhof between around 6am and midnight (Sfr6.40, nine to 14 minutes).

Boat

Lake cruises (☎ 044 487 13 33; www.zsg. ch) run between April and October. They leave from Bürkliplatz. A small circular tour (*kleine Rundfahrt*) takes 1½ hours (adult/child Sfr8.20/4.10) and departs every 30 minutes between 11am to 7.30pm. A longer tour (*grosse Rundfahrt*) lasts four hours (adult/child Sfr24/12). Pick tickets up at ZVV (local transport) ticket windows.

Riverboats (adult/child Sfr4.10/2.90, every 30 min Easter–mid-October) run by the same company head up the Limmat river and do a small circle around the lake (one hour). Board at the Schweizerisches Landesmuseum stop.

Car & Motorcycle

Parking is tricky. The two most useful car-parking garages (www.parkhaeuser.ch; up to Sfr43 a day) are opposite the main post office and at Uraniastrasse 3.

Lake Constance (p221)

Public Transport

Zürich's ZVV (www.zvv.ch) public transport system of buses, S-Bahn suburban trains and trams is completely integrated. Services run from 5.30am to midnight, and tickets must be bought in advance. Every stop has a dispenser. Either type in the four-figure code for your destination or choose your ticket type: a short single-trip *Kurzstrecke* ticket valid for five stops (Sfr2.60), a single ticket for greater Zürich valid for an hour (Sfr4.10) or a 24-hour city pass for the centre, Zone 10 (Sfr8.20).

AROUND ZÜRICH
Winterthur

POP 98,200 / ELEVATION 447M

Switzerland's sixth-largest city gave its name to one of Europe's leading insurance companies and is equally known for its high-quality museums.

 Sights

Winterthur owes much of its eminence as an art mecca to collector Oskar Reinhart, a scion of a powerful banking

OCEAN / CORBIS ©

and insurance family. His collection was bequeathed to the nation and entrusted to his hometown when he died in 1965. Consider picking up the Winterthur Museumspass (Sfr20 for one day excluding Technorama and Sfr30 for two days with Technorama).

SAMMLUNG OSKAR REINHART AM RÖMERHOLZ
Gallery

(www.bundesmuseen.ch/roemerholz; Haldenstrasse 95; adult/student Sfr12/9; ⏰10am-5pm Tue & Thu-Sun, to 8pm Wed) The collection, housed in a charming country estate (equipped with a pleasant cafe), is particularly fascinating in the way it seeks to bridge the gap between traditional and modern art, juxtaposing the likes of Goya, Rembrandt and Rubens with Monet, Picasso, Renoir, Cézanne and Van Gogh. Take bus 3 to Spital or get the Museumsbus.

MUSEUM OSKAR REINHART AM STADTGARTEN
Art Museum

(http://museumoskarreinhart.ch; Stadthausstrasse 6; adult/student Sfr12/8; ⏰10am-8pm Tue, to 5pm Wed-Sun) Reinhart's 500-strong collection of Swiss, German and Austrian works of art from the 18th and 19th centuries is on show in a museum on the edge of the central city's park.

FOTOMUSEUM
Museum

(www.fotomuseum.ch; Grüzenstrasse 44; permanent collection adult/concession Sfr8/6; ⏰11am-6pm Tue & Thu-Sun, to 8pm Wed) Winterthur's outstanding Photography Museum is another highlight. The vast collection includes many great names and styles from the earliest days of this art in the 19th century to the present. There's more in the **Fotostiftung** (Photo Foundation; 📞052 234 10 30; www.fotostiftung.ch; Grüzenstrasse 45; adult/concession Sfr7/5; ⏰11am-6pm Tue & Thu-Sun, to 8pm Wed) over the road. The combined price for these and other related photo exhibitions is Sfr17 for an adult and Sfr13 for a concession ticket.

If You Like...
Castles

If you like big old castles like Winterthur's Schloss Kyburg (p215), you'll enjoy these other old fortresses scattered about the northeast of Switzerland:

1 SCHLOSS ARBON
This 16th-century castle watches over the historic centre of Arbon. The castle's **Historisches Museum** (Alemannenstrasse 4; adult/child Sfr4/2; ⏰2-5pm May-Sep, Sun only Mar-Apr & Oct-Nov) races you through 5500 years of history, from the Stone Age to the 18th-century linen trade. On one lane, centuries-old houses display frescos depicting trades of yore. Arbon is on the train line between Zürich and Rorschach.

2 SCHLOSS WARTEGG
(📞071 858 62 62; http://wartegg.ch; Rorschacherberg; s Sfr145-155, Sfr220-270; 🅿) This magnificent fantasy palace is a 10-minute drive from central Rorschach on the hillside above town. This 16th-century former royal Austrian castle is set in leafy grounds with towering sequoias and Lake Constance views.

KUNSTMUSEUM
Art Museum

(www.kmw.ch, in German; Museumstrasse 52; adult/concession Sfr15/12; ⏰10am-8pm Tue, to 5pm Wed-Sun) For a satisfying stroll through a solid collection of the 19th- and 20th-century classics, the city's main Art Museum is worth some of your time. Many of the standard suspects, from Kandinsky to Klee, are represented, along with an impressive slew of contemporary creators.

SCHLOSS KYBURG
Castle

(www.schlosskyburg.ch; adult/child Sfr8/3; ⏰10.30am-5.30pm Tue-Sun) Just outside the city, Kyburg weaves interactive fun into the texture of its ancient castle buildings (try on a suit of armour – but not the torture instruments!). The 15th-century murals in the castle's chapel showing Christ as the judge at the Last Judgment are especially vivid. Out the back, a vegetable and herb garden flourishes, much as in past centuries.

Take the S-Bahn to Effretikon, then the bus to Kyburg. Ask the tourist office for the Kyburg leaflet, with transport timetables. The journey takes 30 minutes each way.

Eating

Bars and cheap restaurants are clustered along Neumarkt, offering a wide array of different ethnic cuisines.

GASTHAUS RÖSSLI Swiss, German **$$**
(**052 213 66 44; Steiggasse 1; mains Sfr22-34; lunch & dinner Tue-Sat**) For typical Swiss-German fare in a mountain-style, wood-clad eatery, you can't go past the Little Horse. The Wiener schnitzel is a house classic that is prepared at your table and the *Hackbraten* (meatloaf) is famous across town.

Information

Discount Card A Museumspass costs Sfr20 for one day and Sfr30 for two days and gives you entry to almost all the sights.

Tourist office (**052 267 67 00; www.winterthur-tourismus.ch; near platform 1, Hauptbahnhof; 8.30am-6.30pm Mon-Fri, to 4pm Sat**)

Getting There & Around

Four to five trains an hour run to Zürich (Sfr11.80, 21 to 28 minutes). The A1 freeway goes from Zürich, skirts Winterthur and continues to St Gallen and Austria.

As local bus tickets to Oberwinterthur cost Sfr4.10, it's better to get a 24-hour pass for Sfr8.20 instead.

A Museumsbus minivan shuttle (Sfr5) leaves the train station hourly between 9.45am and 4.45pm for the Sammlung Oskar Reinhart am Römerholz, the Museum Oskar Reinhart am Stadtgarten and the Kunstmuseum.

SCHAFFHAUSEN CANTON

Cyclists love touring this relatively flat region, and lower-end accommodation is booked up swiftly on weekends. Excellent public transport and manageable distances make it an easy day trip from Zürich too.

Schaffhausen

POP 34,600 / ELEV 404M

Schaffhausen is the kind of quaint medieval town one more readily associates with Germany – no coincidence, given how close it is to the border. Ornate frescos and oriel bay windows grace the pastel-coloured houses lining the pedestrian-only **Altstadt** (Old Town).

Fronwagplatz, Schaffhausen
AGE FOTOSTOCK / ROBERT HARDING ©

⊙ Sights

Opening hours are given for high season (April through October); many sights have reduced hours at other times.

VORSTADT
Neighbourhood

Schaffhausen is often nicknamed the *Erkerstadt* because of its 170 *Erkers* (oriel bay windows), which citizens built as a display of wealth. One of the most noteworthy windows belongs to the 17th-century **Zum Goldenen Ochsen** (Vorstadt 17), whose frescoed facade displays, among other things, an eponymous Golden Ox. The 16th-century **Zum Grossen Käfig** (Vorstadt 45) presents an extraordinarily colourful tale of the parading of Turkish sultan Bajazet in a cage by the triumphant Mongol warrior leader Tamerlane. The centuries-old frescos were freshened up in 1906.

A block east, the eye-catching **Haus zum Ritter** (Vordergasse 65), built in 1492, boasts a detailed Renaissance-style fresco depicting, you guessed it, a knight.

FRONWAGPLATZ
Square

Vorstadt meanders south past the 16th-century **Mohrenbrunnen** (Moor Fountain) into the old market place, Fronwagplatz. At the southern end stands the **Metzgerbrunnen** (Butcher's Fountain) and there's also a William Tell–type figure and a large clock tower. Facing the latter is the late baroque **Herrenstube** (Fronwagplatz 3), which was built in 1748 and was once the drinking hole of Schaffhausen nobles.

ALLERHEILIGEN MÜNSTER
Cathedral

(All Saints' Cathedral; Münsterplatz; ☺10am-noon & 2-5pm Tue-Sun) Schaffhausen's church was completed in 1103 and is a rare and largely intact specimen of the Romanesque style in Switzerland. It opens to a beautifully simple **cloister** (☺7.30am-8pm Mon-Fri, from 9am Sat &

♥ If You Like…
Swiss Food

If you like the hearty cheesy Swiss fare at restaurants like Zürich's Alpenrose and Raclette Stube (p209), you'll like the great local food at these places:

1 GERBERSTUBE
(☎052 625 21 55; www.gerberstube.ch; Bachstrasse 8, Schaffhausen; mains Sfr45-70; ☺lunch & dinner Tue-Sat) Behind its 1708 rococo facade, Gerberstube serves carefully prepared traditional cooking in opulent dining rooms. In medieval times it was a guildhall; today it's a tempting setting to tuck into rich oxtail soup with port wine, or less-traditional curry scampi.

2 BURG HOHENKLINGEN
(☎052 741 21 37; www.burghohenklingen.ch; Hohenklingenstrasse 1, Stein am Rhein; mains Sfr39-58 ☺10am-10.30pm Tue-Sat, to 5pm Sun) For medieval atmosphere, you can't beat this 12th-century hilltop fortress, with superb views over Stein am Rhein. Tuck into Swiss classics in the Rittersaal (Hall of Knights). It's a 30-minute uphill walk from the Old Town.

3 APPENZELLER SCHAUKÄSERIE
(www.showcheese.ch; Stein; ☺8.30am-6.30pm Mon-Sun) Cheese-lovers could pop into this Stein-based dairy, which runs through the manufacturing process, explaining how cheeses like the famous Räss get their sweaty-socks smell (a coating of herbs and brine). From Appenzell, there is a frequent bus service to Stein (Sfr6.80, 12 minutes).

Sun), which has gardens that seem like a tangled forest.

HERRENACKER
Square

Framed by pastel-coloured houses with steep tiled roofs, this is one of Schaffhausen's prettiest squares.

MUNOT
Fortress

(☺8am-8pm May-Sep, 9am-5pm Oct-Apr) East of the Haus zum Ritter, Vordergasse becomes Unterstadt, where you'll find stairs through vineyards to the 16th-century fortress. The

Freewheeling along the Rhine

The Rhine flows swiftly through the heart of Schaffhausen and there's no better way to explore further afield than by hiring your own set of wheels. A number of well-marked trails shadow the river and weave through the surrounding countryside. Scenic rides include the 20km Rheinfall–Rheinau route, which leads past the thundering Rheinfall to the Benedictine monastery Kloster Rheinau. Or you can quaff wine as you peddle through vineyards and past half-timbered houses on the 43km Klettgau Wine Route. Details of these and other routes are given on www.veloland.ch.

At the train station, **Rent a Bike** (☎051 223 42 17; www.rentabike.ch, in German) rents out Flyer e-bikes, city bikes and tandems for Sfr50, Sfr33 and Sfr80 respectively per day. Book online or by calling ahead.

unusual circular battlements were built with forced labour following the Reformation. Climb the spiral staircase for views over a patchwork of rooftops and spires to the Rhine and wooded hills fringing the city.

 Activities

ALTSTADT WALKS Walking Tour
(adult/child Sfr14/7; ☾10am Tue & 2pm Sat May–mid-Oct) These one-hour tours of the Old Town kick off at the tourist office. The well-informed guides speak German, English and French.

UNTERSEE UND RHEIN Boat Tour
(☎052 634 08 88; www.urh.ch, in German; Freier Platz; one-way Sfr46.20; ☾Apr–Oct) The 45km boat trip from Schaffhausen to Konstanz via Stein am Rhein and Reichenau is one of the Rhine's more-beautiful stretches. The journey takes 3¾ hours downstream to Schaffhausen and 4¾ hours the other way. See the website for timetables.

Sleeping

PARK VILLA Hotel $$
(☎052 635 60 60; www.parkvilla.ch; Parkstrasse 18; s/d from Sfr170/190, without bathroom from Sfr80/130; P) The eclectic furniture in this faintly gothic house resembles a private antique collection, with an array of four-poster beds, Persian carpets, chandeliers, patterned wallpaper and fake Ming vases in rooms. Dine in Louis XVI splendour in the banquet room.

HOTEL KRONENHOF Hotel $$
(☎052 635 75 75; www.kronenhof.ch; Kirchhofplatz 7; s Sfr125-145, d Sfr175-205, ste Sfr265; 🛜) A guesthouse since 1489, the Kronenhof has welcomed the likes of Goethe and Tsar Alexander. A recent makeover has spruced up the historic interior, with the best rooms now flaunting dark wood floors, crimson walls and bold art. The Ox bistro does a good steak. Rates drop 20% Friday to Sunday.

Eating

Stadthausgasse is takeaway street, rolling out quick eats from pizza to Thai. Head to Fronwagplatz for bakeries, delis, gelatarias and alfresco cafes.

FISCHERZUNFT Fusion $$$
(☎052 632 05 05; www.fischerzunft.ch; Rheinquai 8; mains Sfr54-75; ☾lunch & dinner Wed-Sun) André Jaeger and Jana Zwesper entice with European–Asian taste sensations at this Michelin-starred restaurant by the Rhine, with an elegant beamed dining room and riverside terrace. Match perfectly spiced fish dishes and handmade desserts with top wines from the cellar.

WIRTSCHAFT ZUM FRIEDEN Swiss $$
(☎052 625 47 67; www.wirtschaft-frieden.ch; Herrenacker 11; mains Sfr39-48; ☺lunch & dinner Tue-Sat; ✎) Locals have been eating, drinking and making merry at this cosy wood-panelled inn since 1445. Join them today for good, honest regional fare, such as braised veal cheeks with potato-celery puree or lake fish as well as vegetarian specials such as curries and dumplings prepared with market-fresh vegetables.

CAFÉ VORDERGASSE Cafe $
(Vordergasse 79; snacks & light meals Sfr10-20; ☺6am-7pm Mon-Fri, 7am-5pm Sat, from 10am Sun) This art nouveau–style tearoom spills out onto an ever-popular pavement terrace. Try sandwiches, salads and quiches with a homemade lemonade or smoothie.

❶ Information

Tourist office (☎052 632 40 20; www.schaff hauserland.ch; Herrenacker 15; ☺9.30am-6pm Mon-Fri, 9.30am-12pm & 1.30-6pm Sat & Sun).

❶ Getting There & Away

Direct hourly trains run from Zürich (Sfr18.60, 55 minutes). Local trains head half-hourly to Stein am Rhein (Sfr7.80, 25 minutes). Trains to St Gallen (Sfr28, 1½ to two hours) usually involve a change at Winterthur or Romanshorn.

Stein am Rhein
POP 3200 / ELEV 407M

Stein am Rhein looks as though it has leaped out of the pages of a Swiss fairytale, with its miniature steam train, leafy river promenade and gingerbready houses. The effect is most overwhelming in its cobblestone Rathausplatz, where houses of all shapes and sizes, some half-timbered, others covered in

frescos, line up for a permanent photo op. Why isn't this place on Unesco's World Heritage list?

◎ Sights & Activities

Look out for daredevil kids diving from the bridge into the Rhine as you wander along the leafy river promenade.

RATHAUSPLATZ Square
Often hailed Switzerland's most beautiful town square (no mean feat!), the elongated Rathausplatz is picture-book stuff. The fresco-festooned **Rathaus** (town hall) soars above the 16th-century houses named according to the pictures with which they are adorned, like *Sonne* (Sun) and *Der Weisse Adler* (The White Eagle).

MUSEUM LINDWURM Museum
(www.museum-lindwurm.ch; Unterstadt 18; admission Sfr5; ☺10am-5pm Mon-Sun Mar-Oct) A four-storey house has been converted into this museum, whose living rooms, servants' quarters and kitchen replicate

Frescoed facade on Rathausplatz, Stein am Rhein
DAMIEN SIMONIS / GETTY IMAGES ©

BOB KRIST / CORBIS ©

Don't Miss **Rheinfall**

Ensnared in wispy spray, the thunderous Rheinfall might not give Niagara much competition in terms of height (23m), width (150m) or even flow of water (700 cu metre per second in summer), but it's a stunning sight nonetheless.

Most views of the falls are free, but to get close up to the rushing waters on the south side of the falls, you pay an entry fee at the Schloss Laufen souvenir shop to descend the staircase to the Känzeli viewing platform.

During summer, ferries flit in and out of the water at the bottom of the falls. Some merely cross from Schloss Laufen to Schlössli Worth, but the round-trip that stops at the tall rock in the middle of the falls, where you can climb to the top and watch the water rush all around you, is far more fun.

To get to the Rheinfall, you can catch bus 1 or 6 from Schaffhausen train station to Neuhausen Zentrum (Sfr3, 13 minutes), then follow the yellow footprints.

THINGS YOU NEED TO KNOW

Rhine Falls (www.rheinfall.ch; entry to Känzeli viewing platform adult/child Sfr5/3.50; ⊗daily); **Ferries** (www.maendli.ch; Schloss Laufen to Schlössli Worth adult/child Sfr2/1, round-trip Sfr8/4)

the conditions enjoyed in the mid-19th century by a bourgeois family.

Sleeping & Eating

Half-timbered houses serving Swiss grub line the Rhine, but the quality can be hit or miss.

HOTEL ADLER Hotel $$
(☎052 742 61 61; www.adlersteinamrhein.ch; Rathausplatz 2; s/d Sfr130/185; ☎) Behind the frescoed exterior lie simple yet comfortable rooms. The location on Rathausplatz is the big draw. The dining areas have a pleasingly old-fashioned feel about them and the grub, while nothing outlandishly creative, hits the spot. Local fish is a safe bet.

LA P'TITE CRÊPERIE Creperie $
(Unterstadt 10; crêpes Sfr6.90-12.90; ⏰11am-7pm) Mary-Ann is the crêpe queen at this hole-in-the-wall place with a Boho feel. Feast away on her fabulously light crêpes with cheese and *Bündnerfleisch* (air-dried beef), maple syrup or – what could be more Swiss? – Toblerone. It's closed Tuesdays and Wednesdays during low season.

ⓘ Getting There & Away

Stein am Rhein is on the direct hourly train route that links Schaffhausen (Sfr7.80, 25 minutes) with St Gallen (Sfr29, 1½ hours).

LAKE CONSTANCE

Before package holidays began whisking the locals and their beach towels abroad in the '70s and '80s, Lake Constance (Bodensee) was the German Mediterranean, with its mild climate, flowery gardens and palm trees. The 'Swabian Sea', as it's nicknamed, is Central Europe's third largest lake, straddling Switzerland, Germany and Austria. It's a relaxed place to wind down for a few days, whether cycling through apple orchards and vineyards, heron-spotting in the lake's wetlands, or taking to its glassy waters by canoe.

Come in spring for blossom, summer for lazy beach days and autumn for new wine. Almost everything shuts from November to February.

ⓘ Information

The **Bodensee Erlebniskarte** (www.bodensee -erlebniskarte.de; 3/7/14 days Sfr102/131/181) discount card is sold from mid-April to mid-October. In its most expensive version, it entitles the holder to free unlimited ferry travel, entrance to many museums and attractions, including the Zeppelin Museum in Friedrichshafen and Insel Mainau, and a return journey up the Säntisbahn (p226).

ⓘ Getting There & Away

Good rail services link Zürich to Konstanz (Sfr30, 80 minutes) and Munich (Sfr89, 4¼ hours) in Germany. Trains (Sfr8, 15 minutes) run between Bregenz in Austria and St Margrethen in Switzerland.

ⓘ Getting Around

Various ferry companies, including Switzerland's **SBS Schifffart** (www.sbsag.ch, in German), Austria's **Vorarlberg Lines** (www.bodensee schifffahrt.at) and Germany's **BSB** (www.bsb -online.com), travel across, along and around the lake from mid-April to late October, with the more-frequent services starting in late May. A Swiss Pass is valid only on the Swiss side of the lake.

Trains tend to be the easiest way to get around on the Swiss side, buses on the German bank.

Kreuzlingen
POP 19,000 / ELEV 404M

Kreuzlingen, in the Swiss canton of Thurgau, is often eclipsed by its prettier, more vivacious sister, Konstanz in Germany. That said, its lakefront location is charming. Otherwise the most sensible option is to change trains at Kreuzlingen station and head straight to Konstanz (Sfr3, three minutes). Direct trains run every 30 minutes between Kreuzlingen and Schaffhausen (Sfr17.20, 55 minutes).

ST GALLEN & APPENZELL CANTONS

The cultural high point of a journey around the extreme northeast of the country is a visit to St Gallen's legendary abbey, with its extraordinary rococo library.

Locals go to great lengths to preserve their heritage and this green, hilly region is sprinkled with beautiful, timeless villages. Both cantons are criss-crossed by endless hiking, cycling and mountain-biking trails.

St Gallen
POP 72,700 / ELEV 670M

St Gallen's history as the 'writing room of Europe' is evident in its principal attraction today: the sublime rococo library of its huge Catholic abbey, which rises gracefully above a fountain-dotted courtyard.

Local lore has it that St Gallen began with a bush, a bear and an Irish monk who should have watched where he was going. In AD 612, the tale goes, itinerant Gallus fell into a briar and considered the stumble a calling from God. After a fortuitous encounter with a bear, in which he persuaded it to bring him a log, take some bread in return and leave him in peace, he used the log to begin building the hermitage that would one day morph into St Gallen's cathedral.

◉ Sights

Many houses of Old St Gallen boast elaborate *Erker* (oriel bay windows), especially around Gallusplatz, Spisergasse,

Schmiedgasse and Kugelgasse. The city's tourism folk have counted them all up and reckon there are 111 oriel windows! Some bear the most extraordinary timber sculptures – a reflection of the wealth of their one-time owners, mostly textile barons.

Multilingual guided tours of the Old Town (Sfr20 per person) kick off at the tourist office at 2pm Monday to Saturday from May to October.

DOM Cathedral
(Klosterhof; ⊙9am-6pm Mon, Tue, Thu & Fri, 10am-6pm Wed, 9am-4pm Sat, noon-5.30pm Sun) The twin-towered cathedral is only slightly less ornate than the library, with dark and stormy frescos and aqua-green stucco

A Spin of the Lake

Hopping across the Swiss–German border from Kreuzlingen brings you to the high-spirited, sunny university town of **Konstanz** (www.konstanz.de), well worth a visit for its Romanesque cathedral, pretty Old Town and tree-fringed harbour. Edging north of Konstanz, you reach the Unesco-listed Benedictine monastery of **Reichenau** (www.reichenau.de), founded in AD 724. Close by is **Insel Mainau** (www.mainau.de; adult/child €15.90/8.50; ⊙dawn-dusk), a pleasantly green islet with 45 hectares of Mediterranean-style gardens, including rhododendron groves, a butterfly house and a waterfall-strewn Italian garden.

Stepping across to the lake's northern flank you arrive in the wine-growing town of **Meersburg** (www.meersburg.de), where cobbled lanes thread past half-timbered houses up to the perkily turreted medieval castle. Just east of here is **Friedrichshafen**, forever associated with the Zeppelin, the early cigar-shaped craft of the skies, which made its inaugural flight in 1900. The **Zeppelin Museum** (www.zeppelin-museum.de; adult/child €7.50/3; ⊙9am-5pm Mon-Sun) traces the history of this bombastic, but ill-fated, means of air transport. Still on German turf is the postcard-perfect island town of **Lindau** (www.lindau.de), with its lavishly frescoed houses, palm-speckled promenade and harbour watched over by a lighthouse and Bavarian lion. For further information, head to shop.lonelyplanet.com to purchase a downloadable PDF of the Germany chapter from Lonely Planet's *Western Europe* guide.

Lindau sits just a few kilometres north of Austria and the town of **Bregenz** (www.bregenz.ws). Rising dramatically above the town is the Pfänder (1064m). A **cable car** (adult/child return €11/5.50; ⊙8am-7pm Apr-Oct) glides to the summit, where panoramic views of Lake Constance and the not-so-distant Alps unfold.

Even if you don't have your own car, getting around by bike or boat is a breeze. Well-signposted and largely flat, the 273km **Bodensee-Radweg** (Lake Constance Cycle Route; www.bodensee-radweg.com) encircles the lake, weaving through fields of ripening wheat, vineyards, orchards and shady avenues of chestnut and plane. Most train stations in the region rent out bikes.

STUART DEE / GETTY IMAGES ©

Don't Miss **Stiftsbibliothek**

St Gallen's 16th-century library is one of the world's oldest and the finest example of rococo architecture in Switzerland. Along with the rest of the monastery complex surrounding it, the library forms a Unesco World Heritage Site.

Filled with priceless books and manuscripts painstakingly handwritten by monks during the Middle Ages, it's a dimly lit confection of ceiling frescos, stucco, cherubs and parquetry. Only 30,000 of the total 150,000 volumes are in the library at any one time, and only a handful in display cases, arranged into special exhibitions. If there's a tour guide in the library at the time, you might see the monks' filing system, hidden in the wall panels.

THINGS YOU NEED TO KNOW

www.stiftsbibliothek.ch; Klosterhof 6d; adult/child Sfr10/7; ⏰10am-5pm Mon-Sat, to 4pm Sun

embellishments. Entry is by two modest doors on the north flank – there is no door in the main facade, which is actually the cathedral's apse! Concerts are sometimes held – see www.kirchenmusik.ch. The cathedral is closed during services.

ST LAURENZEN-KIRCHE   Church
(Zeughausgasse; ⏰9.30-11.30am & 2-4pm Mon, 9.30am-6pm Tue-Fri, to 4pm Sat) St Gallen's cathedral gets all the attention, but this Protestant neo-Gothic church is also beautiful, with its mosaic-tiled roof, delicate floral frescos and star-studded

ceiling resembling a night sky. Climb the **tower** (adult/child Sfr5/2.50; ⏰10am & 3pm) for views over the town's terracotta rooftops and spires.

 **Sleeping**

St Gallen is a business town, which can make beds scarce and prices high.

HOTEL DOM   Boutique Hotel **$$**
(☎071 227 71 71; www.hoteldom.ch; Weber-gasse 22; s/d Sfr175/245; P 🛜) An almost

223

startlingly modern hotel, plonked in the middle of the Old Town. The room decor is razor-sharp with clean lines, backlit walls and bold colours. Genuinely friendly staff and a generous breakfast buffet sweeten the deal.

EINSTEIN HOTEL   Historic Hotel $$$
(071 227 55 55; www.einstein.ch; Berneggstrasse 2; s Sfr175-225, d Sfr300-450; P @) Silk curtains, cherry-wood furnishings and plush lambs'-wool rugs grace the spacious rooms at this grand 19th-century pile. Relax with a swim in the strikingly lit atrium pool or a massage in the spa. The panoramic rooftop restaurant (mains Sfr26 to Sfr48) emphasises regional cuisine.

HOTEL VADIAN   Hotel $$
(071 228 18 78; www.hotel-vadian.com; Gallusstrasse 36; s Sfr99-150, d Sfr150-240;) You can't get much closer to the heart of St Gallen at these prices. The hotel was recently given an overhaul and varied modern rooms are in perfect nick. Some have nice touches, like ceiling beams.

Eating & Drinking

St Gallen is noted for its *Erststock-Beizli*, traditional taverns situated on the 1st floor of half-timbered houses.

BÄUMLI   Swiss $$
(071 222 11 74; Schmiedgasse 18; mains Sfr22-47; lunch & dinner Tue-Sat) A late-medieval building houses a timeless eatery that showcases all the typical 1st-floor specialities, from bratwurst with fried onions (Sfr12.80) to lamb cutlets, Wiener schnitzel, *Cordon bleus* (pork schnitzel stuffed with ham and cheese), *Geschnetzeltes* (a sliced pork or veal dish) and *Mostbröggli* (smoked beef jerky).

WIRTSCHAFT ZUR ALTEN POST   Fusion $$
(071 222 66 01; Gallusstrasse 4; mains Sfr22-47; lunch & dinner Tue-Sat) Things are a little ritzy at this upmarket but historical *Beizl* (tavern), where St Gallen specialities like fat veal sausages with rösti are complemented by more-original creations such as Pyrenean milk-fed lamb in an olive-herb crust.

METZGEREI GEMPERLI   Sausages $
(Schmiedgasse 34; sausages from Sfr6.50; 8am-6.30pm Mon-Fri, 7am-5pm Sat) Bite into the best OLMA bratwurst, served plain in a *Bürli* (bun), at this butcher–sausage stand combo.

CHOCOLATERIE   Cafe $
(071 222 57 70; Gallusstrasse 20; 1-6.30pm Mon, 9am-6.30pm Tue-Fri, to 5pm Sat) For exquisite chocolate in liquid and solid forms, this half-timbered place opposite the cathedral is surely the devil's work. Try a smooth, cocoa-rich hot or cold chocolate.

Colourful facades of Appenzell
GAVIN HELLIER / ALAMY ©

Detour:
Braunwald

The attractive car-free mountain resort of Braunwald basks in sunshine on the side of a steep hill, gazing at the snowcapped Tödi Mountain (3614m) and overlooking valley pastures and fir forests below. The **Braunwaldbahn** (one-way/return Sfr7.80/15.60) climbs the hill from the Linthal Braunwaldbahn station.

Braunwald is a terrific base for hiking in summer, and you'll find pamphlets at the funicular station outlining several routes, including to the **Oberblegisee**, a green-tinted Alpine lake. Trains run roughly hourly from Linthal Braunwaldbahn to Zürich (Sfr28, 1½ hours) via Ziegelbrücke (Sfr10.40, 40 minutes). It's a 1¼-hour drive from Zürich along the A3.

ℹ Information

Tourist office (📞 071 227 37 37; www.st.gallen-bodensee.ch; Bahnhofplatz 1a; ⊗9am-6pm Mon-Fri, 10am-4pm Sat) There's another self-service information point, where you can pick up brochures, in the Chocolaterie.

ℹ Getting There & Away

St Gallen is a short train or bus ride from Romanshorn (Sfr9, 25 minutes). There are also regular trains (only four of them direct) to Bregenz in Austria (Sfr18, 35 to 50 minutes), Chur (Sfr33, 1½ hours) and Zürich (Sfr28, 65 minutes via Winterthur).

Appenzell
POP 5700 / ELEV 785M

Appenzell is a feast for both the eyes and the stomach. Behind the gaily decorative pastel-coloured facades of its traditional buildings lie cafes, *confiseries* (sweet and cake shops), cheese shops, delicatessens, butchers and restaurants offering local specialities. It's absolutely perfect for a long lunch and a lazy wander along the crystal-clear Sitter river.

◎ Sights & Activities

Countless hiking trails thread up into the Alps from Appenzell; see www.appenzell.info for inspiration. A great family walk is the 5km Barfusspfad (barefoot trail), which skips through meadows and over mountain brooks to Gonten.

Trekking bikes and e-bikes can be rented at the train station for Sfr25 and Sfr45 per day respectively.

Opening hours are given for high season; many sights have reduced hours from November to March.

ALTSTADT   Neighbourhood
The centrepiece of the Old Town is photogenic **Landsgemeindeplatz**, with elaborately painted hotels and restaurants around its edges. The open-air parliament takes place on this square on the last Sunday of April, with locals wearing traditional dress and voting (in the case of the men, by raising a short dagger).

The buildings along **Hauptgasse** are also admirable. The village **church** has gold and silver figures flanking a baroque altar.

BRAUEREI LOCHER   Brewery
(Industriestrasse 12; beer tasting Sfr1.50; ⊗10am-12.15pm & 1-5pm, closed Mon Nov-Mar) Pure local spring water goes into the refreshing Appenzeller Bier brewed here. The hands-on visitor centre whisks you through brewing history and processes. At the front you can taste three mini beers and buy beers like hoppy Vollmond (full moon) and alcohol-free Leermond (empty moon).

Detour:
Säntis

Small in Swiss terms, the jagged Säntis peak (2503m) is the highest in this part of Switzerland. It offers a marvellous panorama encompassing Lake Constance, Zürichsee, the Alps and the Vorarlberg Mountains. Take the train from Appenzell to Urnäsch and transfer to the bus (approximately hourly) to Schwägalp (Sfr9). From Schwägalp, the cable car, **Säntisbahn** (www.saentisbahn.ch; one-way/return Sfr29/41; ⏰7.30am-6pm Jun–mid-Oct, 8.30am-5pm mid-Oct–May) glides to the summit every 30 minutes.

NATUR-MOORBAD   Spa
(☎071 795 31 21; www.naturmoorbad.ch, in German; Gontenbad) At this moor bath, dating to 1740, you can dip in mud-laden water from the moors (Sfr30) to help with stress or skin conditions (adding in nettles, ferns and other plants), or luxuriate in a pampering rose bath (Sfr109 for two).

🛏 Sleeping & Eating

The tourist office can advise on B&Bs, holiday apartments and farmstays in the area. Most restaurants charge roughly Sfr12 to Sfr14 for *Käseschnitte* (cheese on toast) and other snacks, and Sfr20 to Sfr40 for main courses.

GASTHAUS HOF   Guesthouse $
(☎071 787 40 30; www.gasthaus-hof.ch; Engelgasse 4; s/d/tr/q Sfr85/130/180/220; 🛜) Just off Landsgemeindeplatz, this cheap-sleep option has simple but spacious rooms with timber-clad walls. The old-school restaurant comes with plenty of local bonhomie.

HOTEL APPENZELL   Historic Hotel $$
(☎071 788 15 15; www.hotel-appenzell.ch; Landsgemeindeplatz; s/d Sfr130/220; @) With its broad, brightly decorated facade, this typical Appenzeller building houses generously sized rooms with wooden beds. Decor combines gentle pinks and blues with frilly lace on the picture windows. The restaurant offers a wide-ranging seasonal menu that includes vegetarian dishes.

GASTHAUS LINDE   Swiss $
(071 787 13 76; Hauptgasse 40; mains Sfr18-30; ⏰lunch & dinner Fri-Wed) This warm, wood-panelled tavern oozes local character and does excellent Appenzell beer fondue. More adventurous diners can tuck into offal specialities.

ℹ Information

The **tourist office** (☎071 788 96 41; www.appenzell.info, in German; Hauptgasse 4; ⏰9am-noon & 1.30-6pm Mon-Fri, 10am-5pm Sat) has details on the Appenzeller Ferienkarte.

ℹ Getting There & Away

From St Gallen, the narrow-gauge train to Appenzell (Sfr13.20, 45 minutes) leaves from the front and to the right of the main train station. Departures from St Gallen are approximately every half-hour, via Gais or Herisau (where you must occasionally change trains).

Around Appenzell

Scattered with Alpine dairy farms and quaint villages, the countryside surrounding Appenzell makes for some highly scenic driving along narrow, winding roads.

⦿ Sights & Activities

WERDENBERG   Village
Blink and you'll miss this village and that would be a shame! Founded in 1289, it is said to be the oldest settlement of timber houses in Switzerland. This huddle of some 40-odd houses lies between an

oversized pond and a grapevine-covered hill topped by the **Schloss Werdenberg** (www.schloss-werdenberg.ch; adult/child Sfr6/5; ⏲11.30am-6pm Tue-Fri, 10am-6pm Sat & Sun).

ℹ Getting There & Away

Trains run from St Gallen to Buchs (Sfr19.80, 55 minutes), where you can pick up local buses to Werdenberg.

Walensee

Walensee is a long finger of a lake along the A3 freeway (and railway line) that connects Zürich with Graubünden. The limestone Churfirsten mountains rise spectacularly above its north flank, occasionally interrupted by a coastal hamlet or upland pasture and, about halfway along the lakefront, seemingly cracked open by Switzerland's highest waterfall.

◉ Sights & Activities

FLUMSERBERG   Mountain
(www.flumserberg.ch) For a little Alpine fun, take the winding mountain road westward from Flums to a series of villages and Flumserberg, perched high above the lake and facing the impenetrable rock wall of the Churfirsten range.

SEERENBACHFÄLLE   Waterfall
This series of three colossal waterfalls, thundering down 585m from top to bottom, is fuelled by a complex network of underground rivers running through the mountain rock from as far away as the peak of Säntis. The middle waterfall, a 305m drop, is considered Switzerland's highest. The closest you can reach by car is Betlis, a 30-minute hike away.

**SCHIFFSBETRIEB
WALENSEE**   Boat Tour
(www.walenseeschiff.ch) Boats regularly cross Murg and Quinten. From April to mid- October there are also regular boats between Weesen and Walenstadt, calling in at various spots along the way (including Betlis and Quinten).

🛏 Sleeping & Eating

LOFTHOTEL MURG   Boutique Hotel **$$**
(☎081 720 35 75; www.lofthotel.ch; Murg; s Sfr120-180, d Sfr180-240; 🛜) A 19th-century cotton mill has been reincarnated as the Lofthotel, affording fine views of the Churfirsten mountains and Walensee. Clean lines, polished concrete and bold artworks define the industrial-chic rooms, which sport flat-screen TVs and iPod docks. Farm-fresh produce and homemade preserves are served at breakfast (Sfr20).

**PARKHOTEL
SCHWERT**   Historic Hotel **$$**
(☎055 616 14 74; www.parkhotelschwert.ch; Hauptstrasse 23, Weesen; s/d Sfr129/190; 🛜) Looking back on 600 years of history, this elegantly restored hotel has individually decorated rooms with parquet floors. Market-fresh fish, meat and French classics are on the menu in the brasserie and on the lake-facing terrace.

FISCHERSTUBE   Swiss **$$**
(☎055 616 16 08; Marktgasse 9, Weesen; mains Sfr30-50; ⏲lunch & dinner Thu-Tue) Snowy white linen and bottle-green wood panelling create a refined backdrop for well-executed fish dishes here. Pair fine wines with local whitefish and perch.

ℹ Getting There & Away

By train from Zürich, get off at Ziegelbrücke (Sfr21, 45 minutes), which is a 15-minute walk from central Weesen, or change for trains on to Walenstadt.

GLARUS CANTON

The spiky, glacier-capped peaks of the Glarus Alps rise above stout wooden farmhouses and lush pastures in this little-explored canton, linked to the centre of the country by the vertiginous Klausenpass. Its northern boundary touches Walensee and provides much of the Alpine beauty that can be observed from the lake's north shore. For more information, contact **Glarner Tourismus** (☎055 610 21 25; www.glarus.ch, in German; Niederurnen).

St Moritz, Graubünden & the Southeast

Flit from glitz to raw beauty to Italian charm. While you've probably heard about St Moritz' glamour, Davos' sensational downhill skiing and the tales of Heidi (fictionally born here), vast swathes of Graubünden remain little known and ripe for exploring. Strike into the Alps on foot or follow the lonesome passes that corkscrew high into the mountains, where only the odd marmot or chamois and your own little gasps of wonder break the silence.

The Ticino Alps are as magnificent as elsewhere in Switzerland, but here you can admire them while sipping a full-bodied merlot at a pavement cafe, enjoying a hearty lunch at a chestnut-shaded *grotto* (rustic Ticino-style inn or restaurant), or floating in the mirror-like lakes of Lugano and Locarno. The southeast tempers its classic Alpine looks with Italian good-living.

Lago di Lugano (Lake Lugano; p259)

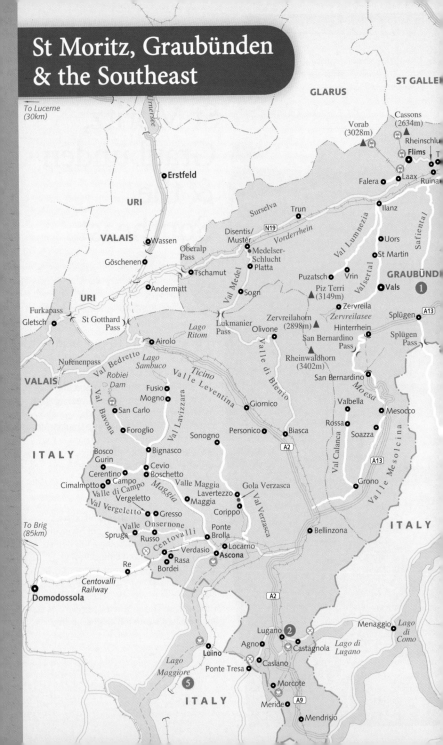

LIECHTENSTEIN

Heididorf
gans
Fläsch
Is
Maienfeld
ad Ragaz
Jenins
Malans
Landquart
Zizers
Chur
Domat/Ems
Reichenau

Bündner
Herrschaft

Sulzfluh
(2817m)

AUSTRIA

Küblis

Samnaun

Prättigau
Valley

N28

Fünf
Dörfer

A13

6

Gotschnagrat
(2285m)
Weissfluh
(2844m)

Weissfluh
(2653m)

Klosters
Selfranga

Wolfgang
Davos

7

Weisshorn
(2653m)

Arosa
Hörnli (2496m)

Piz Buin
(3312m)

Pischahorn
(2980m)

Bos-cha

Guarda

Vereina
Tunnel

Lavin

Motta
Naluns
Ftan

N27

Scuol
Vulpera

Schloss
Tarasp

Untersengadin

Inn
River

Domleschg

A13

Valbella

Parpaner
Rothorn
(2865m)

Lenzerheide

Schiesshorn
(2605m)

Jakobshorn
(2590m)

N28

Flüela
Pass

Rinerhorn
(2528m)

Sagliains
Susch

Zernez

Thusis
Via
Mala
Tiefencastel
Zillis

Lenz

Wiesen

Filisur

Monstein

Chamanna
Cluozza

Il Fuorn

Ofen
Pass

N28

Müstair

4

Andeer

Bergün

Savognin

Albulatal

Parc
Ela

N3

Albula
Pass

Oberengadin

N27

S-chanf
Zuoz
La Punt

Swiss
National
Park

Alp
Trupchun

Val Müstair

Piz Nair
(3057m)

Celerina
St Moritz

Samedan

Muottas Muragl (2453m)
Piz Languard (3262m)

Bivio

Julier Pass

3

Val Bernina

Pontresina

ITALY

Silvaplana
Sils-Maria

Juf

September
Pass

Maloja

Morteratsch
Surlej

Val Fex

Diavolezza
(2973m)

Piz Lagalb
(2959m)

N29

Casaccia

Maloja
Pass

Val
Bregaglia

Piz
Corvatsch
(3451m)

Bernina
Pass

Alp Grüm
(2091m)

Soglio

N3

Piz
Bernina
(4049m)

Val Poschiavo

Poschiavo

Lago di
Poschiavo

Grosotto

Castasegna

Stampa
Promontogno

Chiavenna

Pizzo Badile
(3308m)

Brusio

ITALY

ITALY

1 Graubünden

2 Lugano

3 St Moritz

4 Müstair

5 Lago Maggiore

6 Chur

7 Davos

N

0   10 km
0   6 miles

St Moritz, Graubünden & the Southeast's Highlights

① Graubünden Outdoors

Hundreds of miles of ski runs lace the mountains of this vertiginous canton, and no skill or desire is not catered for. Resorts include the fabled Klosters and Laax, which is one of the top Swiss resorts for snowboarders. In summer, the country's only national park offers natural wonder.

Need to Know

BEST TIME TO VISIT Winter's obvious; summer for exploring the countryside. **TOP TIP** Reserve Glacier Express seats ahead in high season. **For further coverage, see p242.**

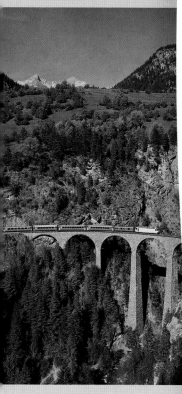

Graubünden Outdoors Don't Miss List

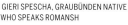

GIERI SPESCHA, GRAUBÜNDEN NATIVE
WHO SPEAKS ROMANSH

1 WILDLIFE WATCHING

Wander through the biggest conservation areas in Switzerland, the **Swiss National Park** (p247), which is Switzerland's only national park and one of the best-protected natural environments in Europe. The Alpine landscape remains much the same as it was 5000 years ago. The best place for watching deer is **Val Trupchun**, where you can witness the rutting season in September.

2 RIDING THE GLACIER EXPRESS

Travel through spectacular scenery on panoramic train coaches on the **Glacier Express** (p245), which transports you through the Alpine heartland from St Moritz to Zermatt.

3 RHINE GORGE

A real treat for nature lovers and white-water river rafting enthusiasts, this imposing gorge is often called Switzerland's **Little Grand Canyon**, and has boundless beauty. It's about 5km north of Laax.

4 LAAX: FREESTYLE PARADISE

Hone your existing skills and try out new ones in areas geared to every skill at **Laax's mountain bike areas** (p251). Challenge yourself on log rides and stone and root sections on the downhill and freeride runs through the region. In winter Laax more than lives up to its winter sports reputation. In addition to Europe's first Freestyle Indoor Base, there are **four snowparks** offering something for all ability levels. Everything is possible – be it initial attempts in the Beginner Park, getting a feel for the kickers and rails, jibbing with ease, maxing out in the Ils Plauns Park or perfecting style.

5 HORSE-DRAWN CARRIAGE RIDE

Enjoy a fun horse-drawn carriage ride through the **Klosters countryside** (p250). It's especially romantic in winter to snuggle up under blankets beneath the night sky and then enjoy a fondue afterwards.

Lugano Region

Italian flair is never far away in the canton of Ticino and that's especially true in its main city of Lugano (p255). With sun-washed villas lining its namesake lake, Lugano makes a good starting point for excursions across the water and over the mountains of the region. Bottom right: Bellinzona's Castelgrande (p254)

Need to Know

BEST TIME TO VISIT
Beautiful weather starts sooner and lasts longer in temperate Lugano – April to October at least. Winter can be bleak. **For further coverage, see p255.**

Lugano Region Don't Miss List

PATRICIA CARMINATI,
GUIDE

1 MARKET FOOD & PARKS

Visit Lugano's **street market** (Tuesday, Friday and Saturday) and at lunch time, do as local people do – buy some polenta with gorgonzola cheese sold by one local farmer who cooks it on **Piazza della Riforma** (p257). Take it away and go to **Ciani Park** where you can eat under the trees with a wonderful view of the lake. After lunch, relax at the 'Park and read' open-air library where you can borrow a book and a comfortable chair.

2 BOAT & SWIM LAKE LUGANO

Take a **boat** (p259) to **Cantine di Gandria**; after 20 minutes you will be on the opposite shore of the lake. You can swim in the clear waters of Lake Lugano and then enjoy a typical lunch in one of the grottos there.

3 TREKKING

If you like trekking, take the cable car to **Monte Brè** and then walk to **Monte Boglia** (this is only one of the many trekking paths in the Lugano area). Don't miss the lakeside Gandria walking path, which takes about one hour, and is nice and easy.

4 BELLINZONA'S CASTLES

After 30 minutes by train from Lugano, you get to **Bellinzona** (p253) with its three medieval **castles**. If possible, travel here on Saturday morning when the colourful **food market** takes place, people speak dialect and farmers sell their products from the valleys. Enjoy the local atmosphere and the market menu (restaurants offer low-priced menus on Saturdays that feature food made with seasonal local products), then discover *bissolo*, a typical chocolate of Bellinzona (chestnut paste covered with chocolate) that is sold in two local bakeries.

5 TRAIN TO CASLANO

Take the little orange train in front of Lugano's train station to the nearby village of **Caslano**. Here you'll find local handicrafts. Afterwards, you can go trekking around **Monte Caslano** or swim in the lake.

Skiing St Moritz

The world's original ski resort hasn't lost a step (or should we say a slalom) over the decade. St Moritz (p242) continues to draw the famous but it's still a place where they rub shoulder with humbler folks just there for the incredible skiing. After dark, the nightlife is some of the best in the country.

3

4 ## Müstair & Hidden Villages

Müstair (p248) is nearly lost on the border with Italy. It's a fine reminder of how Switzerland has always been in the way of somebody trying to get from here to there. Charlemagne may well have taken time out from taking over Europe to found a monastery here in the 8th century. And there are more villages awaiting your discovery (p249).

Lago Maggiore

Most of the beautiful waters of Lake Maggiore (p259) stretch into Italy but right at the top is Locarno. Here you can stroll the Città Vecchia, the city's Old Town, and easily mistake it for Lombardy to the south. Head out on the water and enjoy views of palm trees along the sun-drenched shore. Back on land, tuck into the region's fine cuisine.

5

GLENN VAN DER KNIJFF / GETTY IMAGES ©

MICHAEL TUREK / GETTY IMAGES ©

Chur

6

Chur (p248) is the oldest city in the nation, with a history dating back 5000 years. You can feel some of those centuries in St Martinskirche, which dates back to the 8th. Meanwhile you keep catching glimpses of beautiful Alpine backdrops as you wander the Old Town. Feet a little tired? Catch a train 15 minutes to the famous spa at Bad Ragaz (p250).

Winter Davos

7

Every January, Davos (p251) makes the news when world luminaries gather to think big thoughts and make proclamations. Important stuff yes, but everyone would have more fun if they did the smart thing and hit the slopes. Davos may not have quite the fabled rep as its resort sibling St Moritz but it counters with some of the best ski runs in a nation of incredible ski runs.

St Moritz, Graubünden & the Southeast's Best...

Natural Spots

- **Müstair** (p248) Hidden away near the Italian border is this Unesco-listed treasure.

- **Swiss National Park** (p247) See the raw, natural side of Switzerland.

- **Lago di Lugano** (p259) Cruise the beautiful lake by boat while spotting palm trees on the shore.

- **Klosters** (p250) More than 700km of footpaths radiate out through one perfect Alpine vista after another.

Food & Drink

- **Lugano** (p258) You'll be spoiled for choice, but lake fish with Italian flavours are tops with regional wines.

- **Locarno** (p260) The place for Italian-flavoured fare; try anything with polenta.

- **St Moritz** (p244) In season the range of cafes, restaurants and bars is dizzying – and it's not the altitude.

- **Davos** (p252) Draws Italian inspiration from Ticino plus there are plenty of hearty mountain meals that are perfect post-ski.

Skiing

- **St Moritz** (p242) Famous for being famous, and also for fantastic skiing.

- **Davos** (p251) If you can take your eyes off the fabled powder, you'll see magnificent scenery in all five ski areas.

- **Pontresina** (p245) Shares many of St Moritz' pistes but also has its own stunners.

- **Madrisa** (p250) The sweet spot of the region's skiing is accessible from Davos and Klosters.

Need to Know

Beautiful Towns

○ **Bellinzona** (p253) Fortresses and castles dominate this strategic old town at the confluence of valleys.

○ **Pontresina** (p245) Lovely old 13th-century town a beautiful train ride away from St Moritz.

○ **Chur** (p248) Old fortress towers still protect the Old Town and its cobblestone streets.

○ **Klosters** (p250) What a mountain Swiss village should look like – and it's authentically so.

ADVANCE PLANNING

○ **Four months before** Book your rooms for peak-season winter-sports fun at the big-name resort towns like St Moritz, Klosters and Davos. Otherwise, the region is so relaxed that you can just turn up and enjoy.

RESOURCES

○ **Graubünden Tourism** (www.graubuenden.ch) Tourism info across the canton.

○ **Ticino Tourism** (www.ticino.ch) Tourism info across the canton.

○ **Wine** A big part of the Ticino experience is wine; get the *Le Strade del Vino* map-guide at tourist offices, which details wineries around the canton.

GETTING AROUND

○ **Train** Some of Switzerland's most famous and beautiful railways can be found in this region, including Rhätische Bahn's Glacier Express and the Bernina Express (p249) over the Bernina Pass. Otherwise, all the main towns are well-served by trains.

○ **Cable Cars & Gondolas** Like their brethren to the north, the Alps in this region are laced by cables conveying people to dizzying heights for dizzying views as well as superb hiking and skiing.

BE FOREWARNED

○ **Shoulder season** When it's not summer and prime time for hiking and other outdoor pleasures, or winter sports time (December to April), resort towns such as St Moritz all but shut down (May and November can be very quiet). A few places in St Moritz do stay open for people arriving off the Glacier Express.

○ **Davos** The World Economic Forum – which only adds to the region's peak ski-season mania in late January – has spawned other forums through the year that can soak up rooms like a sponge. Check dates here: www.weforum.org.

Left: Glacier Express (p245);
Above: Lakeside Lugano (p255)

St Moritz, Graubünden & the Southeast Itineraries

Spend days exploring the many pleasures – visual and edible – in Ticino, Switzerland's Italian side. Then enjoy the contrasts of Graubünden, where the raw beauty of nature is punctuated by posh world-famous resorts.

3 DAYS — **BELLINZONA TO LOCARNO**
Ticino

If the French accent of Valais comes as a surprise for many who think of Switzerland in purely Germanic terms, the Italian accent *and* flavour of Ticino will come as a very lovely surprise. Start in **(1) Bellinzona**, which lies at a confluence of lakes and is dominated by fortresses that date back to Roman times. Head up the suitably named **Castelgrande** (Grand Castle!) and survey your domain. Next up is **Castello di Montebello**, which ticks off every necessary castle feature right down to the drawbridge. Finally hike up to the most formidable castle: **Castello di Sasso Corbaro**.

Next up is **(2) Lugano**. Beautifully set on its namesake lake, its sinuous streets are ideal for wandering, lined with shops and restaurants, and punctuated by the odd little square with cafes. Stop and get drawn into the richly detailed frescoes at **Chiesa di Santa Maria degli Angioli**, then board a **boat** for a trip on the water. When the spirit moves you, pause for some delicious local fare.

Finally, don't even bother counting the palm trees in **(3) Locarno** – it's just about the sunniest Swiss destination and the perfect place to put your motor in neutral.

CHUR TO ST MORITZ
Graubünden

Viewing Alps all around you is reason enough to visit **(1) Chur**. The evocative Old Town and great restaurants are just a bonus. Given you're on holiday, you should try to be as relaxed as possible, and an afternoon spent letting your cares bubble away at the spa at **(2) Bad Ragaz** will be well worth it. Whether it's winter or summer, you'll find plenty to keep tension from returning at **(3) Klosters**: the skiing and hiking here and at nearby **(4) Davos** are legendary. While Davos is renowned for its high-profile World Economic Forum, Klosters retains a rural Swiss mountain-chalet flavour with an overlay of posh.

Leave the luxe behind and head over the Flüela Pass (one of many spectacular mountain passes in the region) to little **(5) Zernez**. This tidy rural village is the gateway to the **(6) Swiss National Park**, where you can get close to raw Alpine nature in this beautiful but manicured country.

Once you've had your fill of marmots, you can shift gears and make the short jaunt to the most fabled Swiss resort of them all: **(7) St Moritz**. The myriad pleasures range from the natural to the sybaritic. Enjoy!

Castelgrande (p254), Bellinzona
PAOLO CORDELLI / GETTY IMAGES ©

Discover St Moritz, Graubünden & the Southeast

View of the lake at St Moritz
MASSIMO RIPANI / 4CORNERS ©

ST MORITZ

POP 5200 / ELEV 1856M

Switzerland's original winter wonderland and the cradle of Alpine tourism, St Moritz (San Murezzan in Romansch) has been luring royals, celebrities and moneyed wannabes since 1864. With its shimmering aquamarine lake, emerald forests and aloof mountains, the town looks a million dollars.

Yet despite the string of big-name designer boutiques on Via Serlas and celebs bashing the pistes (Kate Moss and George Clooney included), this resort isn't all show. The real riches lie outdoors with superb carving on Corviglia, hairy black runs on Diavolezza and miles of hiking trails when the snow melts.

Activities

Winter Activities

With 350km of slopes, ultramodern lifts and spirit-soaring views, skiing in St Moritz is second to none, especially for confident intermediates. For groomed slopes with big mountain vistas, head to **Corviglia** (2486m), accessible by funicular from Dorf. From Bad a cable car goes to **Signal** (shorter queues), giving access to the slopes of Piz Nair. There's varied skiing at **Corvatsch** (3303m), above nearby Silvaplana, including spectacular glacier descents and the gentle black run Hahnensee. Silhouetted by glaciated four-thousanders, **Diavolezza** (2978m) is a must-ski for freeriders and fans of jaw-dropping descents. A general ski pass that covers all the slopes, including Silvaplana, Sils-Maria, Celerina, Zuoz, Pon-

St Moritz

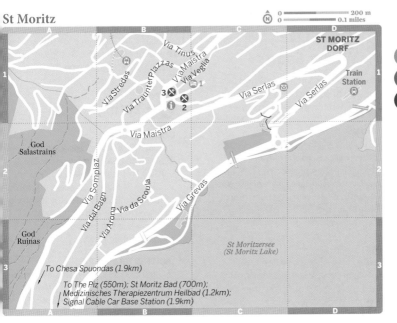

St Moritz map. Scale: 0 – 200 m / 0 – 0.1 miles. ST MORITZ DORF, Train Station, St Moritzersee (St Moritz Lake), God Salastrains, God Ruinas. Streets: Via Tinus, Via Maistra, Via Veglia, Via Stredas, Via Trauterplazzas, Via Serlas, Via Maistra, Via Somplaz, Via dal Bagn, Via Arona, Via da Scuola, Via Grevas. To Chesa Spuondas (1.9km); To The Piz (550m); St Moritz Bad (700m); Medizinisches Therapiezentrum Heilbad (1.2km); Signal Cable Car Base Station (1.9km).

tresina and Diavolezza, costs Sfr410/137 for adults/children for seven days in high season. Visit the website www.engadin.stmoritz.ch for the low-down on skiing facilities and services.

Skiing or snowboarding group tuition (adult/child Sfr85/55 per day) can be arranged at the **Schweizer Skischule** (☎081 830 01 01; www.skischool.ch; Via Stredas 14; ⏰8am-noon & 2-6pm Mon-Sat, 8-9am & 4-6pm Sun).

Summer Activities

In summer, get out and stride one of the region's excellent hiking trails, such as the Corvatsch *Wasserweg* (water trail) linking six mountain lakes. Soaring above St Moritz, **Piz Nair** (3057m) commands views of the jewel-coloured lakes that necklace the valley below.

MEDIZINISCHES
THERAPIEZENTRUM HEILBAD   Spa
(☎081 833 30 62; www.heilbad-stmoritz.ch; Plazza Paracelsus 2; admission to mineral baths Sfr35; ⏰8am-7pm Mon-Fri, 8am-12.30pm Sat) After exerting yourself on the slopes, rest

St Moritz

⌂ Sleeping
1 Hotel Eden C1

⊗ Eating
2 Chesa Veglia B1
3 Hatecke B1

in a mineral bath or with an Alpine herb pack here.

 Sleeping

CHESA SPUONDAS   Family Hotel $$
(☎081 833 65 88; www.chesaspuondas.ch; r incl half board Sfr202-282; P @) This family hotel nestles amid lush meadows at the foot of forest and mountains. Rooms are in keeping with the Jugendstil villa, with high ceilings, parquet floors and the odd antique. Kids are the centre of attention here, with dedicated meal times, activities, play areas and the children's ski school a 10-minute walk away. Bus 1 from St Moritz stops nearby.

If You Like... Winter Sports

If you like the skiing action you'll find at big names like St Moritz (p242), you might also like these winter sports havens:

1 CELERINA

Sunny Celerina is a 45-minute amble northeast of St Moritz and shares the same ski slopes. It's known for its 1.6km **Olympic bob run** (📞081 830 02 00; www.olympia-bobrun.ch), which is the world's oldest – dating to 1904 – and made from natural ice. A 135km/h run costs Sfr250, but the buzz is priceless.

2 LAAX

(www.laax.com) A snowboarding mecca, Laax boasts both Europe's smallest and largest half-pipe, excellent freestyle parks and many off-piste opportunities. Skiers are equally content to bash 220km of slopes at several interlinked resorts. Slaloming downhill, you'll probably spy the unfortunately named Crap da Flem (*crap* means 'peak' in Romansch). Laax is also a hotspot for mountain biking. Postal buses make the 20km run from Chur in the east.

3 AROSA

(www.arosa.ch) Beginner and intermediate skiers enjoy 70km of red and blue runs, rising as high as Weisshorn at 2653m. Big air fans should check out the half-pipe and fun park. Reach Arosa from Chur: take the hourly narrow-gauge train (Sfr14.20, one hour). It's a lovely, winding journey.

HOTEL EDEN   Hotel $$

(📞081 830 81 00; www.edenstmoritz.ch; Via Veglia 12; s Sfr159-186, d Sfr266-314; P 🛜) Right in the heart of town, the Eden cen-tres on an attractive central atrium and antique-strewn lounge where a fire crack-les in winter. The old-style, pine-panelled rooms are cosy and those on the top floor afford terrific lake and mountain views.

JUGENDHERBERGE ST MORITZ Hostel $

(📞081 836 61 11; Via Surpunt 60; www.youth hostel.ch/st.moritz; dm/d Sfr59/146; P 🛜)

On the edge of the forest, this hostel has clean, quiet four-bed dorms and doubles. There's a kiosk, children's toy room, bike hire and laundrette. Bus 9 stops in front of the hostel in high season.

 Eating

CHESA VEGLIA   Italian $$$

(📞081 837 28 00; Via Veglia 2; pizza Sfr22-36, mains Sfr40-70, 🕐Mon-Sun Dec-Mar & Jul-Sep) This slate-roofed, chalk-white chalet is St Moritz' oldest restaurant, dating from 1658. The softly lit interior is all warm pine and creaking wood floors, while the terrace affords lake and mountain views.

MATHIS BRASSERIE   Swiss $$

(📞081 833 63 55; www.mathisfood.ch; Cor-viglia; mains Sfr22.50-36.50; 🕐Mon-Sun) Swiss celebrity chef Reto Mathis has seriously upped the ante in slope-side dining. Spectacularly perched at 2486m, this panoramic brasserie is the most casual of his culinary ventures. Enjoy wide-screen mountain views over fresh pasta, rösti or polenta with venison sausage.

HATECKE   Cafe $

(Via Maistra 16; snacks & mains Sfr15-25; 🕐9am-6.30pm Mon-Fri, to 6pm Sat) Organic, locally sourced *Bündnerfleisch* and melt-in-your-mouth venison ham are carved into wafer-thin slices on a century-old slicing machine in this speciality shop. Take a seat on a sheepskin stool in the cafe next door to lunch on delicious En-gadine beef carpaccio or *Bündnerfleisch* with truffle oil.

ℹ Information

Uphill from the lakeside train station on Via Serlas is the post office, and five minutes further on is the **tourist office** (📞081 837 33 33; www. stmoritz.ch; Via Maistra 12; 🕐9am-6.30pm Mon-Fri, 9am-12.30pm & 1.30-6.30pm Sat, 4-6pm Sun in peak season, shorter hours rest of year). Audioguide city tours are available for Sfr10.

ⓘ Getting There & Away

St Moritz Bad is about 2km southwest of the main town, St Moritz Dorf. Local buses and postal buses shuttle between the two.

The Glacier Express (www.glacierexpress.ch) links St Moritz to Zermatt (adult/child Sfr136/68) via the 2033m Oberalp Pass. The majestic route takes 7½ hours to cover the 290km and crosses 291 bridges. Seat reservation costs an additional Sfr33 in summer and Sfr13 in winter.

Regular trains, as many as one every 30 minutes, run from Zürich to St Moritz (Sfr70, 3½ hours) with one change (at Landquart or Chur).

BERNINA PASS ROAD

Bare, brooding mountains and glaciers that sweep down to farmland give the landscape around the Bernina Pass (2323m; Passo del Bernina in Italian) austere grandeur. The road twists spectacularly from Celerina southeast to Tirano in Italy, linking Val Bernina and Val Poschiavo.

From St Moritz, as many as 10 trains run via Pontresina (Sfr5, 10 minutes) direct to Tirano (Sfr33, 2½ hours) in northern Italy. This stretch of track, known as the **Bernina Line** (www.rhb-Unesco.ch), was added to the Unesco World Heritage list in 2008 along with the Albula Pass. Constructed in 1910, it is one of the world's steepest narrow-gauge railways, negotiating the highest rail crossing in Europe and taking in spectacular glaciers, gorges and rock pinnacles.

Pontresina & Around
POP 2000 / ELEV 1800M

At the mouth of the Val Bernina and licked by the ice-white tongue of Morteratsch Glacier, Pontresina is a low-key alternative to St Moritz. Check out the pentagonal Moorish tower and the Santa Maria Chapel, with frescos dating from the 13th and 15th centuries.

Pontresina's own mountain, **Piz Languard** (3262m), is well suited to families and novice skiers. Use the resort as a base to explore slopes further down the valley at **Piz Lagalb** (2959m) and **Diavolezza** (2973m), with its phenomenal 10km glacier descent. In summer, it's worth taking the cable cars to either for views. The walk from Diavolezza to Morteratsch affords striking glacier close-ups.

The legendary slopes of Graubünden

❶ Information

From the train station, west of the village, cross the two rivers, Rosegg and Bernina, for the centre and the tourist office (📞081 838 83 00; www.pontresina.ch; Rondo Bldg, Via Maistra; ⏰8.30am-6pm Mon-Fri, 8.30am-noon & 3-6pm Sat & 3-6pm Sun, closed Sun mid-Oct–mid-Dec).

THE ENGADINE

The almost-3000km-long Inn River (En in Romansch) springs up from the snowy Graubünden Alps around the Maloja Pass and gives its name to the Engadine. The valley is carved into two: the Oberengadin (Upper Engadine), from Maloja to Zernez; and the Unterengadin (Lower Engadine), stretching from Zernez to Martina, by the Austrian border.

Oberengadin is dominated by the ritzy ski resort of St Moritz, while Unterengadin, home to the country's only national park, is characterised by quaint villages with sgraffito-decorated houses and pristine countryside.

Zernez
POP 1100 / ELEV 1474M

One of the main gateways to the Swiss National Park, Zernez is an attractive cluster of stone chalets, outlined by the profile of its baroque church and the stout medieval tower of its castle, Schloss Wildenberg.

The village is home to the hands-on **Swiss National Park Centre** (📞081 851 41 41; www.nationalpark.ch; adult/child Sfr7/3; ⏰8.30am-6pm Jun-Oct, 9am-noon & 2-5pm Nov-May), where an audioguide gives you the low-down on conservation, wildlife and environmental change.

🛏 Sleeping & Eating

HOTEL BÄR & POST   Hotel $$
(📞081 851 55 00; www.baer-post.ch; Zernez; dm Sfr19, s Sfr87-115, d Sfr140-220) Welcoming all-comers since 1905, these central digs have inviting rooms with lots of stone pine and downy duvets, plus basic bunk rooms. There's also a sauna and a rustic restaurant (mains Sfr15 to Sfr43), dishing up good steaks and pasta.

Skiier on the lower slopes of Piz Nair, above St Moritz

MARTIN MOOS / GETTY IMAGES ©

Don't Miss Swiss National Park

The Engadine's pride and joy is the **Swiss National Park** (www.nationalpark.ch), easily accessed from villages such as Scuol, Zernez and S-chanf. Created in 1914 and spanning 172 sq km, Switzerland's only national park is a nature-gone-wild swathe of dolomitic peaks, shimmering glaciers, larch woodlands, pastures, waterfalls and high moors strung with topaz-blue lakes. It's a remote and totally enchanting place to step off the beaten track for a few days. Bear in mind that the park goes into hibernation in winter.

Still largely untouched, the park is a glimpse of the Alps before the dawn of tourism. Some 80km of well-marked hiking trails lead through the park, where, with a little luck and a decent pair of binoculars, ibex, chamois, marmots and golden eagles can be sighted. The **National Park Centre** (☎ 081 851 41 41; www.nationalpark.ch; ◷ 8.30am-6pm Jun-Oct, 9am-noon & 2-5pm Nov-May) in Zernez should be your first port of call for information on activities and accommodation. It sells an excellent 1:50,000 park map (Sfr20), which covers 21 different walks through the park.

Entry to the park and its car parks is free. Conservation is paramount here, so stick to footpaths and respect regulations prohibiting camping, littering, lighting fires, cycling, picking flowers and disturbing the animals.

IL FUORN Guesthouse $$
(☎ 081 856 12 26; www.ilfuorn.ch; Il Fuorn; s/d/tr/q Sfr95/150/195/220; ◷ mid-Jun–Oct) Bang in the heart of the national park, this guesthouse shelters light, comfy rooms with pine furnishings. Fresh trout and game are big on the restaurant menu.

ⓘ **Getting There & Away**

Trains run regularly from Zernez to St Moritz (Sfr18, 50 minutes), stopping at S-chanf, Zuoz and Celerina. For the latter and St Moritz, change at Samedan.

Detour: Müstair

Squirreled away in a remote corner of Switzerland, just before the Italian border, Müstair is one of Europe's early Christian treasures and a Unesco World Heritage Site. When Charlemagne supposedly founded a monastery and a church here in the 8th century, this was a strategically placed spot below the Ofen Pass, separating northern Europe from Italy and the heart of Christendom.

Vibrant Carolingian (9th century) and Romanesque (12th century) frescos smother the interior of the church of Benedictine **Kloster St Johann** (St John's Convent; www.muestair.ch; admission free; ☉7am-8pm May-Oct, 7am-5pm Nov-Apr).

Postal buses run along the valley between Zernez and Müstair (Sfr20.20, one hour).

CHUR

POP 33,400 / ELEV 585M

The Alps rise like an amphitheatre around Chur, Switzerland's oldest city, inhabited since 3000 BC. Linger more than an hour or two and you'll soon warm to the capital of Graubünden.

⊙ Sights & Activities

ALTSTADT Neighbourhood
Near the Plessur River, the **Obertor** marks the main medieval entrance to Chur's cobblestone Old Town. Alongside the stout **Maltesertor** (once the munitions tower), and the **Sennhofturm** (nowadays the city's prison), it's all that remains of the old defensive walls.

The city's most iconic landmark is **St Martinskirche** (Kirchgasse 12) with its distinctive spire and clock face. The 8th-century church was rebuilt in the late-Gothic style in 1491 and is dramatically lit by a trio of Augusto Giacometti stained-glass windows. St Martin presides over a burbling stone fountain in front of the church.

Follow Kirchgasse uphill to reach **Kathedrale St Maria Himmelfahrt** (Hof; ☉6am-7pm Mon-Sat, 7am-7pm Sun), a 12th-century cathedral with a late 1400s Jakob Russ high altar containing a splendid triptych.

🛏 Sleeping

ROMANTIK HOTEL STERN Historic Hotel $$
(☎081 258 57 57; www.stern-chur.ch; Reichsgasse 11; s/d Sfr150/290; 🅿@🛜) Part of Switzerland's romantic clan, this centuries-old hotel has kept its flair, with vaulted corridors and low-ceilinged, pine-filled rooms. Call ahead and they'll pick you up from the station in a 1933 Buick.

ZUNFTHAUS ZUR REBLEUTEN Historic Hotel $
(☎081 255 11 44; www.rebleuten.ch; Pfisterplatz 1; s Sfr70-85, d Sfr128-148) Housed in an imposing frescoed building on a pretty square, the Zunfthaus zur Rebleuten looks proudly back on 500 years of history. The 12 rooms are fresh and inviting. Especially romantic (watch your head) are those in the loft.

🍴 Eating

BÜNDNER STUBE Swiss $$
(☎081 258 57 57; Reichsgasse 11; mains Sfr25-42; ☉lunch & dinner Mon-Sun) Candlelight and wood panelling create a warm atmos

248

phere in Romantik Hotel Stern's highly regarded restaurant. The chef keeps it fresh and seasonal, serving asparagus in spring, game in autumn. Bündner specialities like *Capuns, Maluns* and *Gerstensuppe* are beautifully cooked and presented.

HOFKELLEREI Swiss $$
(📞081 252 32 30; Hof 1; mains Sfr19-39; 🕐lunch & dinner Tue-Sun) Wooden floorboards creak as you enter this vaulted Gothic restaurant. Take a pew to feast on regional flavours like *Pizokel* with plums and *Capuns* under the wrought-iron chandeliers.

Shopping

KERAMIK RUTH Handicrafts
(Obere Gasse 31; 🕐1.30-5.30pm Tue & Thu, 11am-4pm Sat) Ruth displays her sweet-shop-bright pottery at this hobbit-sized shop – from hand-thrown pots to polka-dotty teapots.

RÄTISCHE GERBEREI Handicrafts
(Engadinstrasse 30; 🕐1.30-6.30pm Mon, 8am-noon & 1.30-6pm Tue-Fri) Upstairs are mountains of fluffy sheepskins, downstairs are genuine cowbells for a fraction of the price you'd pay elsewhere.

ⓘ Information

Tourist office (📞081 252 18 18; www.chur tourismus.ch; Bahnhofplatz 3; 🕐7.30am-8pm Mon-Fri, 8am-6pm Sat & Sun) Has stacks of info and maps on the region and can arrange city tours.

ⓘ Getting There & Away

There are rail connections to Klosters (Sfr21, 1¼ hours) and Davos (Sfr27, 1½ hours), and fast trains to Sargans (Sfr10.40, 20 minutes), with onward connections to Liechtenstein and Zürich (Sfr38, 1¼ to 1½ hours). Postal buses leave from the terminus above the train station.

Chur is the departure point for one of Switzerland's most memorable rail journeys, the **Bernina Express** (www.rhb.ch) to Lugano.

♥ If You Like... Villages

If you like the beautiful ancient town of Müstair (p248), you'll love these little Swiss villages with their timeless charms:

1 GUARDA
With its twisting cobbled streets and hobbitlike houses in candy shades, Guarda has storybook appeal. Six kilometres east of Susch, Guarda is a 30-minute uphill hike from its valley-floor train station, or you can take the hourly postal bus (Sfr3).

2 MAIENFELD
Dominated by a colourfully frescoed Rathaus (town hall) and haughty church, it's worth hanging out for the local cuisine and wine from the surrounding vineyards. Catch a train from Chur (Sfr7.80, 15 minutes).

3 MORCOTE
With its narrow cobbled lanes and endless nooks and crannies, this peaceful former fishing village on Lake Lugano clusters at the foot of Monte Abostora. Narrow steps lead 15 minutes uphill to Chiesa di Santa Maria del Sasso, which commands dazzling lake views. Get here on a postal bus from Lugano.

The four-hour route takes in 55 tunnels and 196 bridges. A one-way ticket costs Sfr82; seat reservation is an additional Sfr12/9 in summer/winter.

KLOSTERS & DAVOS

Following the N28 road east from Landquart, you enter the broad Prättigau Valley, which stretches east to . Several valley roads spike off the highway before Klosters, and the one leading to **St Antönien** is the most attractive. This high Alpine country is punctuated by villages and burned-wood Walser houses raised by this rural folk since migrating here from eastern Valais from the 13th century onward.

Detour:
Bad Ragaz

After days enjoying hikes or downhill runs, take your weary bones to the graceful little spa town of Bad Ragaz (population 530), a couple of kilometres west of Maienfeld, which opened in 1840.

Bad Ragaz' ultra-sleek **Tamina Therme** (☎081 303 27 40; www.taminatherme.ch; Hans-Albrecht-Strasse; day ticket adult/child Sfr34/21; ⊙8am-10pm Mon-Sun, to 11pm Fri), a couple of kilometres south of town, has several pools for wallowing in the 34°C thermal waters, as well as massage jets, whirlpools, saunas and an assortment of treatments and massages.

Bad Ragaz is on the Chur–Zürich train line. Trains from Chur via Maienfeld run hourly (Sfr8.40, 15 minutes).

Klosters

POP 3900 / ELEV 1194M

No matter whether you come in summer to hike in the flower-speckled mountains or in winter when the log chalets are veiled in snow and icicle-hung – Klosters is postcard stuff. Indeed, the village has attracted a host of slaloming celebrities and royals with its chocolate-box looks and paparazzi-free slopes.

 **Activities**

Winter Activities

Davos and Klosters share 320km of ski runs, covered by the Regional Pass (adult/child/youth Sfr69/28/48 per day), as well as some glorious off-piste terrain. **Parsenn** beckons confidence-building novices, while experts can tackle black runs like panoramic Schlappin and Gotschnawang. **Madrisa** is a great all-rounder, with long, sunny runs, mostly above the treeline for intermediates, a kids' club, tubing and skidoo park, and a fun park with kickers and rails.

Summer Activities

Hikers hit the trail on one of the region's 700km of well-maintained footpaths, which range from gentle family strolls to high- altitude, multiday treks. Would-be climbers can tackle the rope bridges and climbing trees at Madrisa.

🛏 Sleeping & Eating

GASTHAUS BARGIS   Guesthouse $$
(☎081 422 55 77; www.bargis.ch, in German; Kantonsstrasse 8; apt Sfr100-190) Erika is your kindly host at this quaint dark-wood chalet on the road into Klosters Dorf, run by the Ambühl family since the 18th century. The sunny, immaculate apartments brim with homely touches from ornamental ducks to open fireplaces. The pine-clad restaurant (mains Sfr24 to Sfr32.50, open from Wednesday to Sunday) is a cosy spot for Bündner specialities.

**HOTEL CHESA
GRISCHUNA**   Historic Hotel $$$
(☎081 422 22 22; www.chesagrischuna.ch; Bahnhofstrasse 12; s/d/ste Sfr259/439/549) An archetypal vision of a Swiss chalet, this family-run pad has toasty pine rooms with antique flourishes and ornately carved ceilings. The lantern-lit restaurant (mains Sfr42 to Sfr60) is an Alpine charmer, too.

ℹ Information

In the centre of the village is the tourist office (☎081 410 20 20; www.klosters.ch; Alte Bahnhofstrasse 6; ⊙8.30am-6pm Mon-Fri, 9am-6pm Sat, 9am-1pm Sun).

ⓘ Getting There & Away

Klosters is split into two sections. Klosters Platz is the main resort, grouped around the train station. Two kilometres to the left of the station is smaller Klosters Dorf and the Madrisa cable car.

See Davos for more info, as Klosters is on the same train route between Landquart and Filisur. Klosters and Davos are linked by free buses for those with Guest Cards or ski passes.

Davos

POP 11,300 / ELEV 1560M

Unlike its little sister Klosters, Davos is more cool than quaint. But what the resort lacks in Alpine prettiness, it makes up for with seductive skiing, including monster runs descending up to 2000m, and après-ski parties. It is also the annual meeting point for the crème de la crème of world capitalism, the World Economic Forum.

Davos comprises two contiguous areas, each with a train station: Davos Platz and the older Davos Dorf.

🤸 Activities

Winter Sports

Naturally blessed with awesome scenery and great powder, Davos has carved out a name for itself as a first-class skiing destination, with varied runs in five different areas. The vast **Parsenn** area reaches as high as Weissfluhjoch (2844m), from where you can ski to Küblis, more than 2000m lower and 12km away. Alternatively, take the demanding run to Wolfgang (1629m) or the scenic slopes to Klosters.

Summer Activities

Together, Davos and Klosters provide 700km of marked hiking paths and 600km of mountain bike tracks, including some challenging descents and single-track trails; see www.bike-davos.ch for routes, maps and rental outlets.

🛏 Sleeping

HOTEL ALPENHOF Hotel **$$**
(☏ 081 415 20 60; www.alpenhof-davos.ch; Hofstrasse 22; s/d Sfr148/276; 🛜) You'll feel right at home in the Alpenhof's light-filled rooms with chunky pine furnishings, downy duvets and DVD players. The restaurant places the emphasis on fresh, regional fare and has a kids' menu. Family reductions are available. The hotel is 1.5km south of the centre; buses 428 and 432 to Crestannes stop close by.

WALDHOTEL BELLEVUE Historic Hotel **$$$**
(☏ 081 415 15 15; www.waldhotel-bellevue. ch; Buolstrasse 3; s Sfr205-275, d Sfr390-460; 🅿🛜♨) The Magic Mountain in Thomas Mann's eponymous 1924 novel, this

Castello di Montebello (p253), Bellinzona
CRAIG PERSHOUSE / GETTY IMAGES ©

sanatorium turned hotel has recently been given a stylish facelift. Even standard rooms come with sunny balconies and luxuries like fruit, mineral water and bathrobes.

 Eating

HÄNGGI'S   Italian $$
(✆081 416 20 20; Mattastrasse 11; pizza Sfr16-26, mains Sfr33-51; ⊙lunch & dinner) Wood-fired pizza, crisp and delicious, is what this cosy beamed restaurant is known for. Or go for well-executed Italian-inspired dishes such as basil risotto with fresh tomatoes, market-fresh fish and tangy homemade sorbet.

BISTRO GENTIANA   Swiss $$
(✆081 413 56 49; Promenade 53; mains Sfr25-42; ⊙5-10.30pm Thu-Tue summer, 11am-2pm & 5pm-midnight Mon-Sun winter) This art deco bistro specialises in snails (*Schnecken*) and rich cheese fondues. A dish of six

juicy snails oven-cooked in mushroom heads costs Sfr29.80.

STRELA-ALP   Swiss $
(www.strela-alp.ch; mains Sfr15-30; ⊙9am-5pm Sun-Thu, 9am-11pm Fri & Sat) Expansive mountain views, a sunny terrace and Swiss grub like *rösti* and fondue await at this rustic haunt near Schatzalp funicular top station.

ⓘ Information
The most central branch of the **tourist office** (✆081 415 21 21; www.davos.ch; Bahnhofstrasse 8; ⊙8.30am-6.30pm Mon-Fri, 1-5pm Sat, 9am-1pm Sun) is in Davos Dorf. Hours are reduced in low season (spring and autumn).

ⓘ Getting There & Away
For trains to Chur (Sfr27, 1½ hours) or Zürich (Sfr52, 2½ hours), you will change at Landquart. For St Moritz (Sfr27, 1½ hours), take the train at Davos Platz and change at Filisur.

The Guest Card allows free travel on local buses and trains, as does the general ski pass (and the Swiss Pass).

TICINO

The summer air is rich and hot. Vespas scoot along palm-fringed promenades. A baroque campanile chimes. Italian weather. Italian style. And that's not to mention the Italian gelato, Italian pasta, Italian architecture, Italian language. It's Italy Swiss style, with the kinds of peaks and valleys commonly associated with the cantons to the north.

Bellinzona

POP 17,300 / ELEV 230M

Placed at the convergence point of several Alpine valleys, Bellinzona is visually unique. Inhabited since Neolithic times, it is dominated by three grey-stone medieval castles that have attracted everyone from Swiss invaders to painters like William Turner.

The main castle, Castelgrande, stands upon a rocky central hill, which was a Roman frontier post and Lombard defensive tower, and was later developed as a heavily fortified town controlled by Milan.

◉ Sights & Activities

The city's three imposing castles are the main draw. Read up on them at www.bellinzonaunesco.ch. To visit all three, get a general ticket (adult/concession Sfr10/4), valid indefinitely.

CASTELLO DI MONTEBELLO   Castle
(Salita ai Castelli; admission to castle free, museum adult/child Sfr5/2; ⊙ castle 8am-8pm mid-Mar–Oct, museum 10am-6pm mid-Mar–Oct)
On cloudless days, you can see Lago

CRAIG PERSHOUSE / GETTY IMAGES

Don't Miss Castelgrande

Rising dramatically above the Old Town, this medieval stronghold is Bellinzona's most visible icon. Head up Scalinata San Michele from Piazza della Collegiata, or take the lift, buried deep in the rocky hill in an extraordinary concrete bunker-style construction, from Piazza del Sole.

After wandering the grounds and the museum, stroll west along the **Murata** (admission free; ⊘10am-7pm), the castle's snaking ramparts, with photogenic views of vine-streaked mountains and castle-studded hills.

THINGS YOU NEED TO KNOW

Monte San Michele; admission to grounds free; ⊘9am-midnight Tue-Sun, to 6pm Mon

Maggiore from this 13th-century hilltop fortification. The fortress is one of Bellinzona's most impressive with its drawbridges, ramparts and small museum catapulting you back to medieval times.

CASTELLO DI SASSO CORBARO Castle (adult/child Sfr5/2; ⊘10am-6pm mid-Mar–Oct) From Castello di Montebello, it's a 3.5km climb to the last in Bellinzona's castle trilogy. Perched high on a wooded hillside, the castle is an austere beauty with its impenetrable walls and sturdy towers.

 **Sleeping**

Charming digs are few and far between. Many functional hotels are strung out along Viale della Stazione.

HOTEL INTERNAZIONALE Hotel $$
(☎091 825 43 33; www.hotel-internazionale.ch; Viale della Stazione 35; s Sfr135-150, d Sfr200-260, tr Sfr285-315; ✳🛜) Sitting opposite the train station, this candyfloss-pink hotel seamlessly blends turn-of-the-20th-century features like wrought iron and stained glass with streamlined 21st-

century design. Many of the light, contemporary rooms have castle views.

OSTELLO DELLA GIOVENTÙ   Hostel $
(☏091 825 15 22; www.youthhostel.ch/bellinzona; Via Nocca 4; dm Sfr38-41, s Sfr63-73, d Sfr94-100; ☎) Housed in Villa Montebello, at the foot of the eponymous castle, the youth hostel occupies what for 100 years was a high-class girls' school.

 Eating

RISTORANTE CASTEL GRANDE   Italian $$
(☏091 814 87 87; www.ristorantecastelgrande. ch; Castelgrande; mains Sfr35-60; ⊙lunch & dinner Tue-Sun) It's not often you get the chance to eat inside a Unesco World Heritage Site. The medieval castle setting alone is enough to bewitch. Seasonal Ticino specialities like guinea fowl in a chestnut-beer sauce with white polenta are married with top-notch wines.

GROTTO CASTELGRANDE   Italian $$
(☏091 814 87 87; Salita al Castelgrande; mains Sfr27-32; ⊙lunch & dinner Tue-Sun) For the best view of Bellinzona's castles illuminated, book a table on the vine-strewn terrace of this atmospheric vaulted cellar. Dishes like potato gnocchi with Ticino sausage and wild fennel strike a perfect balance.

ℹ Information

Tourist office (☏091 825 21 31; www.bellinzo naturismo.ch; Piazza Nosetto; ⊙9am-6.30pm Mon-Fri, to noon Sat) In the restored Renaissance Palazzo del Comune (town hall). Has city audioguides (Sfr7).

ℹ Getting There & Away

Bellinzona is on the train route connecting Locarno (Sfr8.40, 27 minutes) and Lugano (Sfr12.20, 30 minutes). It is also on the Zürich-Milan route. Up to six postal buses head northeast to Chur (Sfr49, 2¼ hours), departing from beside the train station.

Lugano
POP 55,100 / ELEV 270M

Ticino's lush, mountain-rimmed lake isn't its only liquid asset. The largest city in the canton is also the country's third most important banking centre. Suits

Great Rail Journeys

Graubünden's rugged, high-alpine terrain is harnessed by some of Switzerland's greatest railways. The panoramic **Rhätische Bahn** (Rhaetian Railway; www.rhb.ch) is a staggering feat of early 20th-century engineering, traversing viaducts and tunnels and commanding wide-screen views of forested slopes, jewel-coloured lakes and snowcapped peaks. See the website for advance bookings, seat reservations and special deals. The Half Fare, Swiss Card and Swiss Pass give substantial discounts.

    The Rhaetian Railway's two flagship routes are the Glacier Express (p245) and the Bernina Express (p249). The Glacier Express from St Moritz to Zermatt is a once-in-a-lifetime journey, scaling the Furka, Oberalp and Bernina passes, and taking in highlights such as the canyon-like Rhine Gorge and the six-arched, 65m-high Landwasser Viaduct. The Bernina Express from Chur to Lugano climbs high into the glaciated realms of the Alps and skirts Ticino's palm-fringed lakes. The stretch from Thusis to Tirano is a Unesco World Heritage Site.

Lugano

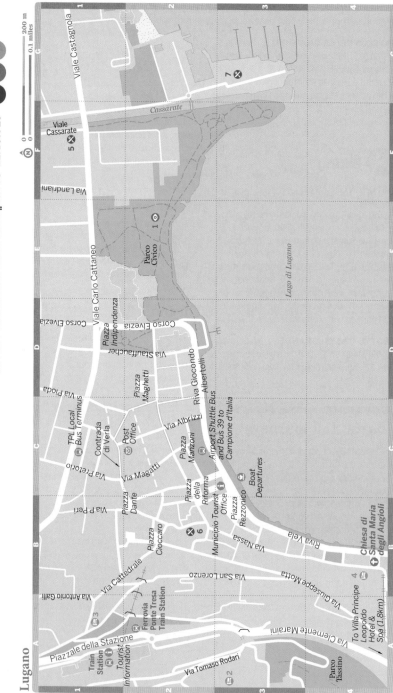

Lugano

aside, Lugano is a vivacious city, with chic boutiques, bars and pavement cafes huddling in the spaghetti maze of steep cobblestone streets that untangle at the edge of the lake and along the flowery promenade.

Sights

Take the stairs or the funicular (Sfr1.10, open 5.20am to 11.50pm) down to the centre, a patchwork of interlocking *piazze*. Porticoed lanes weave around the busy main square, Piazza della Riforma, which is presided over by the 1844 neoclassical Municipio (town hall) and is even more lively when the Tuesday and Friday morning markets are held.

CHIESA DI SANTA MARIA DEGLI ANGIOLI   Church
(St Mary of the Angels; Piazza Luini; ⊙7am-6pm) This simple Romanesque church contains two frescos by Bernardino Luini dating from 1529. Covering the entire wall that divides

the church in two is a grand didactic illustration of the crucifixion of Christ. The closer you look, the more scenes of Christ's Passion are revealed. The power and vivacity of the colours are astounding.

MUSEO DEL CIOCCOLATO ALPROSE   Museum
(www.alprose.ch; Via Rompada 36, Caslano; adult/child Sfr3/1; ⊙9am-5.30pm Mon-Fri, to 4.30pm Sat & Sun) Chomp into some cocoa culture at this choc-crazy museum – a sure-fire hit with kids. Whiz through chocolate history, watch the sugary substance being made and enjoy a free tasting. The shop, cunningly, stays open half an hour longer. Take the Ferrovia Ponte Tresa train (Sfr7).

LUNGOLAGO   Gardens
This lakefront promenade necklaces the shore of glassy Lago di Lugano, set against a backdrop of rugged mountains. Linden and chestnut trees provide welcome shade in summer, while tulips, camellias and magnolias bloom in spring.

Lago di Lugano (Lake Lugano; p259)
MARTIN MOOS / GETTY IMAGES ©

The flower-strewn centrepiece is **Parco Civico** (🕐6am-11pm; admission free), where peach-hued **Villa Ciani** (🕐10am-6pm Tue-Sun) hosts regular art exhibitions.

Activities

Swimming, sailing, wakeboarding and rowing on the lake, as well as hiking in the surrounding mountains and valleys, are popular summer pursuits – the tourist office has details.

🛏 Sleeping

Many hotels close for at least part of the winter.

HOTEL & HOSTEL MONTARINA
Hotel, Hostel $

(📞091 966 72 72; www.montarina.ch; Via Montarina 1; dm Sfr27, s Sfr80-90, d Sfr110-130; P🛜♨♿) Occupying a bubblegum-pink villa dating to 1860, this hotel and hostel duo extends a heartfelt welcome. Choose between the dorms in the vaulted basement, wood-floored antique rooms and contemporary rooms with private bathrooms.

VILLA PRINCIPE LEOPOLDO HOTEL & SPA
Historic Hotel $$$

(📞091 985 88 55; www.leopoldohotel.com; Via Montalbano 5; s Sfr510-670, d Sfr600-790; P❄🛜♨) This red-tiled residence set in sculptured gardens was built in 1926 for Prince Leopold von Hohenzollern, of the exiled German royal family. It oozes a regal, nostalgic atmosphere. The gardens and many of the splendid rooms offer lake views.

HOTEL INTERNATIONAL AU LAC
Historic Hotel $$

(📞091 922 75 41; www.hotel-international.ch; Via Nassa 68; s Sfr120-185, d Sfr195-330; 🕐Apr-Oct; P❄🛜♨) Choose a front room to gaze out across Lago di Lugano at this century-old hotel on the lakefront. Rooms are comfortable, with a smattering of antique furniture.

HOTEL FEDERALE
Hotel $$

(📞091 910 08 08; www.hotel-federale.ch; Via Paolo Regazzoni 8; s/d Sfr165/230; P🛜) If you can afford the grand top floor doubles with lake views, this curiously shaped pink place beats many multi-stellar places hands down. It's in a quiet spot with immaculately kept rooms, a restaurant with alfresco seating and a little fitness room.

🍴 Eating

AL PORTONE
Italian $$

(📞091 923 55 11; www.ristorantealportone.ch; Viale Cassarate 3; mains Sfr30-50; 🕐lunch & dinner Tue-Sat) Bold artworks grace this contemporary gourmet haunt. Here Silvio and Sabrina ply you with such creative delights as John Dory with beetroot pannacotta, and butter-soft veal shanks infused with pepper and grappa.

GRAND CAFÉ AL PORTO
Cafe $

(Via Pessina 3; light meals Sfr14-24, cakes Sfr4-6; 🕐8am-6.30pm Mon-Sat) Going strong since 1803, this cafe is the vision of old-world grandeur with its polished wood panelling and pineapple-shaped chandeliers. The tortes, pastries and fruit cakes are irresistible. Upstairs is the frescoed Cenacolo Fiorentino, once a monastery refectory.

L'ANTICA OSTERIA DEL PORTO
Italian $$

(📞091 971 42 00; Via Foce 9; mains Sfr29-35; 🕐lunch & dinner Wed-Mon) Set back from Lugano's sailing club, this is the place for local fish and Ticinese dishes like polenta crostini with porcini. The terrace overlooking the Cassarate stream is pleasant, as are the lake views.

 Shopping

Pedestrian-friendly Via Nassa is a catwalk for designers like Bulgari, Louis Vuitton and Versace. Its graceful arcades also harbour jewellery stores, cafes and gelaterias. For one-off gifts, explore

Morcote (p249), on Lago di Lugano

WERNER DIETERICH / GETTY IMAGES ©

steep, curving Via Cattedrale, where boutiques and galleries sell antiques, vintage clothing, crafts and handcrafted jewellery.

ℹ️ Information

Tourist office (www.lugano-tourism.ch) Municipio (☎091 913 32 32; Riva Giocondo Albertolli; ⊙9am-7pm Mon-Fri, 9am-6pm Sat, 10am-6pm Sun); Train Station (⊙2-7pm Mon-Fri, 11am-7pm Sat) Reduced hours November through March.

ℹ️ Getting There & Away

Bus

To St Moritz, postal buses runs direct via Italy (Sfr69, four hours, daily late June to mid-October and late December to early January). All postal buses leave from the main bus depot at Via Serafino Balestra, but you can pick up the St Moritz and some other buses outside the train station 15 minutes later.

Lago di Lugano

Much can be seen in one day if you don't fancy a longer excursion. Boats are operated by the **Società Navigazione del Lago di Lugano** (www.lakelugano.ch). Examples of return fares from Lugano are Melide (Sfr24.20), Morcote (Sfr33) and Ponte Tresa (Sfr40.60). If you want to visit several places, buy a pass: one, three or seven days cost Sfr40, Sfr60 or Sfr71 respectively. There are reduced fares for children.

The departure point from Lugano is by Piazza della Riforma.

Lago Maggiore

Only the northeast corner of Lago Maggiore is in Switzerland; the rest slices into Italy's Lombardy region. **Navigazione Lago Maggiore** (www.navigazionelaghi.it) operates boats across the entire lake.

Locarno

POP 15,200 / ELEV 205M

With its palm trees and much-vaunted 2300 hours of sunshine a year, Locarno has attracted pasty northerners to its warm, Mediterranean-style setting since the late 19th century.

259

Sights

CITTÀ VECCHIA — Neighbourhood
Locarno's Italianate Old Town fans out from **Piazza Grande**, a photogenic ensemble of arcades and Lombard-style houses. A craft and fresh-produce market takes over the square every Thursday. From here, narrow lanes thread north to the baroque-gone-mad **Chiesa Nuova** (Via Cittadella), guarded by a giant bas-relief St Christopher and with cherubs and stucco smothering its pastel-painted interior. Standing proud on fountain-dotted Piazza Sant'Antonio, the **Chiesa di Sant'Antonio** is best known for its altar to the *Cristo Morto* (Dead Christ).

CASTELLO VISCONTEO — Castle
(Piazza Castello; adult/child Sfr7/5; ⏰10am-noon & 2-5pm Tue-Fri, 10am-5pm Sat & Sun Apr–mid-Nov) Named after the Visconti clan that long ruled Milan, this stout 15th-century castle's nucleus was raised around the 10th century. It now houses a museum with Roman and Bronze Age exhibits.

 Activities

The lakefront is made for aimless ambles, or rent an e-bike (Sfr29 per day) from the tourist office to explore further.

Sleeping

CAFFÈ DELL'ARTE — B&B $$
(☎091 751 93 33; www.caffedellarte.ch; Via Cittadella 9; d Sfr149-189; 🛜) Sublime details like gilded Venetian mirrors, chandeliers, frescos and zebra-stripe fabrics lend character to the wood-floored rooms at this B&B.

VECCHIA LOCARNO — Guesthouse $
(☎091 751 65 02; www.vecchia-locarno.ch; Via della Motta 10; s Sfr55-90, d Sfr100-140; @🛜) A sunny inner courtyard forms the centrepiece of this laid-back guesthouse. Rooms are bright and simple, the best with views over the Old Town and hills.

What's Cooking in Ticino?

Switzerland meets Italy in Ticino's kitchen, and some of your most satisfying eating experiences in Ticino will happen in *grotti* – rustic, out-of-the-way restaurants, with granite tables set up under the cool chestnut trees in summer.

Alongside the Ticinese specialities below, perch, whitefish and *salmerino* (a cross between salmon and trout, only smaller) are popular around lakes Lugano and Maggiore. The region's bounty of new wine, chestnuts, game and mushrooms make autumn a tasty season to visit.

- **Polenta** Creamy, savoury maize cornmeal dish.
- **Brasato** Beef braised in red wine.
- **Capretto in umido alla Mesolcinese** Tangy kid-meat stew with a touch of cinnamon and cooked in red wine.
- **Cazzöla** A hearty meat casserole served with cabbage and potatoes.
- **Mazza casalinga** A mixed selection of delicatessen cuts.
- **Cicitt** Long, thin sausages made from goat's meat and often grilled.
- **Robiola** Soft and creamy cow's milk cheese that comes in small discs.

Robiola cheese

CUBOIMAGES SRL / ALAMY ©

Eating

CITTADELLA   Seafood $$
(☏ 091 751 58 85; Via Cittadella 18; mains
Sfr25-44; ☻lunch & dinner Tue-Sun) Fish is as
fresh as it comes at this popular trattoria,
whether you go for whole sea bass or
spaghetti with clams. Choose between
the beamed dining room and the vine-
clad terrace.

OSTERIA CHIARA   Osteria $$
(☏ 091 743 32 96; Vicolo della Chiara 1; mains
Sfr19-42; ☻lunch & dinner Tue-Sat) Tucked
away on a cobbled lane, this has all the
cosy feel of a *grotto*. Sit at granite tables
beneath the pergola or at timber tables
by the fireplace for homemade ravioli and
hearty meat dishes. From the lake follow
the signs up Vicolo dei Nessi.

ℹ️ Information

The **tourist office** (☏ 091 791 00 91; www.
ascona-locarno.com; Largo Zorzi 1; ☻9am-6pm
Mon-Fri, 10am-6pm Sat, 10am-1.30pm & 2.30-
5pm Sun) is nearby.

ℹ️ Getting There & Away

Trains run every one to two hours from Brig
(Sfr52, 2¾ to 3¾ hours), passing through
Italy (bring your passport). Change trains at
Domodossola. There are also runs to and from
Lucerne (Sfr54, 2¾ to three hours). Most trains
to Zürich (Sfr58, 2¾ to three hours) go via
Bellinzona.

Switzerland

In Focus

The hypnotic Matterhorn, near Zermatt (p183)
PHOTOGRAPHER: CHERYL CONLON / GETTY IMAGES ©

Switzerland Today

Grindelwald (p138)

> *Given its overwhelming beauty, it's natural that the Swiss are mad about their land.*

belief systems
(% of population)

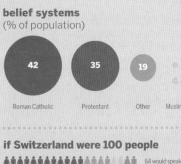

42 Roman Catholic **35** Protestant **19** Other Muslim

if Switzerland were 100 people

64 would speak German
20 would speak French
7 would speak Italian
8 would speak another language
1 would speak Romansch

visitors per sq km

🧍 ≈ 34 people

SWITZERLAND USA UK

Victim of its own Success: Franc Matters

Peaceful and prosperous, safe and sound, a magnet for the rich and a safe haven for wealth: this privileged land of quality living and global finance, of outdoor magnificence and Alpine aesthetic, found itself the victim of its own success in 2011. The Swiss franc, long recognised as one of the world's most stable currencies, had become so overvalued it was threatening the traditionally robust Swiss economy. So strong was the franc that Swiss exports were falling along with the number of incoming tourists as price-conscious visitors from abroad suddenly realised just how much a cup of coffee in Switzerland was going to cost them. Even the Swiss were abandoning their local shops and hopping across the border into cheaper France, Germany and Italy to do their weekly shop. So the Swiss National Bank, in an unprecedented move, made the value of the Swiss franc tumble in an instant (by 9% in 15 minutes!) by pegging it at 1.20 to the euro. An

Mad about their Land: Go Green

Given the overwhelming beauty of their country, it's natural that the Swiss are mad about their land. 'Go green' is the dominant vibe and 'sustainable technology' the buzzword for the man on the street and pioneering scientists striving to go around the world Jules Verne–style in solar-powered boats and planes. As recently as September 2011, the Swiss parliament banned the construction of new nuclear-power plants and called for a nuclear phase-out (in favour of hydroelectric power) by 2034. Currently, five nuclear-power plants generate 40% of Switzerland's energy needs.

Reinventing the Alps is the hot topic at higher altitudes. World-class architects are respectfully weaving futuristic apartments clad in larch-wood tiles (Sir Norman Foster in St Moritz) and spiralling hotel towers of ecological dimensions (Herzog & de Meuron in Davos) into Switzerland's quintessential Heidi-postcard landscape with great success. But how to be green and how to burn clean energy are not the most pressing matters. Rather, it is what must be done to keep ski resorts sustainable as the globe warms; experts say we can forget sure-thing snow below 1500m by 2050.

SIEGFRIED EIGSTLER / GETTY IMAGES ©

entire nation waited with bated breath to see if the contrived depreciation would pay off. Critics were not convinced.

To the Polls: Parliamentary Elections

Federal elections, held every four years, saw 49% of the Swiss electorate turn out to cast their vote in the 2011 nationwide ballot. The incumbent Swiss People's Party (SVP; UDC or Union Démocratique du Centre in French) lost the greatest share of votes – a disappointment for the right-wing party who'd hoped to beat the record 29% of votes it had set four years previously. The country's other main political party, left-wing rivals the Social Democrat Party, likewise saw a drop in support, as Swiss punters hedged their bets with smaller, relatively new parties like the Liberal Greens and Conservative Democrats.

History

Château de Morges (p82), Morges

IMAGEBROKER / ALA

Switzerland is unique, and nowhere is this more startlingly explicit than in its history. Commonly regarded as Sonderfall Schweiz (literally 'special case Switzerland'), this small landlocked country in Europe is a privileged and neutral country, with a long history of independence to support this. Despite the presence of global institutions (the UN, Red Cross etc) and moves towards greater international cooperation, modern-day Switzerland remains idiosyncratic, insular and one-of-a-kind.

Clans & Castles: Swiss Roots

Modern Swiss history might start in 1291 but that is not to say that the thousands of years leading up to Switzerland's birth are not significant – this was the period that gave Switzerland the best of its fairy-tale châteaux and *schlösser* (castles).

The earliest inhabitants were Celtic tribes, including the Helvetii of the Jura and the Mittelland Plain, and the Rhaetians

58 BC

Julius Caesar establishes the Celtic tribe, Helvetii, between the Alps and the Jura.

near Graubünden. Their homelands were first invaded by the Romans, who had gained a foothold under Julius Caesar by 58 BC and established Aventicum (now Avenches) as the capital of Helvetia (Roman Switzerland). Switzerland's largest Roman ruins are at Augusta Raurica. By AD 400, Germanic Alemanni tribes arrived to drive out the Romans.

The Alemanni groups settled in eastern Switzerland and were later joined by another Germanic tribe, the Burgundians, in the western part of the country. The latter adopted Christianity and the Latin language, laying the seeds for the division between French- and German-speaking Switzerland. The Franks conquered both tribes in the 6th century, but the two areas were torn apart again when Charlemagne's empire was partitioned in 870.

When it was reunited under the pan-European Holy Roman Empire in 1032, Switzerland was initially left to its own devices. Local nobles wielded the most influence: the Zähringen family, who founded Fribourg, Bern and Murten, and built a fairytale castle with soaring towers and red turrets in Thun in the Bernese Oberland; and the Savoy clan, who established a ring of castles around Lake Geneva, most notably Château de Morges and magnificent Château de Chillon, right on the water's edge near Montreux.

When the Habsburg ruler Rudolph I became Holy Roman Emperor in 1273, he sent in heavy-handed bailiffs to collect more taxes and tighten the administrative screws. Swiss resentment grew quickly.

The Best...
Castles

1 Château de Morges, Morges

2 Schloss Thun, Thun

3 Medieval castles, Bellinzona

4 Burg Hohenklingen, Stein am Rhein

5 Château de Gruyères, Gruyères

Confoederatio Helvetica: Modern Switzerland

Rudolph died in 1291, prompting local leaders to make an immediate grab for independence. On 1 August that year, the forest communities of Uri, Schwyz and Nidwalden – so the tale goes – gathered on Rütli Meadow in the Schwyz canton in central Switzerland to sign an alliance vowing not to recognise any external judge or law. Historians believe this to be a slightly distorted version of events but, whatever the scenario, a pact does exist, preserved in the town of Schwyz. Displayed at the Bundesbriefmuseum in Schwyz, the pact is seen as the founding act of the Swiss Confederation whose Latin name, Confoederatio Helvetica, survives in the 'CH' abbreviation for Switzerland (used, for example, on car number plates and in internet addresses).

AD 1032

Clans in western Switzerland are swallowed up by the Holy Roman Empire.

1273

Habsburg ruler Rudolph I becomes Holy Roman Emperor and takes control of much Swiss territory.

1291

Modern Switzerland officially 'begins' with the independence pact at Rütli Meadow (some claim it was 1307).

William Tell: Man or Myth?

Regardless of whether or not the patriotic William Tell existed or was responsible for even half the deeds attributed to him, the 14th-century crossbow maker from the Uri canton is a key figure in the Swiss identity. A national legend, the man who helped drive out Switzerland's foreign rulers by shooting an apple off his son's head has perfectly embodied the country's rather singular approach to independence throughout the ages.

In 1315, Duke Leopold I of Austria dispatched a powerful army to quash the growing Swiss nationalism. Instead, however, the Swiss inflicted an epic defeat on his troops at Morgarten, which prompted other communities to join the Swiss union. The next 200 years of Swiss history was a time of successive military wins, land grabs and new memberships. The following cantons came on board: Lucerne (1332), Zürich (1351), Glarus and Zug (1352), Bern (1353), Fribourg and Solothurn (1481), Basel and Schaffhausen (1501), and Appenzell (1513). In the middle of all this, the Swiss Confederation gained independence from Holy Roman Emperor Maximilian I after a victory at Dornach in 1499.

No More Stinging Defeats: Swiss Neutrality

Swiss neutrality was essentially born out of the stinging defeat the rampaging Swiss, having made it as far as Milan, suffered against a combined French and Venetian force at Marignano, 16km southeast of Milan, in 1515. After the bloody battle, the Swiss gave up their expansionist dream, withdrew from the international scene and declared neutrality for the first time. For centuries since, the country's warrior spirit has been channelled solely into mercenary activity – a tradition still echoed in the Swiss Guard that protects today's pope at the Vatican.

When the religious Thirty Years War (1618–48) broke out in Europe, Switzerland's neutrality and diversity combined to give it some protection. The Protestant Reformation, led by preachers Huldrych Zwingli and Jean Calvin, made some inroads in Zürich and Geneva, while Central Switzerland (Zentralschweiz) remained Catholic. Such was the internal division that the Swiss, unable to agree even among themselves which side to take in the Thirty Years War, stuck to neutrality.

The French invaded Switzerland in 1798 and established the brief Helvetic Republic, but they were no more welcome than the Austrians before them and internal fighting prompted Napoleon (then in power in France) to restore the former Confederation of

1315
Swiss militias win a surprise victory over Habsburg Austrian forces at the Battle of Morgarten.

1476
Charles the Bold, Duke of Burgundy, is crushed at the Battle of Murten.

1499
The Swiss Confederation wins virtual independence from the Habsburg-led Holy Roman Empire.

Cantons in 1803 – the cantons of Aargau, St Gallen, Graubünden, Ticino, Thurgau and Vaud joined the Confederation at this time.

Swiss neutrality as we know it today was formally established by the Congress of Vienna peace treaty in 1815 that, following Napoleon's defeat by the British and Prussians at Waterloo, formally guaranteed Switzerland's independence and neutrality for the first time. (The same treaty also added the cantons of Valais, Geneva and Neuchâtel to the Swiss confederation.)

Despite some citizens' pro-German sympathies, Switzerland's only involvement in WWI lay in organising Red Cross units. After the war, Switzerland joined the League of Nations, but on a strictly financial and economic basis (which included providing its headquarters in Geneva) – no military involvement.

WWII likewise saw Switzerland remain neutral, the country being largely unscathed bar some accidental bombings on Schaffhausen when Allied pilots mistook the town in northeastern Switzerland for Germany, twice dropping bombs on its outskirts in April 1944. Indeed, the most momentous event of WWII for the Swiss was when Henri Guisan, general of the civilian army, invited all top military personnel to Rütli Meadow (site of the 1291 Oath of Allegiance) to show the world how determined the Swiss were to defend their own soil.

The Best...
Old Towns

1 St Gallen

2 Appenzell

3 Vevey

4 Mürten

5 Schaffhausen

IN FOCUS HISTORY

Give Cantons a Voice: The Constitution

In 1847, civil war broke out. The Protestant army, led by General Dufour, quickly crushed the Sonderbund (Special League) of Catholic cantons, including Lucerne. The war only lasted 26 days, prompting the German chancellor Otto von Bismarck to subsequently dismiss it as 'a hare shoot'. But for the peace-loving Swiss, the disruption and disorder

Switzerland's Würste Affair

Protestant Swiss first openly disobeyed the Catholic Church during 1522's 'affair of the sausages', when a printer and several priests in Zürich were caught gobbling *Würste* on Ash Wednesday when they should have been fasting.

1515

After Swiss forces take Milan and Pavia in Italy in 1512, the Swiss are defeated.

1519

Protestant Huldrych Zwingli preaches 'pray and work' in Zürich; the city adopts his reform proposals.

1590–1600

Some 300 women in Vaud are captured, tortured and burned alive on charges of witchcraft.

were sufficient to ensure they rapidly consolidated the victory by Dufour's forces with the creation of a new federal constitution. Bern was named the capital.

The 1848 constitution, largely still in place today, was a compromise between advocates of central control and conservative forces wanting to retain cantonal authority. The cantons eventually relinquished their right to print money, run postal services and levy customs duties, giving these to the federal government. However, they retained legislative and executive control over local matters. Furthermore, the new Federal Assembly was established in a way that gave cantons a voice. The lower national chamber, the *Nationalrat,* has 200 members, allocated from the 26 cantons in proportion to population size. The upper states chamber, the *Ständerat,* comprises 46 members, two per canton.

Opposition to political corruption sparked a movement for greater democracy. The constitution was revised in 1874 so that many federal laws had to be approved by national referendum – a phenomenon for which Switzerland remains famous today. A petition with 50,000 signatures can challenge a proposed law; 100,000 signatures can force a public vote on any new issue.

Famously Secret: Swiss Banking

Banking confidentiality, dating back to the Middle Ages, was enshrined in Swiss law in 1934 when numbered (rather than named) bank accounts were introduced. The Swiss banking industry has thrived ever since, thanks mainly to the enviable stability that guaranteed neutrality brings. When the Bank for International Settlements (BIS; the

The Magic Formula: Swiss Government

The make-up of Switzerland's Federal Council, the executive government, is determined not by who wins the most parliamentary seats (ie the winning party rules), but by the 'magic formula' – a cosy power-sharing agreement made between the four main parties in 1959.

○ The Federal Council consists of seven ministers.

○ The four largest parties in parliament are guaranteed seats in the Federal Council in accordance with their shares of the popular vote.

○ The president is drawn on a rotating basis from the seven federal ministers, so there's a new head of state each year.

○ Many federal laws must first be approved by public referendum; several are held every year.

1847
Civil war between Protestants and Catholics lasts 26 days, leaving 86 dead and 500 wounded.

1863
Horrified by wartime slaughter, Henri Dunant co-founds the International Red Cross in Geneva.

RED CROSS BUILDING, GENEVA
WALTER BIBIKOW / GETTY IMAGES ©

organisation that facilitates cooperation between central banks) chose Basel as base in 1930 it was for one good reason – Switzerland was a neutral player.

In the late 1990s a series of scandals erupted, forcing Switzerland to start reforming its famously secretive banking industry, born when a clutch of commercial banks were created in the mid-19th century. In 1995, after pressure from Jewish groups, Swiss banks announced that they had discovered millions of dollars lying in dormant pre-1945 accounts and belonging to Holocaust victims and survivors. Three years later, amid allegations they'd been sitting on the money without seriously trying to trace its owners, Switzerland's two largest banks, UBS and Crédit Suisse, agreed to pay US$1.25 billion in compensation to Holocaust survivors and their families.

Switzerland has long been a favourite spot for the wealthy to deposit their fortunes in private banks. Almost one-third of the world's US$7 trillion offshore deposits are said to be in Switzerland – hence the immense pressure on Switzerland in 2009 from the US, Britain, Germany and other high-tax countries to change its 1934 banking law protecting depositors accused of tax evasion by their home countries. The Swiss conceded, prompting critics to triumphantly ring the death knell for Swiss banking

The Federal Charter of Swiss Confederation (p267)

1918
With a sixth of the population in poverty and 20,000 dead from flu, workers strike.

1940
More than 430,000 troops are mobilised in case of German invasion.

1949
Orson Welles delivers line about the Swiss inventing the cuckoo clock in *The Third Man*.

secrecy. This followed hot on the heels of the Swiss decision in 2004 to tax accounts held in Switzerland by EU citizens – again in reaction to external pressure.

Forever Neutral: A Nation Apart

Since the end of WWII, Switzerland has enjoyed an uninterrupted period of economic, social and political stability – thanks, in predictable Swiss fashion, to the neutrality which saw it forge ahead from an already powerful commercial, financial and industrial base while the rest of Europe was still picking up and rebuilding the broken pieces from the war. Zürich developed as an international banking and insurance centre, and the World Health Organization and a stash of other international bodies set up headquarters in Geneva. To preserve its much-vaunted neutrality, however, Switzerland opted to remain outside the UN (although Geneva has hosted its second-largest seat after the main New York headquarters from the outset) and, more recently, the European Union.

A hefty swing to the conservative right in the 2003 parliamentary elections served to further enhance Switzerland's standing as a nation staunchly apart. In 2006, the anti-EU, anti-immigration Swiss People's Party (SVP) called for the toughening up

The UN's second-largest seat is in Geneva (p62)
PHOTOGRAPHER: ANDY CHADWICK / ALAMY ©

1979
Jura (majority French-speaking Catholics) leaves Bern (German-speaking Protestants) to become an independent canton.

1990
The internet is 'born' at Geneva's CERN, which develops the language essential to the web.

JULIA GAVIN / ALAMY © ARCHITECTS: T. BÜCHI AND H. DESSIMOZ

of immigration and political asylum laws; the policies were passed with an overwhelming majority at national referendum. Then there was the rumpus over its bid to ban building new minarets for Muslim calls to prayer – an idea that aroused much anger internationally, but was approved by the constitution after 57.7% of voters said yes to the ban in a national referendum. During the campaign, the SVP published anti-immigrant posters featuring three white sheep kicking one black sheep off the striking white cross of the Swiss flag.

In spite of the SVP's tough conservative line, there have been concrete signs that Switzerland is opening up to the wider world. The country became the 190th member of the UN in 2002 (a referendum on the issue had last been defeated in 1986) and three years later it voted to join Europe's passport-free travel zone, Schengen (finally completing the process at the end of 2008). In another referendum the same year, the Swiss narrowly voted in favour of legalising civil unions for same-sex couples (but not marriage), one more defeat for the SVP.

Yet few expect Switzerland to even consider joining either the EU or the Euro single-currency zone any time soon (if ever). Traditionally, the French-speaking western cantons have long desired both, while the German-speaking cantons (and Ticino) have generally been opposed.

The Best...
History Museums

1 Stiftsbibliothek, St Gallen

2 Schweizerisches Landesmuseum, Zürich

3 Historisches Museum, Arbon

4 Château de Chillon, Montreux

5 Augusta Raurica, Kaiseraugst

2001
Swissair collapses, Zug parliament massacre, canyoning accident and St Gotthard Tunnel fire cause many deaths.

2008
The world financial crisis endangers Switzerland's two biggest banks, UBS and Crédit Suisse.

2012
CERN scientists possibly discover the Higgs boson subatomic particle, a key to understanding the universe.

Family Travel

Ski school in the Jungfrau Region (p149)

INGOLF POMPE / GETTY IMAGES

Orderly, clean and not overly commercial, Switzerland is a dream for family travel and promotes itself heavily as such. Every ski resort works hard at being family-friendly, with good summertime activities on offer, and hotels and B&Bs cater well for families. Check out Swiss Tourism's Families brochure (order or download it online at www.myswitzerland.com). It's jam-packed with ideas, as is the website, which lists child-friendly accommodation, family offers and so on.

Activities

Winter resorts go to great trouble to provide family-friendly plans and activities. Everything from lessons to special non-adult areas are near-universal and programs are varied by ages, so the rebellious young teen need be nowhere near their seven-year-old sibling. A trip to one of the best snowboarding destinations on the planet is rarely going to disappoint.

In summer, adventure-sports companies often have programs just for kids and most have programs designed for the entire family. You can go hike with goats, walk a St Bernard, go on a GPS hiking treasure hunt, spot a marmot, swing like mad on ropes and much, much more.

Transport

Family train travel is good value. Kids under six years old travel for free with **Swiss Railways** (www.rail.ch) and those aged six to 16 years revel in free unlimited rail travel with its annual Junior Card (Sfr30) or – should it be grandparents travelling with the kids – the grandchild travel card (Sfr30). Switzerland's mountain of scenic journeys by train and boat (p285) enchant children of all ages. Upon arrival at point B, dozens of segments of the perfectly signposted hiking, biking, rollerblading and canoeing trails are flagged as suitable for younger children. These are designed strictly for non-motorised traffic by Switzerland Mobility.

It's worth mentioning the travel itself: from railways in every shape and size to lake boats to cable cars and gondolas seemingly out of an adventure flick, just getting around Switzerland is a thrilling adventure.

Hotels

All types of accommodation will have family rooms, and deals geared for families are common at larger places. Resorts will often have childcare facilities or programs designed to allow parents to enjoy their own holiday within the holiday.

Staying in a B&B is family fabulous: little kids can sweetly slumber upstairs while weary parents wine and dine in peace downstairs. Pick a B&B on a farm or kip on straw in the hay barn for adventurous kids.

Additionally, many hotels in resort areas have outdoor playgrounds and a new increasingly popular trend is rooms geared for kids. Bright colours, games on the TV, every channel a child could hope for, pint-sized beds, rubber ducks in the tub and much more. Teens will find night-time clubs in resort areas geared for under-16s, places where they can meet others from around the world.

Restaurants & Food

Children are generally welcome in most restaurants. Some even offer smaller, kid-sized menus and servings. Toddlers are usually fed straight from their parents' plates and if high-chairs aren't available, staff will improvise.

As far as the menu goes, any country with a fondness for cheese and potatoes like Switzerland is bound to be popular with kids of *all* ages (including large ones

Need to Know

- **Car Seats** Switzerland has the toughest child car-seat rules in the world: children age 12 years or under 150cm in height must use car seats or booster seats. Car hire/rental firms charge around Sfr50 for these.
- **Changing facilities** Uncommon in traditional establishments; only really found in modern, major facilities.
- **Cots** Usually available at all accommodation, except perhaps a remote mountain hut.
- **Health** As you would do at home.
- **Highchairs** Usually available.
- **Kids' menus** At many restaurants.
- **Nappies (diapers)** Readily available.
- **Strollers** Larger resorts may have them.
- **Transport** Myriad family passes and kids' discounts available.

The Best...
Places to Delight Kids

1 Verkehrhaus, Lucerne

2 Alimentarium, Vevey

3 Gstaad Ski Resort

4 Interlaken & Grindelwald adventure outfitters

5 Cailler Chocolate Factory

called 'adults'). And there's also the Swiss mania for ice cream in virtually all weather conditions.

Then there's the big elephant in the room, the big cocoa elephant: chocolate. From iconic Alpine-shaped Toblerone to a plethora of bars sold in all sizes and flavours, the country is awash in treats. One final item that should seal the deal for most kids: one of life's great pleasures is sitting outside at a ski resort and drinking the richest, creamiest hot chocolate imaginable.

Towns & Cities

Swiss cities are also child-friendly. There's lots to do in both Zürich (p204) and Geneva (p69) and at every other city and town in between. None are huge and intimidating – even in Zürich you can take the time to admire a white swan gliding past the busiest part of town. Castles abound and you've got ancient and thrilling features like the old wooden bridges in Lucerne.

Up in the Alps, kids can run free in a town like Wengen, where trails set off across the gorgeous countryside but there are few opportunities to get in trouble.

Winter Sports

Snowboarding at Davos (p251)

JAN GREUNE / GETTY IMAGES ©

In a land where every 10-man, 50-cow hamlet has a ski lift, the question is not where you can ski but how. Ritzy or remote, party-mad or picture-perfect, virgin or veteran, black run or blue – whatever your taste and ability, Switzerland has a resort to suit.

Regions

The following winter sports regions are just a glimpse of what's available in the Alps. Switzerland has scores of fantastic resorts and we are unable to cover them exhaustively here. See regional chapters for more.

Bernese Oberland & Central Switzerland

If only all ski resorts were like those in the Bernese Oberland. At its winter wonderland heart is the Jungfrau, an unspoilt Alpine region with dark timber villages and scenery lovely enough to distract anyone from mastering parallel turns.

The region is criss-crossed with 214km of well-maintained slopes, ranging from easy-peasy to hair-raising, which afford fleeting views of the 'Big Three': the Eiger, Mönch and Jungfrau. Grindelwald, Wengen and Mürren all offer varied skiing and have a relaxed,

Online Ski Deals

For last-minute ski deals and packages, check out websites like www.igluski.com and www.j2ski.com. Local tourist offices, **Snowfinders** (www.snowfinders.co.uk) and **My Switzerland** (www.myswitzerland.com) might also have good-value offers.

Speed to the slopes by prebooking your ski and snowboard hire at **Ski Set** (www.skiset.co.uk) or **Snowbrainer** (www.snowbrainer.com), both of which offer discounts of up to 49% on shop rental prices. If you want to skip to the front of the queue, consider ordering your lift pass online, too. Swiss Passes (www.swisspasses.com) gets you a reduction of 5% to 15% on standard lift pass prices.

family-friendly vibe. For more glitz and Gucci, swing west to Gstaad, which has fine downhill on 250km of slopes and pre- and post-season glacier skiing at nearby Glacier 3000, framed by 4000m peaks.

Surprisingly little-known given its snow-sure slopes and staggering mountain backdrop, Engelberg is dominated by the savage rock and ice walls of glacier-capped Mt Titlis. The real treasures here are off-piste, including Galtiberg, a 2000m vertical descent from the glacier to the valley.

Valais & Zermatt

One of Switzerland's most-enduring images is the perfect pyramid-shaped peak of the Matterhorn, soaring 4478m above Zermatt. Snowboarders, intermediates and off-pisters are all catered for in this car-free resort with 300km of eye-poppingly scenic runs. You can even ski over to Cervinia in Italy. Verbier has a cool 412km of slopes and some terrifically challenging off-piste spots for experts. Hard-core boarders favour snow-sure, glacier-licked Saas Fee. Snuggling up to France's mammoth Portes du Soleil ski arena, Champéry has access to 650km of slopes. Queues are few and families are welcome in lesser-known beauties such as Bettmeralp.

St Moritz & Graubünden

Rugged Graubünden has some truly legendary slopes. First up is super-chic St Moritz, with 350km of groomed slopes (intermediates are in heaven), fine glacier descents and freeride opportunities. The twin resorts of (pretty) Klosters and (popular) Davos share 320km of runs; the latter is superb for cross-country and has excellent parks and half-pipes. Boarders also rave about the terrain parks, freeriding and après-ski scene in Laax. Family-oriented Arosa is a scenic pick for beginners, intermediates and cross-country fans. Want to give the crowds the slip? Celerina shares many of the slopes with St Moritz but is low-key and has a famous bob run.

When?

The slopes buzz with skiers and boarders from mid-December until Easter. Unless you're tied by school holidays (Christmas, February half-term and Easter), avoid them to get better deals and avoid crowds.

Passes, Hire & Tuition

Yes, Switzerland is expensive and no, skiing is not an exception. That said, costs can be cut by avoiding school-holiday times and choosing low-key villages over upscale resorts. Ski passes are a hefty chunk out of your budget and will set you back around Sfr70 per day or Sfr350 per week. Factor in around Sfr40 to Sfr70 per day for ski hire and Sfr20 for boot hire, which can be reserved online at www.intersportrent.com. Kids' equipment is roughly half-price.

All major resorts have ski schools, with half-day group lessons typically costing Sfr40 to Sfr50 and a full-day off-piste around Sfr100. **Swiss Snowsports** (www.snowsports.ch) has a clickable map of 180 ski schools across the country.

Ski Run Classifications

Piste maps are available on most tourist-office websites and at the valley stations of ski lifts; runs are colour-coded according to difficulty as follows:

Blue Indicates easy, well-groomed runs that are suitable for beginners.

Red Indicates intermediate runs that are groomed but often steeper and narrower than blue runs. Skiers should have a medium level of ability.

Black For expert skiers with polished technique and skills. They are mostly steep and not always groomed, and may have moguls and steep vertical drops.

Safety on the Slopes

○ Avalanche warnings should be heeded and local advice sought before detouring from prepared runs.

Top Slopes for...

○ **Snowboarding** Freeriders seeking deep powder, big air and, like, totally *awesome* terrain parks, head to Saas Fee, Laax and Davos.

○ **Families** Picture-book pretty Arosa, Bettmeralp and Klosters for their fine nursery slopes, kids' clubs and slope-side activities ranging from sledding to skidooing.

○ **Off-piste** Explore the virgin powder in the glorious backcountry of Engelberg, Andermatt, Verbier and Davos.

○ **Glacier skiing** For pre- and post-season skiing, schuss across to Glacier 3000 near Gstaad, glacier-encrusted Mt Titlis in Engelberg and the snow-sure slopes of Saas Fee.

○ **Scenic skiing** Zermatt for its legendary Matterhorn views and the Jungfrau region to slalom in the shadow of the Eiger, Mönch and Jungfrau.

○ **Scary-as-hell descents** Dare to ski the near-vertical Swiss Wall, the mogul-riddled Mont-Fort in Verbier and the Inferno, a 16km black-run marathon from Schilthorn to Lauterbrunnen.

○ **Cross-country skiing** Master your classic or skating technique on the twinkling *Loipen* in Davos, Arosa and Kandersteg.

○ **Non-skiers** Still ski-shy? Try Gstaad or Grindelwald, where off-piste fun like ice skating, curling, airboarding, horse-drawn sleigh rides, winter hiking and husky sledding keeps non-skiers amused.

The Best...
Famous Ski Resorts

1 Verbier

2 Zermatt

3 St Moritz

4 Davos

5 Klosters

◦ If you're going off-piste or hiking in snowy areas, never go alone and take an avalanche pole, a transceiver or a shovel and, most importantly, a professional guide.

◦ Before setting foot in the mountains check the day's avalanche bulletin by calling ☎187 or checking online at www.slf.ch.

◦ The sun is powerful in the Alps and is intensified by snow glare. Wear ski goggles and high-factor sunscreen.

◦ Layers help you to adapt to the constant change in body temperature. Your head, wrists and knees should be protected.

◦ Black run look tempting? Make sure you're properly insured first; sky-high mountain rescue and medical costs can add insult to injury.

Resources

Bergfex (www.bergfex.com) Comprehensive website with piste maps, snow forecasts of the Alps and details of 111 ski resorts in Switzerland.

On the Snow (www.onthesnow.co.uk) Handy website with reviews of Switzerland's ski resorts, plus snow reports, webcams and lift pass details.

If You Ski (www.ifyouski.com) Resort guides, ski deals and info on ski hire and schools.

MadDogSki (www.maddogski.com) Entertaining ski guides and insider tips on everything from accommodation to après ski.

World Snowboard Guide (www.worldsnowboardguide.com) Snowboarder central. Has the lowdown on most Swiss resorts.

Where to Ski and Snowboard (www.wheretoskiandsnowboard.com) Resort overviews and reviews, news and weather.

Summer Sports

Hiking near Grindelwald (p138) with views of the Eiger, Mönch and Jungfrau

GUENTER FISCHER / GETTY IMAGES ©

Switzerland is a sporty nation and it's easy to see why: glacial brooks and thundering waterfalls, colossal peaks and beckoning valleys. The water is mineral pure, the sky a brighter shade of blue, the air piney fresh. No wonder the Swiss can't keep still with that phenomenal backyard. And what's good for the locals is fabulous for visitors. Long summer nights let you pack in as much as possible.

When to Go

Except for the depths of winter – which offers its own options for fun – you can revel in the Swiss outdoors free of winter gear for much of the year.

⊙ **May–June** The crowds are thin and the weather is often fine. Snow patches still linger above 2000m. June is great for hiking with long, warm days and wildflowers carpeting the slopes. Many huts are still closed and mountain transport is limited.

⊙ **July-August** A conga line of high-altitude hikers and cyclists makes its way through the Swiss Alps. All lifts and mountain huts are open (book ahead). The lakes beckon all water-sports fans.

⊙ **September–early October** Pot luck: can be delightful or drab. The larch forests look beautiful in their autumn mantle of gold, and temperatures at lower altitudes are still mild.

Weather Reports

The weather is notoriously fickle in the Alps. Even in August, conditions can skip from foggy to sunny, stormy to snowy in the course of a day, so check the forecast on www.meteoschweiz.ch before embarking on long hikes at high altitudes.

Accommodation prices drop, as do the crowds, but many hotels and lifts close.

○ **Mid-October–November** Days get shorter and the weather is unpredictable. Expect rain, fog and snow above 1500m. Most resorts go into hibernation.

Walking & Hiking

Mighty glaciers and 4000m mountains, remote moors and flower-flecked meadows, limestone ravines and sparkling rivers – Switzerland has an almost indecent amount of natural splendour for its size. More than 60,000km of marked trails criss-cross the country and only by slinging on a backpack and hitting the trail can you begin to appreciate just how *big* this tiny country really is.

Walk Designations

As locals delight in telling you, Switzerland's 62,500km of trails would be enough to stretch around the globe 1.5 times. And with (stereo)typical Swiss precision, the footpaths that criss-cross the country are remarkably well signposted and maintained. That said, a decent topographical map and compass is still recommended for Alpine hikes. Like ski runs, trails are colour-coded according to difficulty:

Yellow Easy. No previous experience necessary.

White-red-white Mountain trails. You should be sure-footed as routes may involve some exposure.

White-blue-white High Alpine routes. Only for the physically fit; some climbing and/or glacier travel may be required.

Pink Prepared winter walking trails.

Regions

Alpine hikers invariably have their sights set high on the trails in the Bernese Oberland, Valais and Graubünden, which offer challenging walking and magnificent scenery. That said, lowland areas such as the vine-strewn Lavaux wine region and the bucolic dairy country around Appenzell can be just as atmospheric and are accessible virtually year-round.

In summer, many tourist offices run guided hikes – free with a local guest card – including Grindelwald and Lugano. Other resorts such as Klosters, Davos and Arosa give you a head start with free mountain transport when you stay overnight in summer.

Accommodation

Want to overnight on your walk? **Wanderland** (www.wanderland.ch) should be your first port of call for hiker-friendly accommodation, with farmstays, hotels, campsites and Swiss Alpine Club (SAC) huts searchable by route and region.

Resources

Local tourist offices are excellent sources of recommendations and info for walking and hiking. Tell them what you want to do and they can set you up. They also have all types of maps for sale.

Websites

Get planning with the routes, maps and GPS downloads on the following websites:

My Switzerland (www.myswitzerland.com) Excellent information on walking in Switzerland, from themed day hikes to guided treks and family-friendly walks. An iPhone app covering 32 walks is available for download.

Wanderland (www.wanderland.ch) The definitive website on hiking in Switzerland, with walks and accommodation searchable by region and theme, plus information on events, guides, maps and packages.

Cycling & Mountain Biking

Routes

Switzerland is an efficiently run paradise for the ardent cyclist, laced with 9000km of cycling trails and 4500km of mountain-biking routes.

Mountain and downhill bikers whizz across to Alpine resorts like Arosa in summer, where cable cars often allow you to take your wheels for free or for a nominal fee. To hone your skills on obstacles, check out the terrain parks in Davos and Verbier.

Bike Hire

Reliable wheels are available in all major towns and many now offer free bike hire from May to October as part of the eco-friendly initiative **Suisse Roule** (www.suisse roule.ch), including Bern, Lausanne, Zürich and Geneva.

Available at all major train stations, **Rent a Bike** (www.rent-a-bike.ch) has city bikes, mountain bikes, e-bikes and tandems for Sfr33, Sfr50, Sfr50 and Sfr80 per day respectively. For a small additional charge, you can pick your bike up at one station

Aletsch Glacier from Eggishorn (p190)

and drop it off at another. Bikes can be reserved online. A one-day bike pass for SBB trains costs Sfr18.

Resources

Veloland (www.veloland.ch) For maps, route descriptions and the lowdown on Switzerland's nine national routes, plus details on bike rental and e-bike stations.

Mountainbikeland (www.mountainbikeland.ch) Useful website for mountain bikers, with details on Switzerland's single-trail and fun tours, and three national routes.

The Best...
Summer
Sports Towns

1 Interlaken

2 Grindelwald

3 Zermatt

4 Klosters

5 Davos

Adventure & Water Sports

Rock Climbing & Mountaineering

Switzerland has been the fabled land for mountaineers ever since Edward Whymper made the first successful ascent of the Matterhorn in 1865, albeit a triumph marred with rope-breaking tragedy. Today, Zermatt's Alpin Center arranges some first-class climbs to surrounding 4000-ers.

The climbing halls in Chur and Interlaken are perfect for limbering up.

Swiss Alpine Club (SAC; www.sac-cas.ch) Browse for information on countrywide climbing halls, tours and courses.

Schweizer Bergführerverband (Swiss Mountain Guide Association; www.4000plus.ch) Search for a qualified mountain guide or climbing instructor.

Via Ferrate

For the buzz of mountaineering but with the security of being attached to the rock face, clip onto a *via ferrata* (*Klettersteig* in German). These head-spinning fixed-rope routes are currently all the rage in Switzerland. Some of our favourites include those in Mürren for scenery and Kandersteg for more of a challenge.

Via Ferrata (www.viaferrata.org) provides maps and routes graded according to difficulty.

Rafting & Hydrospeeding

In summer, the raging Saane, Rhine, Inn and Rhône rivers create a dramatic backdrop for rafting and hydrospeeding (surfing rapids solo on a glorified bodyboard). Memorable splashes include the thundering Vorderrhein through the limestone Ruinaulta gorge and rivers near Interlaken.

Swissraft (www.swissraft.ch) has bases all over the country. Expect to pay around Sfr110 for a half-day rafting tour and Sfr140 for hydrospeeding, including transport and equipment.

Kayaking & Canoeing

Lazy summer afternoons are best spent absorbing the slow, natural rhythm of Switzerland's crystal-clear lakes and rivers (for instance, Lake Constance and fjord-like Lake Uri).

See http://kanuland.myswitzerland.com for routes and paddle-friendly accommodation tips. A half-day canoeing tour will set you back between Sfr85 and Sfr120. Tourist offices can provide details on local outfits.

Trains, Ferries & Cable Cars

Train platform, Zürich (p204)

MARTIN MOOS / GETTY IMAGES ©

The Swiss even have a name for it: the Swiss Travel System. It's an interconnected web of trains, boats, cable cars and postal buses that put almost the entire country within easy car-free reach. You truly can set your watch to the schedules with their easy connections. Even better, many of the rides are show-stoppers and include lake boats, rides up the Alps and world-famous scenic trains.

Boats

Gliding along the clear waters of a Swiss lake aboard a boat is one of the nation's restful pleasures. Scenic rides abound. Many of these are circular journeys aimed at tourists, but in other places they are a great means of transport from one place to another. And in summer, you might find that your boat is a historic steam-driven classic, complete with tooting horn.

The following are some of the best places to try out lake travel:

o **Lake Geneva** There's almost no place on this huge lake without a boat dock. You can mix and match boat and train travel while enjoying mountain and vineyard views.

o **Lake Lucerne** Boats fan out from the heart of Lucerne and you can enjoy views of Alps near and far while you glide along. A classic trip

The Best...
Great Journeys

1 Jungfraujoch

2 Mt Titlis

3 Schilthorn

4 Mt Pilatus

5 Aletsch Glacier

is a circular visit to Mt Pilatus, which includes a beautiful stretch aboard a lake boat.

○ **Lake Lugano** One of the mildest Swiss places climate-wise, you get views of the lush mountains along the lake and there are little villages to explore during a day of boat-hopping.

Cable Cars

It's the stuff of movies (several): dangling cars and tiny gondolas gliding up the side of an impossibly sheer mountainside to a summit with stunning views. Getting there is truly half the fun.

Most run through the year, serving skiiers in winter, hikers in summer and view-lovers year-round. Note: always check what time the last cable car goes down the mountain, as this can be as early as 4pm in some resorts.

Key types of Swiss cable cars include the following:

○ **Cable Car** (*Luftseilbahn* in German, *téléphérique* in French, *funivia* in Italian) Large – often very large – cars that travel between stations dangling from cables, usually passing their counterpart en route.

○ **Funicular** (*Standseilbahn*, *funiculaire* in French, *funicolare*) A car runs on tracks and is pulled by a cable.

○ **Gondola** (*Gondelbahn, télécabine, telecabinoia*) Lots of little cars dangle from a cable and run non-stop in a loop.

Train

The Swiss rail network combines state-run and private operations. The **Swiss Federal Railway** (www.rail.ch, www.sbb.ch/en) covers all the major routes. A plethora of private trains sidle into valleys and along the sides of mountains, linking even tiny burgs to the main train lines.

For more on Swiss trains, see p305 for details.

Scenic Trains

Swiss trains are often more than a means of getting from A to B. Stunning views invariably make the journey itself the destination. Switzerland boasts the following routes among its classic sightseeing journeys. Bear in mind that you can choose just one leg of the trip, and that scheduled services ply the same routes for standard fares. In addition to these journeys, almost any train in the Jungfrau region provides beautiful views.

The first three trains on this list have panoramic coaches with extra-large windows:

Glacier Express (☎ 027 927 77 00; www.glacierexpress.ch; 2nd/1st class Sfr136/226, obligatory seat reservation summer/winter Sfr33/13; ⏱ 7½hr, daily) Spectacular journey between Zermatt and St Moritz, Chur or Davos. The Brig–Zermatt Alpine leg makes for pretty powerful viewing, as does the area between Disentis/Mustér and Brig.

Golden Pass Route (☎ 021 989 81 90; www.goldenpass.ch; one-way 2nd/1st class Sfr70/116) Travels between Lucerne and Montreux. The journey is in three legs, and you must change trains twice. Regular trains, without panoramic windows, work the whole route hourly.

Bernina Express (📞 081 288 65 65; www.rhb.ch; one-way 2nd/1st class Sfr58/96, obligatory seat reservation summer/winter Sfr12/9; 🕐 2½hr, daily) Cuts 145km through Engadine from Chur to Tirano. May and October, you can opt to continue onwards from Tirano to Lugano by bus.

Chocolate Train (www.mob.ch) Return trip in a belle époque Pullman car from Montreux to the chocolate factory at Broc.

Mont Blanc/St Bernard Expresses (www.tmrsa.ch) From Martigny to Chamonix, France, or over the St Bernard Pass.

By Boat & Rail

The **Wilhelm Tell Express** (📞 041 367 67 67; www.wilhelmtellexpress.ch; adult standard/premium Sfr169/209, Swiss Pass free, standard/premium supplement Sfr39/79; 🕐 May-Oct) starts with a wonderful 2½-hour cruise across Lake Lucerne to Flüelen, from where a train winds its way through ravines and past mountains to Locarno.

Travel Passes

Passes are an excellent means of getting around Switzerland. Most offer some combination of free and discounted travel on trains, boats, cable cars and/or postal buses.

Find comprehensive information on the many passes at http://traintickets.myswitzerland.com.

European Rail Passes

Eurail and Inter Rail passes are valid on Swiss national railways. However, you cannot use them on postal buses, city transport, many cable cars and some private train lines (Eurail does offer a 25% discount on the Zermatt route and the Jungfraubahn routes at the heart of the Bernese Oberland).

Swiss Travel Passes

The following national travel passes generally offer better savings than Eurail or Inter Rail passes on extensive travel within Switzerland.

Passes can be purchased in the UK from the **Switzerland Travel Centre** (www.stc.co.uk). In the US, **Rail Europe** (www.raileurope.com) sells the range of passes. In Switzerland, larger train stations sell passes, including the one in the basement at Zürich's airport.

○ **Swiss Pass** The Swiss Pass entitles the holder to unlimited travel on almost every train, boat and bus service in the country, and on trams and buses in 41 towns, plus free entry to 400-odd museums. Reductions of 50% apply on funiculars, cable cars and private railways. Different passes are available, valid between four days and one month.

○ **Swiss Flexi Pass** This pass allows you to nominate a certain number of days (anywhere from three to six) during a month when you can enjoy unlimited travel.

○ **Half-Fare Card** Almost every Swiss owns one of these. As the name suggests, you pay only half the fare on trains with this card, plus you get some discounts on local-network buses, trams and cable cars. An adult one-year Half-Fare Card costs a local Sfr165 (photo necessary).

○ **Family Card** A free Family Card gets free travel (on trains, buses and boats – even on some cable cars) for those aged six to 15 years when travelling with at least one of their parents.

The Swiss Table

Oozing, melting raclette

FOODPHOTOGR. EISING / CORBI

There is far more to Swiss cuisine than chocolate, cheese and Swiss-German rösti, and the very best dining in this essentially rural country is all about the nation's own foods. While the chic city crowd feasts on international fare, the Swiss kitchen is extraordinarily rich thanks to French, German and Italian influences on the local dishes.

Cheese

First things first: not all Swiss cheese has holes. Emmental, the hard cheese from the Emme Valley east of Bern, does – as does the not dissimilar Tilsiter from the same valley. But, contrary to common perception, most of Switzerland's 450 different types of cheese (*käse* in German, *fromage* in French, *formaggio* in Italian) are hole-less. Take the well-known hard cheese Gruyère, made in the town of Gruyères near Fribourg; or the overwhelmingly stinky Appenzeller, used in a rash of tasty, equally strong-smelling dishes in the same-name town in northeastern Switzerland. Or there's Sbrinz, Switzerland's oldest hard cheese and transalpine ancestor to Italian parmesan, ripened for 24 months to create its distinct taste – eat it straight and thinly sliced like carpaccio or grated on top of springtime asparagus.

Another distinctive Swiss cheese with not a hole in sight is hard, nutty-flavoured Tête de Moine (literally 'monks's head') from the Jura, which comes in a small round and is cut with a flourish in a flowery curl using a special handled cutting device known as a *girolle* (great present to take back home – supermarkets sell them).

As unique is L'Etivaz which, in the finest of timeless alpine tradition, is only made up high on lush summer pastures in the Alpes Vaudoises (Vaud Alps). As cows graze outside, shepherds inside their century-old *chalets d'alpage* (mountain huts) heat up the morning's milk in a traditional copper cauldron over a wood fire. Strictly seasonal, the Appellation d'Origine Contrôllée (AOC) cheese can only be made from May to early October using milk from cows that have grazed on mountains between 1000m and 2000m high.

Fondue & Raclette

It is hard to leave Switzerland without dipping into a fondue (from the French verb *fondre,* meaning 'to melt'). And you shouldn't! The main French contribution to the Swiss table, a pot of gooey melted cheese is placed in the centre of the table and kept on a slow burn while diners dip in cubes of crusty bread using slender two-pronged fondue forks. Just the sight of the creamy cheese languidly glistening on the bread is enough to make some diners swoon.

The classic fondue mix in Switzerland is equal amounts of Emmental and Gruyère cheese, grated and melted with white wine and a shot of kirsch (cherry-flavoured liquor); order a side platter of cold meats and tiny gherkins to accompany it.

Switzerland's other signature alpine cheese dish is raclette. Unlike fondue, raclette – both the name of the dish and the cheese at its gooey heart – is eaten year-round. A half-crescent slab of the cheese is screwed onto a specially designed 'rack oven' that melts the top flat side. As it melts, cheese is scraped onto plates for immediate consumption with boiled potatoes, cold meats and pickled onions or gherkins.

Rösti

Be sure not to miss rösti (a shredded, oven-crisped potato bake). Baked to a perfect crisp, the shredded potato is mixed with seasonal mushrooms and bacon bits to create a perfect lunch, paired with nothing more than a simple green salad. This is Swiss Alpine heaven.

Meats

For a quintessential Swiss lunch, nothing beats an al fresco platter of air-dried beef, a truly sweet and exquisitely tender delicacy from Graubünden that is smoked, thinly sliced and served as *Bündnerfleisch.*

Travel east and *Würste* (sausages) become the local lunch feast, typically served with German-speaking Switzerland's star dish: rösti. Veal is highly rated and is tasty thinly sliced and smothered in a cream sauce as *geschnetzeltes Kalbsfleisch* in Zürich.

For true blue-blooded meat lovers there is no better season to let tastebuds rip in this heavily forested country than autumn, when restaurants up and down the country

cook up *Wildspezialitäten/specialités de gibier,* or *chasse/cacciagione* (fresh game). Venison and wild boar are also popular.

Pork

With its fresh game, abundance of wild mushrooms, chestnuts and grape harvests, autumn is exquisitely gourmet in Switzerland and as the days shorten this season only gets better. Fattened over summer, the family pig – traditionally slaughtered on the feast of St Martin (11 November) marking the end of agricultural work in the fields and the start of winter – is ready for the butcher. On farms and in villages for centuries, the slaughter would be followed by the salting of meat and sausage-making. Work done, folk would then pass over to feasting to celebrate the day's toil. The main dish for the feast: pork.

In the French-speaking Jura, in particular, the feasting tradition around Fête de la St-Martin lives on with particular energy and enthusiasm in Porrentruy. Local bars and restaurants organise feasts for several weekends on the trot in October and November. A typical pork feast consists of gorging on seven copious courses.

Pork dishes to look out for year-round include *Rippli* (a bubbling pot of pork rib meat cooked up with bacon, potatoes and beans) in and around Bern, and in the canton of Vaud, *papet vaudois* (a potato, leek, cabbage and sausage stew) and *taillé aux greubons* (a crispy savoury pastry, soft and dotted inside with pork-lard cubes). In the Engadine, sausage is baked with onions and potato to make *pian di pigna*.

Fish

Fish is the speciality in lakeside towns. Perch (*perche,* in French) and whitefish fillets (*féra*) are common, but don't be fooled into thinking the *filets de perche* chalked on the blackboard in practically every Lake Geneva restaurant are from the lake; much comes frozen from Eastern Europe.

Handmade chocolates

Fruit, Sweets & Chocolate

Plump Valais apricots, plums, pears and sweet black cherries fill orchards with a profusion of pretty white blossoms in April and May. For year-round pleasure, the Swiss dry, preserve and distil their abundance of fruit to create fiery liqueurs, winter compotes and thick-as-honey syrups for baking or spreading on bread.

The Botzi pear cultivated around Gruyères is deemed precious enough to have its own AOC. Bite into it as nature intended or try it with local *crème de Gruyères*, the thickest cream ever. *Cuisses de dame* (lady's thighs) are sugary deep-fried thigh-shaped pastries, found in French-speaking cantons next to *amandines* (almond tarts). Apart from the ubiquitous *Apfelstrudel* (apple pie), typically served with runny vanilla sauce, German cantons cook up *Vermicelles,* a chestnut-cream creation resembling something like spaghetti.

Then, of course, there is chocolate...

Swiss Wine

Savouring local wine in Switzerland is an exquisite, increasingly rare gastronomic joy in this globalised world. Switzerland exports little of its wine, meaning that most of its quality reds, whites and rosé vintages, including dozens by small vignerons, can only be tasted and enjoyed in situ.

Lake Geneva & Vaud

The bulk of Swiss wine production takes place in the French-speaking part of the country, where vineyards line the shore of Lake Geneva and stagger sharply up hillsides in tightly-packed terraces knitted together by ancient dry-stone walls.

Most of Lake Geneva's winemaking estates are found on either side of Lausanne in the canton of Vaud. Whites from the pea-green terraced vineyards of the Lavaux wine region between Lausanne and Montreux are so outstanding that the area has been designated a Unesco World Heritage Site. Lavaux's two grands crus are Calamin and Dézaley.

Swiss Chocolate

In the early centuries after Christ's death, as the Roman Empire headed towards slow collapse on a diet of rough wine and olives, the Mayans in Central America were pounding cocoa beans, consuming the result and even using the beans as a system of payment.

A millennium later, the Spanish conquistador Hernando Cortez brought the first load of cocoa to Europe in 1528. He could not have anticipated the subsequent demand for his cargo. The Spaniards, and soon other Europeans, developed an insatiable thirst for the sweetened beverage produced from it. The solid stuff came later.

Swiss chocolate (www.chocolat.ch) built its reputation in the 19th century, thanks to familiar names such as François-Louis Cailler (1796–1852), Philippe Suchard (1797–1884), Henri Nestlé (1814–90), Jean Tobler (1830–1905), Daniel Peter (1836–1919) and Rodolphe Lindt (1855–1909). For factory visits, see p114.

Valais

Drenched in an extra bonanza of sunshine and light from above the southern Alps, much of the land north of the Rhône River in western Valais is planted with vines – and this is where some of Switzerland's best wines are produced.

Dryish white Fendant, the perfect accompaniment to fondue and raclette, and best served crisp cold, is the region's best-known wine, accounting for two-thirds of Valais wine production. Johannisberg is another excellent white and comes from the Sylvaner grape; while Petite Arvine and Amigne are sweet whites.

Dôle, made from Pinot noir and Gamay grapes, is the principal red blend and is as full bodied as an opera singer with its firm fruit flavour.

Ticino

The favourite liquid for lunch in Switzerland's Italianate climes is Merlot, which accounts for almost 90% of Ticino's wine production. The main winemaking areas are between Bellinzona and Ascona, around Biasca and between Lugano and Mendrisio.

Rösti (p289)

Spa Resorts & Treatments

Bad Ragaz (p250)

ARCO IMAGES GMBH / ALAMY ©

The healthy action in Switzerland isn't all in the great outdoors. There's a lot of good stuff – steamy stuff even – going on in the country's renowned spas, saunas and health centres. Many feature mineral baths with natural springs bubbling with water heated deep in the earth. You can go lavish or simple, choose a simple massage or a full-on beauty and health regimen.

Spa Treatments

Here are some of the activities, treatments and blissful interludes you can enjoy at various Swiss spas.

○ **Beauty treatments** A vast category that Switzerland is known for. Many spas have their own branded lines of products and treatments geared towards making you a more beautiful you.

○ **Facials** A standard offering at almost every spa but with myriad variations.

○ **Hay baths** How to get the Swiss cows jealous: you're covered in freshly cut hay, which releases oils through heat and makes you all supple.

○ **Massage** If you're expecting some Asian experience with lots of little candles and bells, think again. Swiss masseuses are incredibly skilled and the focus is on getting that kink out, not creating a mood.

The Best...
Spa
Therapies

○ **Physiotherapy** Popular with visitors from dark northern climes. Light, massage and physical activity are combined.

○ **Roman-Irish bath** A staple of the traditional thermal baths that draw heated water from deep inside the earth. Get naked and enjoy a series of steamy baths from 40°C to 70°C and then nap it all off.

○ **Sauna** Even small hotels often have saunas. Let that 60°C or more heat open your pores and the poisons run right out. Whack yourself with a birch branch if they have one.

○ **Thalasso therapy** Saltwater baths and algae packs combine to nourish the body.

○ **Whirlpool** A fixture at virtually every spa and plenty of resort hotels. After a long day on the slopes, what's better than a bubble in hot water with friends.

○ **Yoga** As popular in Switzerland as elsewhere, common at resorts, large hotels and spas.

Top Spas

The following list includes some of the top spas you'll find in this book. For more spas, **Switzerland Tourism** (www.myswitzerland.com) has comprehensive listings.

○ **Romantik Hotel Schweizerhof** (p141) In Alps-happy Grindelwald, the spa has massage jets, treatment rooms, a teeth-chattering ice grotto and a pool with wide-screen mountain vistas.

○ **Leukerbad** (p191) Europe's largest thermal spa resort is in the heart of Valais. Lindner Alpentherme offers a twinset of pools – one in, one out, both 36°C – with whirlpools, jets, Jacuzzi and mountain views.

○ **Natur-Moorbad** (p226) At this moor bath, dating to 1740, you can de-stress in mud-laden water from the moors. It's well east of Zürich in Appenzell.

○ **Medizinisches Therapiezentrum Heilbad** (p243) After a hard session on the slopes of St Moritz, rest in a mineral bath or with an Alpine herb pack.

○ **Bad Ragaz** (p250) An entire little spa town near Chur, the main event is the chic Tamina Therme, which is renowned for its 34°C thermal waters.

Survival Guide

Countryside around Sion (p181)
PHOTOGRAPHER: DAMIEN DOUXCHAMPS / GETTY IMAGES ©

A-Z

Directory

●●●

Accommodation

Switzerland sports accommodation in every price range and the reviews in this guidebook run from budget to midrange and top end, arranged by author preference. Prices listed are for high season and include breakfast (unless otherwise noted). They are categorised according to the following guidelines:

Budget ($)These generally cost up to Sfr150 for a double, but this can differ slightly, depending on city or countryside addresses.

Midrange ($$) With all the comforts of a private bathroom, TV, telephone and more. Prices go up to approximately Sfr350 for a double, again depending on where you're staying.

Top end ($$$) Where you can wallow in pure unadulterated, time-honoured Swiss luxury; starts at Sfr350 for a double.

Rates in cities and most towns stay constant throughout the year bar the Christmas and New Year periods, when rates rise. In mountain resorts prices are seasonal: low season (mid-September to mid-December and mid-April to mid-June) is the cheapest time to visit, mid-season (January to mid-February and mid-June to early July and September) begins to get pricy, and high season (July to August, Christmas, and mid-February to Easter) is the busy period. Seasonal differences are less marked at budget hotels.

Tourist offices have accommodation listings and most will make a hotel reservation for you, for as little as Sfr5 or no commission. A handy resource for tracking down accommodation is www.myswitzerland.com.

B&BS

Some of Switzerland's most charming accommodation comes in the form of bed and breakfast – a room in a private home (anything from a castle to a farm), which includes breakfast, often made from homemade produce. Some hosts will also, if you order in advance, cook up an evening meal served for an additional Sfr20 to Sfr30 per person, often with wine.

Tourist offices have lists of B&Bs in their areas – urban rarities but plentiful in the countryside areas – and 800-odd can be tracked through **BnB** (www.bnb.ch), which also publishes an annual guide (Sfr28). In rural areas, private houses frequently offer inexpensive 'room(s) vacant' (*Zimmer frei* in German, *chambres libres* in French, *camere libere* in Italian), with or without breakfast.

HOTELS & PENSIONS

The standard at the lower end of the market can vary. **Swiss Budget Hotels** (📞 084 880 55 08; www.rooms.ch) has a downloadable hotel guide of good-quality cheaper hotels and regular special offers.

The cheapest rooms have a sink, but share the toilet and shower in the corridor, costing around Sfr60 for a single and Sfr90 for a double in a small town, and around Sfr80 for a single and Sfr120 for a double in cities or mountain resorts. Pop in a private shower and the nightly rate rises by at least Sfr20.

A *Frühstückspension* or *Hotel-Garni* serves only breakfast. Small pensions with a restaurant often have a 'rest day' when check-in may not be possible except by prior arrangement (telephone ahead).

The **Steinbock Label** (www.steinbock-label.ch, in German) hotels are recognised as eco-hotels and labelled

---

Book Your Stay Online

For more accommodation reviews by Lonely Planet authors, check out http://hotels.lonelyplanet.com. You'll find independent reviews, as well as recommendations on the best places to stay. Best of all, you can book online.

with one to five *Steinböcke* (ibexes) to reflect their sustainability.

RENTAL ACCOMMODATION

Self-caterers can opt for a chalet or apartment, both of which need booking in advance; for peak periods, reserve six to 12 months ahead. A minimum stay of one week (usually Saturday to Saturday) is common.

Useful online resources for bargain-basement deals, particularly out of high season or for last-minute bookings, include **REKA** (Schweizer Reisekasse; ☎ 031 329 66 33; www.reka.ch), **Interhome** (☎ 043 810 91 91; www.interhome.ch) and **Switzerland Tourism** (www.myswitzerland.com).

Business Hours

The reviews in this guidebook won't list hours unless they differ from the hours listed here. Hours are given for high season (April through October) and tend to decrease in low season.

Banks 8.30am to 4.30pm Monday to Friday, usually with late opening hours one day a week.

Offices 8am to noon, 2pm to 5pm Monday to Friday

Restaurants Noon to 2pm, 6pm to 10pm

Shops 9am to 7pm Monday to Friday (sometimes with a one-to two-hour break for lunch at noon in small towns), 9am to 6pm Saturday. In cities,

Climate

Geneva

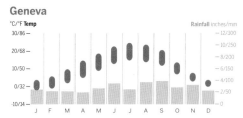

Zermatt

Zürich

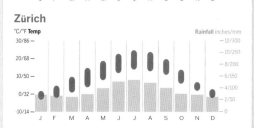

there's often shopping until 9pm on Thursday or Friday. Sunday sees some souvenir shops and supermarkets at some train stations open.

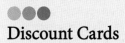

Customs Regulations

Visitors may import 200 cigarettes, 50 cigars or 250g of pipe tobacco. The allowance for alcoholic beverages is 1L for beverages containing more than 15% alcohol by volume, and 2L for beverages containing less than 15%. Alcohol and tobacco may only be brought in by people aged 17 or over.

Gifts up to the value of Sfr100 may also be imported, as well as food provisions for one day.

Discount Cards

SENIOR CARDS

Senior citizens are not entitled to discounts on Swiss railways, but there are various discounts available on museum admission, ski passes and some cable cars, so it's worth asking. The discounts often start for those as young as 62 (proof of age necessary), although sometimes a higher limit is observed. The abbreviation for senior

297

ⓘ Practicalities

○ **Newspapers** For German-language readers, there's Zürich's *Neue Zürcher Zeitung* (www.nzz.ch) and *Tages Anzeiger* (www.tagesanzeiger.ch); Geneva's *Le Temps* (www.letemps.ch) and *La Tribune de Genève* (www.tdg.ch) are available in Suisse Romande; Lugano-based *Corriere del Ticino* (www.cdt.ch, in Italian) is in Italian. Free tabloid *20 Minuten* (www.20min.ch) is available in German and French.

○ **TV & Radio** Largely broken down along linguistic lines: German-language SF-DRS operates three TV and numerous radio stations; French and Italian TV operators are TSR and RTSI, respectively, with RSR and RSI their radio equivalents; and TvR and Radio Rumantsch (RR; www.rtr.ch) are Switzerland's Romansch TV and radio stations. WRS (FM 101.7; www.worldradio.ch) is a Geneva-based English-language station broadcasting music and news countrywide.

○ **Websites** Swissinfo (www.swissinfo.org) is a national news website available in several languages, including English.

○ **Weights & Measures** The metric system is used. Like other continental Europeans, the Swiss indicate decimals with commas and thousands with full points.

230V/50Hz

citizens is AHV in German and AVS in French.

STUDENT & YOUTH CARDS

An International Student Identity Card (ISIC) yields discounts on admission prices, air and international train tickets, and even some ski passes. If you're under 26 but not a student, apply for the IYTC (International Youth Travel Card). Travel agency **STA Travel** (www.statravel.ch, in German & French) issues ISICs (Sfr 20) and both cards should be issued by student unions and by youth-oriented travel agencies in your home country.

SWISS MUSEUM PASS

Regular or long-term visitors to Switzerland may want to buy the **Swiss Museum Pass** (www.museumspass.

ch; adult/family Sfr144/255), which covers entry to the permanent collection (only) of 450 museums.

VISITORS' CARDS

In many resorts and cities there's a visitors' card *(Gästekarte)*, which provides various benefits such as reduced prices for museums, swimming pools or cable cars. Cards are issued by your accommodation.

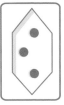

230V/50Hz

●●● Electricity

The electricity current is 220-240V, 50Hz. Swiss sockets are recessed, three-holed, hexagonally shaped and incompatible with many plugs from abroad. They usually, however, take the standard European two-pronged plug.

Food

This guide includes options for all tastes and budgets, reviewed in order of preference and categorised as follows:

Budget ($) Mains less than Sfr25

Midrange ($$) Mains between Sfr25 and Sfr45

Top End ($$$) Mains from Sfr45

Gay & Lesbian Travellers

Attitudes to homosexuality are progressive. Same-sex partnerships are recognised (although gay couples are not permitted to adopt children or have fertility treatment). The age of consent for gay sex is the same as for heterosexuals, 16 years.

Major cities have gay and lesbian bars, and pride marches are held in Geneva (early July) and Zürich (mid-July). **Cruiser magazine** (📞 044 388 41 54; www.cruiser.ch, in German) has extensive listings of organisations, places and events and a searchable online agenda.

The following are some other useful websites:

www.gay.ch (in German)

www.lesbian.ch (in German)

www.myswitzerland.com Information on gay-friendly accommodation and events if you type 'Gay & Lesbian' into the search function.

www.pinkcross.ch (in German and French)

Health

An embassy, consulate or hotel can usually recommend a local doctor or clinic. The quality of health care in Switzerland is generally very high.

ALTITUDE SICKNESS

This disorder can occur above 3000m, but very few treks or ski runs in the Swiss Alps reach such heights – Mont Blanc is one exception – so altitude sickness is unlikely.

TICKS

These small creatures can be found throughout Switzerland up to an altitude of 1200m, and typically live in underbrush at the forest edge or beside walking tracks.

You should always check your whole body if you've been walking through a potentially tick-infested area. If a tick is found attached, press down around the tick's head with tweezers, grab the head and gently pull upwards. Avoid pulling the rear of the body as this may squeeze the tick's gut contents through the attached mouth-parts into the skin, increasing the risk of infection and disease. Smearing chemicals on the tick is not recommended.

LYME DISEASE

This is an infection transmitted by ticks that may be acquired in Europe. The illness usually begins with a spreading rash at the site of the tick bite and is accompanied by fever, headache, extreme fatigue, aching joints and muscles, and mild neck stiffness. If untreated, these symptoms usually resolve over several weeks, but over subsequent weeks or months, disorders of the nervous system, heart and joints may develop. Treatment works best early in the illness. Seek medical help.

TICK-BORNE ENCEPHALITIS

This disease is a cerebral inflammation carried by a virus. Tick-borne encephalitis can occur in most forest and rural areas of Switzerland. If you have been bitten, even having removed the tick, you should keep an eye out for symptoms, including blotches around the bite, which is sometimes pale in the middle. Headache, stiffness and other flu-like symptoms, as well as extreme tiredness, appearing a week or two after the bite, can progress to more serious problems. Medical help must be sought. A vaccination is available.

HYPOTHERMIA

Hypothermia occurs when the body loses heat faster than it can produce it and the core temperature of the body falls. It is surprisingly easy to progress from very cold to dangerously cold due to a combination of wind, wet clothing, fatigue and hunger, even if the air temperature is above freezing. It is best to dress in layers of good insulating materials and to wear a hat and a strong, waterproof outer layer when hiking or skiing. A 'space' blanket for emergencies is essential. Carry basic supplies, including food containing simple sugars and fluid to drink.

Symptoms of hypothermia are exhaustion, numb skin (particularly toes and fingers), shivering, slurred speech, irrational or violent behaviour, lethargy, stumbling, dizzy spells, muscle cramps and violent bursts of energy.

To treat mild hypothermia, get the person out of the wind and/or rain, remove their clothing if wet and replace it with dry, warm clothing. Give them hot liquids – not alcohol – and high-kilojoule, easily digestible food. Do not rub victims; allow them to slowly warm themselves. This should be enough to treat the early stages of hypothermia. The early recognition and treatment of mild hypothermia is the only way to prevent severe hypothermia, which is a critical condition.

Insurance

Free health treatment in Switzerland is very limited; health care generally is very expensive.

If you're skiing, snowboarding or trekking, check whether your policy covers helicopter rescue and emergency repatriation. Mountain rescue is shockingly expensive and most normal policies don't cover many outdoor activities; you'll need to pay a premium for winter-sports cover and further premiums for adventure sports like bungee jumping and skydiving.

Worldwide travel insurance is available at www.lonelyplanet.com/travel_services. You can buy, extend and claim online anytime – even if you're already on the road.

Internet Access

Many hotels have wi-fi (often free), and it's available at lots of cafes and public spaces.

Most hotspots, like those provided by **Swisscom** (080 080 08 00; www.swisscom -mobile.ch), levy a charge – usually around Sfr5 for 30 minutes access over seven days to Sfr125 for 150 hours access over 31 days, payable by credit card or prepaid card sold at Swisscom's 1350 hot spots; locate them with its online hot-spot locator.

Internet cafes can be found in larger towns and cities, but are practically non-existent in small towns and remote areas. Prices range from Sfr5 to Sfr15 per hour.

Public wireless access points can be found at major airports, at 35-odd Swiss train stations and airports, and in 1st-class train carriages on certain routes.

Legal Matters

Swiss police have wide-ranging powers of detention, allowing them to hold a person without charges or a trial. If approached by them, you will be required to show your passport, so always carry it.

Money

A guide to costs and exchange rates can be found on p47.

ATMS

Automated teller machines (ATMs) – called *Bancomats* in banks and *Postomats* in post offices – are common and accessible 24 hours. They accept most international bank or credit cards and they have multilingual instructions. Your bank or credit-card company will usually charge a 1% to 2.5% fee, and there may also be a small charge at the ATM end.

CASH

Swiss francs are divided into 100 centimes (*Rappen* in German-speaking Switzerland). There are notes for 10, 20, 50, 100, 200 and 1000 francs, and coins for 5, 10, 20 and 50 centimes, as well as for one, two and five francs.

Businesses throughout Switzerland, including most hotels and some restaurants and souvenir shops, will accept payment in euros. Change will be given in Swiss francs at the rate of exchange calculated on the day.

CREDIT CARDS

The use of credit cards is slightly less widespread than in the UK or USA and not all shops, hotels or restaurants accept them. MasterCard and Visa are the most popular.

MONEYCHANGERS

Change money at banks, airports and nearly every train station until late into the evening. Banks tend to charge about 5% commission; some money-exchange bureaux don't charge commission at all.

TIPPING

○ Tipping is not necessary, given that hotels, restaurants, bars and even some taxis are legally required to include a 15% service charge in bills.

○ You can round up the bill after a meal for good service, as locals do.

○ Hotel and railway porters expect a franc or two per bag.

○ Bargaining is non-existent.

Public Holidays

New Year's Day 1 January

Good Friday March/April

Easter Sunday & Monday March/April

Ascension Day 40th day after Easter

Whit Sunday & Monday 7th week after Easter

National Day 1 August

Christmas Day 25 December

St Stephen's Day 26 December

Some cantons observe their own special holidays and religious days, eg 2 January, Labour Day (1 May), Corpus Christi, Assumption (15 August) and All Saints' Day (1 November).

Safe Travel

○ Street crime is relatively uncommon. However, watch your belongings; pickpockets thrive in city crowds.

○ The Swiss police aren't very visible, but have a reputation for performing random street searches of questionable necessity on people of non-European background or appearance.

○ Cities such as Zürich, Basel and Bern have a heroin problem, but you generally have to be way off the main thoroughfares to notice it.

Telephone

National telecom provider **Swisscom** (📞 080 080 08 00, from abroad +41 62 286 12 12; www.swisscom.ch) operates one of the world's densest networks of public phone booths. The minimum charge for a call is Sfr0.50, with billing in blocks of Sfr0.10, and phones take coins (Swiss francs or euros) and 'taxcards' (phonecards), sold in values of Sfr5, Sfr10 and Sfr20 at post offices, newsagencies and so on. Some 4000 booths also accept major credit cards and can be used to send SMS worldwide.

The Swiss phone book is searchable online at http://tel.local.ch/en. Dial 📞 1812 (connection charge Sfr.0.80 plus Sfr0.10 a minute) for an automated service, or the pricier 📞 1811 (connection charge Sfr1.70 for two queries, Sfr1.40 for the first minute and Sfr0.22 per minute thereafter) to speak to a real person; the latter can also find international numbers for you. Calls from mobiles for these services cost more.

MOBILE PHONES

Most phones on European GSM networks work perfectly in Switzerland; check with your provider about costs.

Prepaid local SIM cards are available from the three network operators: **Orange** (www.orange.ch; from Sfr10 with Sfr10 credit), **Sunrise** (www.sunrise.ch; from Sfr10 with Sfr10 credit) and **Swisscom Mobile** (www.swisscommobile.ch; from Sfr19.95 with Sfr20 credit). Buy these via the nationwide **Mobile Zone** (www.mobile zone.ch, in German, French & Italian) chain of shops. Prepaid cards must be officially registered, so bring your passport.

PHONE CODES

○ The country code for Switzerland is 📞 41. When calling Switzerland from abroad drop the initial zero from the number; hence to call Bern, dial 📞 41 31 (preceded by the overseas access code of the country you're dialling from).

○ The international access code from Switzerland is 📞 00. To call Britain (country code 📞 44), start by dialling 📞 00 44

○ Telephone numbers with the code 0800 are toll-free; those with 0848 are charged at the local rate. Numbers beginning with 156 or 157 are charged at the premium rate.

○ Mobile phone numbers start with the code 076, 078 or 079.

PHONECARDS

Save money on the normal international tariff by buying a prepaid Swisscom card worth Sfr10, Sfr20, Sfr50 or Sfr100.

> ## Dial All Numbers
>
> Area codes do not exist in Switzerland. Although the numbers for a particular city or town share the same three-digit prefix (for example Bern 031, Geneva 022), numbers always must be dialled in full, even when calling from next door.

Time

The Swiss use the 24-hour clock when writing times. Swiss time is GMT/UTC plus one hour. Daylight-saving time comes into effect at midnight on the last Saturday in March, when the clocks are moved forward one hour, making Switzerland two hours ahead of GMT/UTC; clocks go back again on the last Saturday in October.

Note that in German *halb* is used to indicate the half-hour before the hour, hence *halb acht* (half eight) means 7.30, not 8.30.

The following table shows time difference between Switzerland and in major cities around the world; times do not take daylight saving into account.

CITY	LOCAL TIME
Auckland	11pm
Bern	noon
London	11am
New York	6am
San Francisco	3am
Sydney	9pm
Tokyo	8pm
Toronto	6am

Tourist Information

Make the Swiss tourist board, **Switzerland Tourism** (www.myswitzerland.com), your first port of call. For detailed information, contact local tourist offices, listed under Information in the town and city sections of this guide. Infor-

mation and maps are free and somebody invariably speaks English; many book hotel rooms, tours and excursions for you. In German-speaking Switzerland tourist offices are called *Verkehrsbüro*, or *Kurverein* in some resorts. In French they are called *office du tourisme* and in Italian *ufficio turistico*.

Travellers with Disabilities

Switzerland ranks among the world's most easily navigable countries for travellers with physical disabilities. Most train stations have a mobile lift for boarding trains, and many hotels have disabled access (although budget pensions tend not to have lifts).

The following organisations may be helpful:

Switzerland Tourism (www.myswitzerland.com) Website and tourist offices can offer travel tips for people with physical disabilities.

Mobility International Schweiz (☎ 062 212 67 40; www.mis-ch.ch, in German; Amthausquai 21, CH-4600 Olten) A helpful resource.

Visas

For up-to-date details on visa requirements, go to the **Swiss Federal Office for Migration** (www.bfm.admin.ch) and click 'Services'.

Visas are not required if you hold a passport from the UK, Ireland, the USA, Canada, Australia or New Zealand, whether visiting as a tourist

or on business. Citizens of the EU, Norwegians and Icelanders may also enter Switzerland without a visa. A maximum 90-day stay in a 180-day period applies, but passports are rarely stamped.

Other people wishing to come to Switzerland have to apply for a **Schengen Visa**, named after the agreements that abolished passport controls between 15 European countries: Austria, Belgium, Denmark, Finland, France, Germany, Greece, Iceland, Italy, Luxembourg, the Netherlands, Norway, Portugal, Spain and Sweden. It allows unlimited travel throughout the entire zone for a 90-day period. Apply to the consulate of the country you are entering first, or your main destination.

Transport

Getting There & Away

Flights, cars and tours can be booked online at www.lonelyplanet.com.

ENTERING THE COUNTRY

Formalities are minimal when entering Switzerland by air,

rail or road. In December 2008 Switzerland implemented the Schengen Agreement, so those arriving from the EU don't need to show a passport.

Arriving from a non-EU country, you have to show your passport or EU identity card, and visa if you need one, and clear customs.

✈ AIR

The main airports are **Zürich Airport** (www.zurich-airport.com), **Geneva Airport** (www.gva.ch) and increasingly France-based **EuroAirport** (www.euroairport.com), which serves Basel.

🚗 CAR & MOTORCYCLE

There are well-maintained, fast freeways to Switzerland through all bordering countries. The Alps present a natural barrier to entering Switzerland, so main roads generally head through tunnels. Smaller roads are more scenically interesting, but special care is needed when negotiating mountain passes.

An EU driving licence is acceptable throughout Europe for up to a year, otherwise obtain an International Driving Permit (IDP). Third-party motor insurance is a minimum requirement; get proof of this in the form of a Green Card issued by your insurers.

Car rental firms will take care of mandatory insurance and required safety gear in the car.

🚌 TRAIN

French TGVs from Paris (Gare de Lyon) scoot to Geneva, Lausanne, Bern, Basel, Zürich and more.

Zürich is Switzerland's busiest international terminus, with trains to Germany and Austria. Basel is another hub for trains to Germany. Nearly all connections from Italy pass through Milan before branching off to Zürich, Lucerne, Bern or Lausanne.

Getting Around

Switzerland's fully integrated public transport system is among the world's most efficient. However, travel within Switzerland is expensive and visitors planning to use public transport on intercity routes should consider investing in a Swiss travel pass (p247).

Timetables often refer to *Werktags* (work days), which means Monday to Saturday, unless there is the qualification '*ausser Samstag*' (except Saturday).

✈ AIR

Switzerland's compact size and excellent rail transport render internal flights unnecessary.

🚲 BICYCLE

HIRE

Rent a Bike (📞 041 925 11 70; www.rent-a-bike.ch, in German & French; 🕐 daily) offers bike hire at 100-odd train stations. Prices start from Sfr25 for a half-day and Sfr33 for a full day (returned to the same station) or Sfr40 per day (returned to a different

Climate Change & Travel

Every form of transport that relies on carbon-based fuel generates CO_2, the main cause of human-induced climate change. Modern travel is dependent on aeroplanes, which might use less fuel per kilometre per person than most cars but travel much greater distances. The altitude at which aircraft emit gases (including CO_2) and particles also contributes to their climate change impact. Many websites offer 'carbon calculators' that allow people to estimate the carbon emissions generated by their journey and, for those who wish to do so, to offset the impact of the greenhouse gases emitted with contributions to portfolios of climate-friendly initiatives throughout the world. Lonely Planet offsets the carbon footprint of all staff and author travel.

station); Swiss travel-pass holders and under 16s pay less. In summer, reserve at least a day or two ahead.

There's free bike rental in Bern, Geneva and Zürich.

TRANSPORT

Bikes can be taken on slower trains (for the price of a regular adult 2nd-class ticket), and sometimes even on InterCity (IC) or EuroCity (EC) trains, when there's room in the luggage carriage (one-/six-day bike ticket Sfr18/72, one-day ticket with Swiss Travel Pass Sfr12). Between 21 March and 31 October, you must book (Sfr5) to take your bike on ICN (inter-city tilting) trains.

Trains that don't permit accompanied bikes are marked with a crossed-out pictogram in the timetable. Taking your bike as hand luggage in a transport bag is free.

🚢 BOAT

All the larger lakes are serviced by steamers operated by Swiss Federal Railways (SBB/CFF/FFS), or allied private companies for which national travel passes are valid. These include Geneva, Constance, Lucerne, Lugano, Neuchâtel, Biel and Murten.

Rail passes are often not valid for cruises offered by smaller boat companies.

🚌 BUS

Yellow **Post Buses** (www.postbus.ch) supplement the rail network, following postal routes and linking towns to the less-accessible mountain regions. They are regular, and departures tie in with train arrivals, invariably from next to train stations. Travel is one class only and fares are comparable to train fares.

RESERVATIONS

Tickets are purchased from the driver, though on some scenic routes over the Alps (eg the Lugano–St Moritz run) advance reservations are necessary. See www.postbus.ch for details.

🚗 CAR & MOTORCYCLE

Public transport is excellent in city centres, and parking cars an inconvenience.

FUEL

Unleaded (*bleifrei, sans plomb, senza piombo*) petrol is stand-

ard, found at green pumps, and diesel is also widely available. Expect to pay around Sfr1.75 per litre for unleaded and Sfr1.85 for diesel.

HIRE

It's cheaper to book car hire ahead from your own country. If you're flying into Geneva Airport, it's cheaper to rent a car on the French side. The minimum rental age is usually 25, but falls to 20 at some local firms; you always need a credit card. Rental cars are equipped with winter tyres in winter.

ROAD CONDITIONS

Swiss roads are well built, well signposted and well maintained. Phone 📞163 for up-to-the-hour traffic conditions (recorded information in French, German, Italian and English).

Most major Alpine passes are negotiable year-round, depending on the weather. However, you will often have to use a tunnel instead at the Great St Bernard, St Gotthard and San Bernardino passes. Smaller passes are often closed October to May.

Take your car on trains through these tunnels and passes, open year-round:

Lötschberg Tunnel (📞 0900 553 333; www.bls.ch) From Kandersteg to Goppenstein (car and passengers Monday to Thursday/Friday to Sunday Sfr22/27, 15 minutes) or Iselle in Italy (car and passengers Sfr91, book in advance).

Furka Pass (📞 027 927 70 00; www.mgbahn.ch) From Oberwald to Realp.

Vereina Tunnel (📞 081 288 65 65; www.rhb.ch) Alternative to the Flüela Pass, which is closed in winter; from Selfranga outside Klosters to Sagliains in the Engadine (car and passengers low/mid-/high season Sfr29/36/41).

ROAD RULES

◦ The minimum driving age for cars and motorcycles is 18 and for mopeds, 14.

◦ The Swiss drive on the right-hand side of the road.

◦ Give priority to traffic approaching from the right. On mountain roads, the ascending vehicle has priority, unless a postal bus is involved, as it always has right of way.

◦ The speed limit is 50km/h in towns, 80km/h on main roads outside towns, 100km/h on single-lane freeways and 120km/h on dual-lane freeways.

◦ Car occupants must wear a seatbelt at all times and vehicles must carry a breakdown-warning triangle.

◦ Dipped headlights must be turned on in all tunnels and are recommended for motorcyclists during the day.

◦ Headlights must be used in rain or poor visibility.

◦ Motorcyclists and their passengers must wear crash helmets.

◦ The blood alcohol content (BAC) limit is 0.05%.

◦ If you're involved in a car accident, the police must be called if anyone receives more than superficial injuries.

◦ Proof of ownership of a private vehicle should always be carried.

ROAD TOLLS

There's an annual one-off charge of Sfr40 to use Swiss freeways and semi-freeways, identified by green signs. The charge is payable at the border (in cash, including euros), at petrol stations and from Swiss tourist offices abroad. The sticker (*vignette* in French and German, *contrassegno* in Italian) you receive upon paying the tax can also be bought at post offices and petrol stations. It must be displayed on the windscreen and is valid for one calendar year. If you're caught without it, you'll be fined Sfr100. For more details, see www.vignette.ch. Rental cars come equipped with this.

URBAN PARKING

Street parking in city centres (assuming traffic isn't banned, as it often is) is controlled by parking meters during working hours (8am to 7pm Monday to Saturday). Parking costs around Sfr2 per hour, with maximum time limits from 30 minutes to two hours. Central streets outside these metered areas are usually marked as blue zones, allowing a 1½-hour stay during working hours. Either way, you need to display a parking disc in your window indicating the time you first parked. Discs are free from tourist offices, car-rental companies and police stations.

PUBLIC TRANSPORT

All local city transport is linked via the same ticketing system, so you can change lines on one ticket. Buy tickets before boarding, from dispensers at stops. Single tickets may give a time limit (eg one hour) for travel within a particular zone, and you can only break the journey within that time. Multistrip tickets may be available at a discount (validate them in the on-board machine at the outset of the journey) and one-day passes are even better value.

Inspectors regularly check for people travelling without tickets. On-the-spot fines are Sfr100.

🚃 TRAIN

The Swiss rail network combines state-run and private operations. The **Swiss Federal Railway** (www.rail.ch, www.sbb.ch/en) is abbreviated to SBB in German, CFF in French and FFS in Italian. All major train stations are connected to each other by hourly departures, at least between 6am and midnight, and most long-distance trains have a dining car. For more on Swiss train travel, see p286.

CLASSES

Second-class compartments are perfectly acceptable, but are often close to full. First-class carriages are more comfortable, spacious and have fewer passengers. Power points for laptops let you work aboard and some seats are in wi-fi hotspots – look for the insignia on the carriage.

COSTS

Ordinary fares are relatively expensive, about Sfr38 per 100km; best buy a rail pass. Return fares are only cheaper than two singles for longer trips. Special deals are sometimes available in the low season.

All fares quoted in this guide are for second-class travel unless otherwise stated; first-class fares average 50% to 65% higher.

INFORMATION

All stations can provide advice in English and free timetable booklets. Timetables are also available online and can be personalised and downloaded onto your mobile. Train schedules are revised every December; double-check fares and frequencies quoted here.

For information see www.sbb.ch or call **train information & reservations** (📞 0900 300 300); calls cost Sfr1.19 per minute.

LUGGAGE

Most stations have 24-hour lockers (Sfr6 for a small locker and Sfr9 for a large locker), usually accessible 6am to midnight.

Nearly all stations allow ticket-holders to send their luggage ahead (Sfr20 per item up to 25kg). You dispatch your bag before 9am and collect it at your destination station after 6pm the same day – useful if you're stopping off en route at other places.

RESERVATIONS & TICKETS

Seat reservations (Sfr5) are advisable for longer journeys, particularly in high season.

Some smaller, rural rail routes, marked in the timetable with a yellow eye pictogram, have a 'self-control' ticketing system. On these routes, buy a ticket before boarding or risk a fine. Ticket inspectors appear frequently.

a b c

Language

Switzerland has three official federal languages: French, German and Italian. A fourth language, Romansch (semi-official since 1996), is spoken by less than 1% of the population, mainly in the canton of Graubünden.

Read our pronunciation guides as if they were English, and you'll be understood just fine. The stressed syllables are in italics.

To enhance your trip with a phrasebook, visit **lonelyplanet.com**. Lonely Planet iPhone phrasebooks are available through the Apple App store.

FRENCH

Hello.	*Bonjour.*	bon·zhoor
Goodbye.	*Au revoir.*	o·rer·vwa
Yes.	*Oui.*	wee
No.	*Non.*	non
Please.	*S'il vous plaît.*	seel voo play
Thank you.	*Merci.*	mair·see
Excuse me.	*Excusez-moi.*	ek·skew·zay·mwa
Sorry.	*Pardon.*	par·don
Help!	*Au secours!*	o skoor
Cheers!	*Santé!*	son·tay

Do you speak English?
Parlez-vous anglais?   par·lay·voo ong·glay
I don't understand.
Je ne comprends pas.   zher ner kom·pron pa
How much is this?
C'est combien?   say kom·byun
I'd like ..., please.
Je voudrais ...,   zher voo·dray ...
s'il vous plaît.   seel voo play
Where are (the toilets)?
Où sont (les toilettes)?   oo son (lay twa·let)
I'm lost.
Je suis perdu(e). (m/f)   zhe swee·pair·dew

GERMAN

Hello.	*Guten Tag.*	goo·ten taak
Goodbye.	*Auf Wiedersehen.*	owf vee·der·zey·en
Yes.	*Ja.*	yaa
No.	*Nein.*	nain
Please.	*Bitte.*	bi·te
Thank you.	*Danke.*	dang·ke
Excuse me.	*Entschuldigung.*	ent·shul·di·gung
Sorry.	*Entschuldigung.*	ent·shul·di·gung
Help!	*Hilfe!*	hil·fe
Cheers!	*Prost!*	prawst

Do you speak English?
Sprechen Sie Englisch?   shpre·khen zee eng·lish
I don't understand.
Ich verstehe nicht.   ikh fer·shtey·e nikht
How much is this?
Was kostet das?   vas kos·tet das
I'd like ..., please.
Ich hätte gern ..., bitte.   ikh he·te gern ... bi·te
Where are (the toilets)?
Wo sind   vaw zind
(die Toilette)?   (dee to·a·le·te)
I'm lost.
Ich habe mich verirrt.   ikh haa·be mikh fer·irt

ITALIAN

Hello.	*Buongiorno.*	bwon·jor·no
Goodbye.	*Arrivederci.*	a·ree·ve·der·chee
Yes.	*Sì.*	see
No.	*No.*	no
Please.	*Per favore.*	per fa·vo·re
Thank you.	*Grazie.*	gra·tsye
Excuse me.	*Mi scusi.*	mee skoo·zee
Sorry.	*Mi dispiace.*	mee dees·pya·che
Help!	*Aiuto!*	a·yoo·to
Cheers!	*Salute!*	sa·loo·te

Do you speak English?
Parla inglese?   par·la een·gle·ze
I don't understand.
Non capisco.   non ka·pee·sko
How much is this?
Quanto costa?   kwan·to ko·sta
I'd like ..., please.
Vorrei ..., per favore.   vo·ray ... per fa·vo·re
Where are (the toilets)?
Dove sono   do·ve so·no
(i gabinetti)?   (ee ga·bee·ne·ti)
I'm lost.
Mi sono perso/a. (m/f)   mee so·no per·so/a

Behind the Scenes

Author Thanks

RYAN VER BERKMOES

Thanks to Sally O'Brien and Damien Simonis for generous assistance and everyone listed in the Local Knowledge sections at the start of the chapters. LP's Lynne, Geoff, Moge, Liz, Katie and more came through when the chips were down and before the future looked golden. And a shout-out to the now-retired Felix, who was always hard but never flagged.

Acknowledgments

Climate map data adapted from Peel MC, Finlayson BL & McMahon TA (2007) 'Updated World Map of the Köppen-Geiger Climate Classification', *Hydrology and Earth System Sciences*, 11, 163344.
Geneva Local Knowledge Highlight photograph (p53): PhPache2012
Cover photographs
Front: Aigle Château, Günter Gräfenhain/4corners
Back: Spiez, Dennis Johnson/Lonely Planet Images

This Book

This 1st edition of Lonely Planet's *Discover Switzerland* guidebook was researched and written by Ryan Ver Berkmoes, Nicola Williams, Kerry Christiani, Sally O'Brien and Damien Simonis. This guidebook was commissioned in Lonely Planet's London office, and produced by the following:

Commissioning Editor Katie O'Connell
Coordinating Editors Susie Ashworth, Sam Trafford
Coordinating Cartographer Laura Matthewman
Coordinating Layout Designer Nicholas Colicchia
Managing Editors Anna Metcalfe, Martine Power
Senior Editor Andi Jones
Managing Cartographers Anita Banh, Diana von Holdt
Managing Layout Designer Chris Girdler
Assisting Cartographer Chris Tsismetzis
Cover Research Naomi Parker
Internal Image Research Kylie McLaughlin
Language Content Branislava Vladisavljevic
Thanks to Shahara Ahmed, Sasha Baskett, Ryan Evans, Larissa Frost, Alex Leung, Lucy Monie, Trent Paton, Raphael Richards, Gerard Walker

Index

000 Map pages

000 Map pages

How to Use This Book

These symbols will help you find the listings you want:

⊙	Sights	🎯	Tours	🍷	Drinking
🏖	Beaches	🎉	Festivals & Events	☆	Entertainment
➕	Activities	🛏	Sleeping	🔒	Shopping
⊜	Courses	✖	Eating	ⓘ	Information/Transport

These symbols give you the vital information for each listing:

☏	Telephone Numbers	🛜	Wi-Fi Access	🚌	Bus
⊙	Opening Hours	🏊	Swimming Pool	⛴	Ferry
Ⓟ	Parking	🥗	Vegetarian Selection	Ⓜ	Metro
⊖	Nonsmoking	📖	English-Language Menu	Ⓢ	Subway
✳	Air-Conditioning	👶	Family-Friendly	🚋	Tram
@	Internet Access	🐾	Pet-Friendly	🚆	Train

Reviews are organised by author preference.

Look out for these icons:

FREE No payment required

🌿 A green or sustainable option

Our authors have nominated these places as demonstrating a strong commitment to sustainability – for example by supporting local communities and producers, operating in an environmentally friendly way, or supporting conservation projects.

Map Legend

Sights
- 🏖 Beach
- ⛩ Buddhist
- 🏰 Castle
- ✝ Christian
- 🕉 Hindu
- ☪ Islamic
- ✡ Jewish
- ⊙ Monument
- 🏛 Museum/Gallery
- ⊙ Ruin
- 🍷 Winery/Vineyard
- 🐾 Zoo
- ⊙ Other Sight

Activities, Courses & Tours
- 🤿 Diving/Snorkelling
- 🛶 Canoeing/Kayaking
- ⛷ Skiing
- 🏄 Surfing
- 🏊 Swimming/Pool
- 🚶 Walking
- 🏄 Windsurfing
- ➕ Other Activity/Course/Tour

Sleeping
- 🛏 Sleeping
- ⛺ Camping

Eating
- ✖ Eating

Drinking
- 🍷 Drinking
- ☕ Cafe

Entertainment
- 🎭 Entertainment

Shopping
- 🛍 Shopping

Information
- 📮 Post Office
- ⓘ Tourist Information

Transport
- ✈ Airport
- ⊗ Border Crossing
- 🚌 Bus
- 🚡 Cable Car/Funicular
- 🚲 Cycling
- ⛴ Ferry
- 🚝 Monorail
- Ⓟ Parking
- Ⓢ S-Bahn
- 🚕 Taxi
- 🚉 Train/Railway
- 🚋 Tram
- ⊖ Tube Station
- Ⓤ U-Bahn
- Ⓜ Underground Train Station
- • Other Transport

Routes
- Tollway
- Freeway
- Primary
- Secondary
- Tertiary
- Lane
- Unsealed Road
- Plaza/Mall
- Steps
- Tunnel
- Pedestrian Overpass
- Walking Tour
- Walking Tour Detour
- Path

Boundaries
- International
- State/Province
- Disputed
- Regional/Suburb
- Marine Park
- Cliff
- Wall

Population
- ⊗ Capital (National)
- ⊙ Capital (State/Province)
- ⊙ City/Large Town
- ⊙ Town/Village

Geographic
- 🏠 Hut/Shelter
- 🗼 Lighthouse
- 👁 Lookout
- ▲ Mountain/Volcano
- ⊙ Oasis
- ⊙ Park
-)(Pass
- ⊙ Picnic Area
- ⊙ Waterfall

Hydrography
- River/Creek
- Intermittent River
- Swamp/Mangrove
- Reef
- Canal
- Water
- Dry/Salt/Intermittent Lake
- Glacier

Areas
- Beach/Desert
- Cemetery (Christian)
- Cemetery (Other)
- Park/Forest
- Sportsground
- Sight (Building)
- Top Sight (Building)

Our Story

A beat-up old car, a few dollars in the pocket and a sense of adventure. In 1972 that's all Tony and Maureen Wheeler needed for the trip of a lifetime – across Europe and Asia overland to Australia. It took several months, and at the end – broke but inspired – they sat at their kitchen table writing and stapling together their first travel guide, *Across Asia on the Cheap*. Within a week they'd sold 1500 copies. Lonely Planet was born.

Today, Lonely Planet has offices in Melbourne, London and Oakland, with more than 600 staff and writers. We share Tony's belief that 'a great guidebook should do three things: inform, educate and amuse'.

Our Writers

RYAN VER BERKMOES

Coordinating Author Ryan first visited Switzerland in 1984 as part of a year-long backpacking trip through Europe. He designated the American Express office in Lucerne as his mail drop and thus happily – and regularly – passed through. His awe at the beauty of the town has never faded. Myriad trips since have taken him to every corner and peak. He once wrote a book at a table with a view of the Alps in Wengen and he learned the value of a Swiss franc in Gimmelwald when his coin-op shower clicked off and the water went from hot to glacial.

Read more about Ryan at:
lonelyplanet.com/members/ryanverberkmoes

KERRY CHRISTIANI

Bernese Oberland, Ticino, Northeastern Switzerland, Graubünden Post-grad stints on a vegetable farm near Bern and snowbound winters in Arosa and Wengen sparked Kerry's passion for this boundlessly beautiful country. Since then, she has returned to Switzerland as often as possible to hike in the Alps, sail on Lake Constance and dig out the craziest Alpine events. Kerry's wanderlust has taken her to six continents, inspiring numerous articles and some 20 guidebooks, including Lonely Planet's guides to Germany, Austria, Sardinia and France.

Read more about Kerry at:
lonelyplanet.com/members/kerrychristiani

SALLY O'BRIEN

Fribourg, Neuchâtel & Jura, Mittelland, Central Switzerland A Lonely Planet writer for more than 10 years, Sally has called Vaud Canton home for the last five years. In the course of her research for this guidebook, she visited 11 of the confederation's 26 cantons and, most importantly, ate a whole lot of cheese.

DAMIEN SIMONIS

Basel & Aargau, Zürich Having spent years shuttling back and forth between Switzerland and elsewhere – often to update books for Lonely Planet – fate finally took Damien to gentle Geneva, where he is now ensconced. That does not preclude the occasional foray across the Röstigraben, which is always a treat!

Read more about Damien at:
lonelyplanet.com/members/damiensimonis

NICOLA WILLIAMS

Geneva, Lake Geneva & Vaud, Valais Ever since Nicola moved to a village on the southern side of Lake Geneva, she has never been able to shake off that uncanny feeling that she is on holiday – a garden tumbling down the hillside towards that same glittering lake and Switzerland's mysterious Jura mountains beyond is her wake-up call. Nicola has lived and worked in France since 1997 and when not flitting to Geneva, skiing or dipping into the Swiss countryside (or fondue), she can be found at her desk writing. She has worked on numerous titles for Lonely Planet. She blogs at tripalong.wordpress.com and tweets as @Tripalong.

Read more about Nicola at:
lonelyplanet.com/members/nicolawilliams

Published by Lonely Planet Publications Pty Ltd
ABN 36 005 607 983
1st edition – Jan 2013
ISBN 978 1 74321 527 2
© Lonely Planet 2013   Photographs © as indicated 2013
10 9 8 7 6 5 4 3 2 1
Printed in China